# WHO'S AFRAID OF THE RELIGIOUS RIGHT?

I am a contemptible—a thoroughly despicable—human being.

According to former Texas Gov. Ann Richards, I am a "hate-monger." The chairman of the Democratic Congressional Campaign Committee indicts me as a "fire-breathing radical." The Anti-Defamation League condemns me for crimes against "tolerance and pluralism in America." Democratic consultant Mark Mellman unmasks me as a "card-carrying member of the flat earth society." The Reverend Jesse Jackson suggests that people like me ran the Third Reich—or perhaps it was me.

And no less a personage than William Jefferson Clinton, president of the United States of America, says I'm a "fanatic" spreading a message of "hate and fear."

Apparently, there is no end to my depravity.

If you haven't already guessed it, let me confess the awful truth: I am part of the notorious religious right.

According to the Democratic Party, the news media, and People for the American Way, I am an intolerant fundamentalist, a Bible-brandishing holy warrior who would shred the Bill of Rights, demolish the mythical wall of separation 'twixt church and state, and (in the words of *New York Times* columnist Anthony Lewis)

institute "a Christian version of the Ayatollah Khomeini's Iran."
Praise the Lord and pass the chadors.

I keep asking myself, where did I go wrong? I wasn't always a
theocrat.

Truth be known, I am a member of a certified religious minority, one that has been persecuted more than any other in the course
of history.

My maternal grandfather (of blessed memory) emigrated to
America to escape religious oppression in czarist Russia.

I came of age a libertarian in the 1960s. I have both a bachelor
of arts in government and a law degree, and make a decent living
as a syndicated columnist and speaker. Apologies to the *Washington Post*, but I am not poor, uneducated, or easily influenced—
except, of course, by my wife.

Why then am I considered a threat to democracy, a menace to
life, liberty, and the pursuit of tax-deferred retirement accounts?

Because I refuse to accept conventional wisdom. Because—like
millions of other Americans—I agonize over the direction in
which my country is headed and believe there's a better way.

I believe 1.5 million abortions a year in this nation are an unmitigated tragedy. "Choice" is when you pick Coke over Pepsi. The
deliberate destruction of an unborn child with a heartbeat and
brain waves and a distinct genetic code is not the exercise of a
"choice." It is, to be blunt, a defiance of the Creator and an affront
to a political system based on the defense of innocent life.

I believe gay rights are neither. So sue me; I cannot accept the
fantastic notion that two men who met the evening before in a
leather bar constitute a family with the same legitimacy as a man
and a woman whose union is sanctified by tradition and faith, raising their children in the time-honored fashion.

Heather should have only one mommy. Daddy doesn't need a
new roommate.

The effort to separate morality from sexuality isn't enlightened or tolerant; it is pernicious and has resulted in untold human suffering.

I don't see why a student wearing a T-shirt with an obscenity emblazoned thereon is a celebration of First Amendment freedom but a child engaged in a moment of silent meditation on his Creator is a clear and present danger to the same.

As the father of four, I know that parents are the best judge of what's good for their own children, that when public schools undercut parental values and engage in wholesale indoctrination they are emulating Nazi Germany and Soviet Russia.

I don't see why taxpayers can subsidize obscene art but not educational choice.

I reject the notion that any values are a legitimate basis for political action except those derived from traditional religion. Why are the doctrines of John Dewey, or Shirley MacLaine, or Hillary Clinton, or Karl Marx, or Groucho Marx an acceptable basis for influencing government, but not that book which our forefathers revered and which has served as a moral guide and foundation for successful living throughout the course of history?

Deriving political principles from religious values isn't intolerant or undemocratic but entirely consistent with our national heritage.

Religious conservatives—including the Pilgrims and Puritans, the Quakers in Pennsylvania and Catholics in Maryland—were among our earliest settlers.

Our Republic was founded by their intellectual heirs. Of the fifty-five men who met in Philadelphia in 1787 to draft the Constitution, fifty-two were Orthodox Christians.

The religious right of that era helped to shape our institutions. A later generation of Christian activists launched the abolitionist movement. *Uncle Tom's Cabin* and *The Battle Hymn of the Republic* ("Mine eyes have seen the glory of the coming of the Lord") were both written by ministers' daughters. Abraham Lincoln declared the first national day of prayer and thanksgiving in 1863.

The Republican Party, which we are told is in danger of being "hijacked" by evangelicals, was founded by evangelicals, among others.

The church/state debate is loaded with double standards. Is the combination of politics and religion a mortal danger to democracy? But isn't that what happened during the Civil Rights era? The movement's preeminent organization was the Southern Christian Leadership Conference. Today it would be castigated as exclusionary.

And what of the ministers, rabbis, priests, and nuns who marched in antiwar demonstrations during the sixties—an ominous commingling of political activism and faith to be shunned by all right-thinking people?

No group better epitomizes the establishment's schizophrenia here than the National Catholic Bishops Conference. When the bishops oppose welfare cuts, they are hailed as men of conscience who are compelled by their faith to speak out for justice. When they oppose abortion, they are scorned as extremists who would force their church's dogma on a cringing populace.

The Democrats too would have it both ways. Speaking at a black church in 1994, President Clinton suggested that God wanted Congress to pass his anti-crime bill. (Even Pat Robertson doesn't get direct communications from the Almighty on specific legislation.) By the standard he and his party apply to the religious right, isn't the president a threat to the First Amendment? Political hypocrisy has no limits.

To summarize the views that have made me an outcast and a pariah, I couldn't put it better than House Speaker Newt Gingrich, who cautions us: "You can not maintain a civilization with 12-year-olds having babies, 15-year-olds killing each other, 17-year-olds dying of AIDS, and 18-year-olds getting diplomas they can't read. It is impossible."

Now, I'll tell you a secret: If holding these views condemns me,

I'm in good company. The secular left is terrified lest the public discover how much ordinary people have in common with such dangerous extremists as Ralph Reed and Beverly LaHaye. The average American may not realize it, but when he looks in the mirror he comes face to face with the dread religious right.

Americans have always been a deeply religious people. Forty-three percent of us attend church or synagogue services at least once a week, the highest percentage in the industrialized world.

Seventy-three percent believe God is the all-powerful, all-knowing, and perfect Creator of the universe who rules the world today. The Bible is God's written word and is accurate in every detail say 56 percent of adult Americans.

A majority of the American people would allow abortion only to save the mother's life or in cases of rape or incest; in other words, they would ban over 93 percent of the abortions performed in this country each year.

Fifty-three percent say homosexual relations between consenting adults are morally wrong. Sixty-four percent oppose same-sex marriage, and 61 percent reject gay adoption.

A constitutional amendment to permit nondenominational school prayer is favored by 69 percent.

Furthermore, 70 percent think there's too much sex and offensive language on television, and 83 percent agree with Dan Quayle's unremarkable conclusion that a child is better off in a two-parent family.

As I said, most Americans don't know how much they have in common with us—just yet. But there is a growing perception that we don't have horns and tails.

In its June 27, 1994, issue, *Time* magazine (no friend of conservatives—religious or otherwise) published the results of a survey that must have given its editors acid indigestion. The question? "Are the positions taken by Christian conservatives on social issues too extreme?" Some 40 percent agreed, but even more, 43 percent

said no, the social stands of religious conservatives sound emi-
nently reasonable to us.

If there was one message the media and Democrats tried to
drum into our heads during the 1994 congressional campaign, it
was this: The religious right will destroy the Republican Party.

Association with these fanatics, they told us again and again,
would alienate millions of moderates and doom GOP prospects.
Typical of this wishful thinking was an Al Hunt column in the
*Wall Street Journal* headlined "The Religious Right Is a GOP
Albatross."

Guess what? On Election Day 1994, the albatross soared like an
eagle. Of the fifty-two House seats Republicans picked up on
November 8, 1994, thirty-eight went to traditional-values candidates who welcomed the support of Christian conservatives, as did
nine of eleven freshmen Republican senators elected that year.

As organized labor was to the Democrats for most of this century, so the religious right is to the GOP today. Exit polling
showed these voters now constitute 33 percent of the electorate, up
from 18 percent in 1988. In House races, they voted 69 percent
Republican: 68 percent in Senate races and 71 percent in guber-
natorial contests. Without their solid support, Newt Gingrich
would be the minority leader of the House.

The term *religious right* suggests that those of us so labeled can
be easily categorized—that we are cookie-cutter standardized. Our
critics would have the public believe that we're all white, evangelical Protestants. And of course they're right. The establishment is
always right.

We're all white evangelical Protestants like Roy Innis of the
Congress for Racial Equality, Olga Gomez, Rabbi Shea Hecht,
Howard Hurwitz of the Family Defense Council, and Cardinal
John O'Connor, leaders of the successful effort to defeat the Chil-
dren of the Rainbow Curriculum in New York City.

We're all white, evangelical Protestants like Agudath Israel, the

Union of Orthodox Rabbis, and the Rabbinical Council of America, all of which defend the biblical perspective on homosexuality.

We're all white, evangelical Protestants like movie critic Michael Medved (author of *Hollywood vs. America* and an Orthodox Jew), Rabbi Daniel Lapin (president of Toward Tradition and sponsor of the first national conference of Jewish conservatives, which took place in Washington, D.C., in October 1994), and Marshal Wittman, who was, for several years, the legislative director of the Christian Coalition and a practicing Jew.

We're all white, evangelical Protestants like Bishop Knox, the African American high school principal from Jackson, Mississippi, who stood up for a student-initiated prayer.

We're all white, evangelical Protestants like former Education Secretary Bill Bennett (who happens to be a Roman Catholic) and former Vice President Dan Quayle (who happens to be a Presbyterian).

We're all white, evangelical Protestants like the seventy-five Jewish intellectuals and activists who signed an ad in the *New York Times* on August 2, 1994, repudiating the Anti-Defamation League's smear of the religious right.

We're all religious fanatics like First Amendment author James Madison, who wrote that the founding of our Republic revealed the "finger of that Almighty hand," like liberal Supreme Court Justice William O. Douglas, who confessed: "We are a religious people, and our institutions presuppose a Supreme Being," and like Alexis de Tocqueville, who warned in his classic *Democracy in America:* "America is great because she is good, and if America ever ceases to be good, America will cease to be great."

I could go on at length, but I believe you get the point.

So that's who we are—in all of our glorious diversity—but what do we want and why does the cultural elite find our agenda so intimidating?

Quite simply, we want to return to the moral climate of the 1940s and 1950s. Now I was born in 1946, grew up in the 1950s, and came of age in the sixties, so my knowledge of that era comes not from revisionist history or television reruns, but personal experience.

America in the 1950s wasn't a theocracy. Religious minorities weren't persecuted. There were no forced conversions or religious tests for public office.

People weren't marched off to church at gunpoint on Sunday morning. There were no pogroms. No one's conscience was violated.

On the other hand, there was a lot—and I stress the adjective— a *lot* less crime, promiscuity, illegitimacy, divorce, and venereal disease. Drug abuse was something that happened to bohemians in B-movies. An ethical reversion to that era would be an absolute blessing for this nation.

It's said the religious right wants to force its faith on the public. But whose faith are we talking about? Pat Robertson's? Cardinal O'Connor's? Rabbi Lapin's? These individuals are light years apart theologically, but march shoulder to shoulder on morality.

Which brings me to the next point. To one charge I will readily confess: It is absolutely true, we do want to legislate our morality. And so does everyone else, except anarchists and the politically apathetic.

Everyone who operates in the political arena wants to see their morals reflected in our laws and governmental institutions— including the National Organization for Women, the National Abortion Rights Action League, and the American Civil Liberties Union, whether or not they are willing to admit it.

I challenge our opponents to name one statute or ordinance that isn't based on someone's conception of right and wrong, of virtue and justice. To cite two examples (ordinarily considered far removed from the realm of ethics), the progressive income tax law rests on the assumption of the equity of income redistribution, itself an ethical concept. Our traffic laws are based on the value judgment that it's immoral to recklessly endanger others.

What secularists object to isn't morality legislation per se but the legislation of our morality. Starting from radically different premises, they have wholly rejected the Judeo–Christian world-view.

We believe in the divine origins of man; they believe mankind is a gigantic cosmic accident resulting from the random collision of molecules in a prehistoric sea. We believe in free will; they believe in determinism. We believe humanity is basically flawed. They believe mankind is innately good and infinitely perfectible.

They believe man is corrupted by society; we believe man is corrupted by himself. We believe in rights balanced by responsibilities; they believe in rights infinitely extended. We believe in punishment; they believe in rehabilitation. We believe in the death penalty; they believe in gun control.

We believe in productivity; they believe in equality of outcome. We believe in the family; they believe in social parenting. We believe sex has a moral dimension; they believe it has none, beyond the requirement of consent.

We believe in God; they believe in Freudian psychology or the Marxist class struggle or Keynesian economics, or feminine-centered spirituality, or success conditioning or New Age mantras.

Our values work. For the consequences of theirs, visit any VD clinic, drug rehab center, inner-city public school, or tune in to the *Oprah Winfrey Show*.

When they talk about morality legislation, it's a smoke screen. They are eager to have their values legislated and equally determined that ours (which happen to be the morality of the majority) shall be confined to Sunday sermons.

One final question: Why all the fuss? Why this intense media focus on the religious right? Why all of the wild accusations, distortions, fear-mongering, and hysteria?

The answer: to deflect public attention from the ongoing social revolution in this country. So people won't ask why eight out of every ten Americans can expect to be a victim of violent crime at least once in their lives.

Or why, if current trends continue, by the turn of this century 40 percent of all births in this country will be out of wedlock. Why over 60 percent of the children born today will spend at least part of their childhood in a single-parent home. Why the divorce rate has more than doubled since 1960. Why SAT scores dropped seventy-three points in thirty-four years.

Incredible as it may seem, none of this is attributable to school prayer proposals, public display of religious symbols, or opposition to condom distribution in schools.

Under the Clinton administration, the Democrats and their media auxiliary are especially eager to shift the spotlight from what's happening in national government.

In Bill and Hillary we have our first dysfunctional first family, a co-presidency committed to a social agenda abhorrent to a majority of Americans.

Here is a president who appointed as the nation's top public health official a woman (removed only after his party's debacle in the 1994 election) who says she's every bit as much in favor of gay adoption as adoption by heterosexual couples, a lady who thinks prophylactics should be bestowed on—I kid you not—third graders, a person of immense compassion who orders right-to-lifers to "get over their love affair with the fetus," and an ideologue who urges us to consider legalizing drugs.

And Bill Clinton says the middle-class folks in Topeka who contribute to *The 700 Club* or *Focus on the Family* are radicals whose beliefs pose a mortal danger to this nation!

The media, the Democratic Party, the ADL, People for the American Way, and Bill Clinton just don't get it. This isn't about denominations, or race, or ethnicity, or gender, or one particular region of the country, or small town America.

It is much bigger than an organization, a television ministry, or a campaign slogan. It's about our nation, our families, our churches and synagogues, and our future as a people.

We will not be silenced. We will not be intimidated. You want to dispute our positions? Fine. But don't tell us our very existence poses a threat to democracy. Don't tell us our values put us beyond the pale. And please don't tell us that we don't have the same right to free expression and full participation in the political process that the U.S. Constitution guarantees to every American.

I recall the words of another minister from the Deep South who wasn't afraid to mix politics and religion and who concluded one of his fire-breathing sermons with this confession: "I still believe that standing up for the truth of God is the greatest thing in the world. This is the end of life. The end of life is not to be happy. The end of life is not to achieve pleasure and avoid pain. The end of life is to do the will of God, come what may."

So said Dr. Martin Luther King Jr., in Atlanta, in November of 1956.

A word to the secular left: We're here to stay. Get used to it.

# chapter two

# WHAT IN HEAVEN'S NAME IS A JEWISH CONSERVATIVE?

I f you ask the Jewish establishment, they'll tell you "Jewish conservative" is an anomaly.

Everyone knows Jews are liberal. After all, what other group is said to have the incomes of Episcopalians and the voting habits of Puerto Ricans? As Ruth Wisse, professor of Yiddish literature at Harvard, once wrote, "Jews are associated with liberalism the way the French are associated with wine: It is considered native to their region." To cite but two statistics, 91 percent of Jewish women, in one survey, agreed that there should be an absolute right to an abortion. Among the general population, the figure is less than 50 percent. Over half of Jewish women identify strongly with feminism, compared to 16 percent of non-Jews.

Pick an issue, any issue—gun control, gay rights, welfare reform—and, with honorable exceptions (the Orthodox and Hasidim in particular), you'll find the American Jewish community lurching to the left.

That being the case, are those of us who call ourselves Jewish conservatives out of the mainstream and beyond the pale? Yes and no. Yes, with regard to the values of the majority of secularized, assimilated Jews—those who have substituted Oprah for Torah. No, in terms of the eternal ethos of Judaism.

I have been involved in the conservative movement one way or another for thirty years, and I have the scars to prove it. Early on, I began noticing an impressive number of Jewish activists and intellectuals in conservative ranks. However, in terms of their religious commitment, they were very similar to Jews on the other side of the political spectrum.

This phenomenon is not confined to Jewish conservatives. For most activists, politics fills the void created by the absence of spirituality. Except for the religious right, that's generally as true for conservatives as it is for liberals.

By and large, political people worship the deities of political dogma. The secular left idolizes activist government, income redistribution, equality, multiculturalism, and freestanding rights.

The secular right adores individualism, the free market, national security, occasionally Western culture, and the Laffer curve. Both ignore the source of life, values, rights, and responsibilities.

The key question for Jewish conservatives of the 1990s thus becomes: Are we merely Jew-ish or are we Jews? Are we "conservatives of Jewish extraction" or are we Jews whose souls resonate to three millennia of Jewish teaching—Jews animated by the vision of Sinai, Jews who understand that loyalty to that lofty vision requires them to be conservatives of the spirit?

Those of us who choose to be genuinely Jewish and genuinely conservative have at our disposal a Written and Oral Law that contains all the agenda we'll ever need. We must seek the wisdom, courage, and tenacity to apply those principles consistently to the modern world.

To be true to this heritage, we can't be multicultural or even very tolerant. Tolerance is vastly overrated. Our tradition calls on us not to tolerate the intolerable.

When we entered the Promised Land under Joshua, we found a

multicultural paradise, a beautiful values mosaic. And we proceeded to destroy it.

We could have been tolerant. We could have said, "These Canaanites, sure they sacrifice their children to idols, engage in ritual prostitution, sodomize little boys—but, hey, that's their lifestyle, their choice. We may not understand them, but we must respect them."

We didn't. We smashed their temples, stopped their sacrifices, overturned their idols, and established a hegemony of our values. Jews faithful to the mandate of heaven have been fighting a culture war for the past thirty-three hundred years—ever since a group of nomadic shepherds stepped out of the desert and onto the stage of history and started something that came to be known as Western civilization.

In those days, we were an army that got its marching orders directly from GHQ. The Torah specifically enjoined us: "According to the ways of the land of Egypt in which you dwelt, you shall not follow. And according to the ways of the land of Canaan, whither I bring you, you shall not go. You must not go in their ways.... For I am the Lord your God. You shall keep my laws and statutes and live by them."

An update of Leviticus might read: "And according to the ways of the land of Hollywood (the land of Times Square, the land of San Francisco, the land of D.C., the land of Barney Frank and Bella Abzug), you shall not go."

But just rejecting the ethos of our age isn't enough. We are called upon to bear witness and take action. We can't remain true to the calling of Sinai unless we grapple with the paramount moral issues of our times.

After all, we are the people who taught humanity about the value of life. We told the Canaanites not to "make their children pass through fire." The Greeks thought us barbarians because we didn't kill our children with birth defects. Obviously, we didn't appreciate the centrality of the quality of life.

We gave the world sexual ethics. Prior to the advent of the Torah, to speak of sexual morality was a non sequitur—it didn't compute—like someone today talking about moral aerobics or ethical snack food.

When it came to satisfying sexual urges, the ancient Near East was exceedingly nonjudgmental, scrupulously respectful of differing lifestyles. If a man wanted to have intercourse with a concubine, or a camel, or another man, or a child, that was inconsequential.

Of course, women were treated as breeding stock and children were routinely exploited. It took sexual exclusivity, restraint, and a commitment to heterosexual monogamy to make the family possible.

It was the Jews who proclaimed to the world that not all sexual acts are equal, that only relations between a man and a woman—bound to each other by commitment and tradition—are *kadosh*, or holy. Everything else is wrong, to one degree or another. In so doing, we sanctified the mundane (raising human intercourse from an animal to a spiritual plane) and contained the genie of sexuality within the receptacle of monogamy.

Today, our society is regressing at an alarming rate. The Torah-faithful Jew (with a memory stretching back across the centuries) must ask himself: "Isn't this where I came in?"

America allows the killing of one and one-half million unborn children a year in this country under the guise of reproductive rights. But abortion is the opposite of reproduction. And absent grave necessity, deliberately ending a nascent human life isn't right.

We know who put the child in the womb. Unless and until events reveal otherwise, we must assume that He wants the birth of each unborn child.

I could not put it better than George Weigel and Bill Kristol, who wrote in the August 15, 1994, issue of the *National Review*: "America cannot indefinitely sustain itself as a law-governed democracy when 1.5 million innocents are annually the victims of privately authorized lethal violence. Abortion on demand is morally corrupting in ways that gravely undermine the future of the American experiment."

Once you accept the premise that all innocent life isn't worthy of respect and protection, you open a Pandora's coffin. You can't have reproductive rights alone. Along with these pseudo rights come infanticide, assisted suicide, involuntary euthanasia, and the demise of the Judeo-Christian ethic.

So, too, with gay rights. It is utter unscientific claptrap—and absolutely contrary to Jewish law—to say that homosexuality is a genetically programmed sexual response that individuals are powerless to transcend.

It defies logic to believe that God made certain people "gay" and then (in his Torah) told them that to act according to their nature is "an abomination"—a term of opprobrium that the Bible reserves exclusively for idolatry, human sacrifice, ritual prostitution, and homosexuality.

As Dennis Prager, author of *Nine Questions People Ask About Judaism,* has so cogently observed in his newsletter *The Ultimate Issues:* "It is impossible for Judaism to make peace with homosexuality because homosexuality denies many of Judaism's most fundamental values. It denies life; it denies God's express desire that men and women cohabit; and it denies the root structure of Judaism's wish for all mankind, the family."

Why should only one type of sexual behavior be involuntary? Perhaps promiscuity is also genetically programmed. Maybe God made some people pedophiles and others sadomasochists. Try living in a society where sexuality is divorced from morality and considered nonvolitional. Try it, but you won't like it.

Of course the free market is vital. And of course limited government, the rule of law, a coherent culture, and national security are essential.

But, face it, you can't have a strong economy without strong families. (Successful capitalism presupposes biblical morality.) And you can't have effective national defense without men willing to fight and die for families worth preserving. And you won't have either without a society that upholds the sanctity of life and the sanctity of intimate relations.

We stand for this or we stand for nothing at all. As the Jewish philosopher Abraham Joshua Heschel so poignantly declared: "We are God's stake in human history. We are the dawn and the dusk, the challenge and the test. How strange to be a Jew and go astray on God's perilous errands." How strange and how sad.

What in heaven's name is a Jewish conservative? A Jew who is a conservative in the name of Heaven.

# chapter three

# THE SECULAR JIHAD

## Left to the Public: Pay Up and Shut Up
*September 13, 1995*

I would like to gain a wider audience for my views. To this end, I want you to empty the contents of your wallet or purse into an envelope and mail it to me.

If you were to refuse and if I were—God forbid—a liberal, I would accuse you of censoring my ideas by not facilitating their dissemination.

Liberalism's mutating definition of censorship defies both logic and precedent. In this regard, a recently published book, *Art Under Attack: Artists Reveal the Real Life Toll of Censorship,* is most revealing.

The volume recounts the unendurable anguish of public-trough artists who have had their grants attacked or, worse, been denied the opportunity to commit their art at your expense.

Culture flourished in the centuries before the establishment of the National Endowment for the Arts. Shakespeare was a huge commercial success in his day.

Nothing prevents avant-garde artists from selling their works to whomever they choose, displaying their opuses in any venue that will have them, and finding sponsors and admirers where they will.

Yet, according to indignant arts advocates, any objection taxpayers might make to being compelled to subsidize the aesthetic vision of a Robert Mapplethorpe is comparable to imposing upon artists the cultural hegemony of a Stalinist state.

An even more egregious instance of crying wolf to stifle dissent is People for the American Way's (PAW) annual report on what it chooses to call censorship in public education.

"Censorship attempts remain high," cautions a media advisory heralding the report's release. PAW ("your voice against intolerance") claims to have documented 458 bids to ban books and ideas in the public schools.

These pedagogic purges aren't limited to parents trying to influence curriculum decisions (imagine, the public having a say in public education—scandalous!).

According to PAW, included in the ranks of censors are school committees that reject gay-advocacy instruction or approve abstinence education.

Parental-rights legislation, which would allow families to exempt their children from lifestyle indoctrination, is yet another weapon in the arsenal of censorship, PAW warns.

Initially, the liberal lobby contended that a school board's curriculum decision is synonymous with individual expression and any attempts to reverse the same are the equivalent of the Chinese government gagging dissidents. This was convenient at a time when most board members shared PAW's agenda.

But the definition of censorship has evolved and expanded. Now, when conservatives manage to elect a majority to a school committee and proceed to select course materials that reflect a pro-family perspective, that too is censorship.

Parents who seek to shield their own children from the more

corrosive effects of sex education are another Comstockian nightmare, says PAW.

All of this is light years removed from real censorship, a word which evokes images of Hitler Youth circling a bonfire, consigning to the flames any work whose ideas didn't conform to their own.

Now suppose the Nazis had announced that instead of banning artwork they deemed decadent, they simply would refuse to fund it, that instead of controlling education with a Prussian hand (turning schools into adjuncts of the party), they simply wanted an opportunity to influence the educational process. Such "fascism" would be unworthy of the name.

What PAW and the NEA whiners are really saying is that if we don't provide the money for their curious culture and acquiesce to the proselytizing of our children, they will scream "fascism" at us until they turn blue in the face or our shirts turn brown.

Moreover, they are asserting that they are the only rightful arbiters of state-subsidized art and publicly funded education— that these facets of our culture are their exclusive domain. That, henceforth and forevermore, these institutions shall be exempt from the democratic process.

For liberals, the opposite of censorship isn't unfettered expression, the right to duke it out in the arena of ideas. It's having their ideas enshrined—in the case of art, having their creative vision financed with our taxes and given the imprimatur of state sponsorship; in the case of education, having exclusive say over what is taught and how.

They are the real censors.

What's the First Amendment got to do with it? Absolutely nothing. We're not talking about censorship; we're talking about a demand for special status that directly contravenes democracy. And yet after telling us, ad nauseam, that our role is to cough up and shut up, they wonder why the public is increasingly alienated from government.

## School Prayer: A Hill in the Culture War
*December 5, 1994*

I n the culture war, school prayer is one more hill to be retaken—albeit a crucial piece of symbolic terrain.

Let's be honest: In and of itself, a bland, thirty-second prayer won't have much of an impact. Young hellions will not be supernaturally transformed into cherubs who leave the classroom chanting excerpts from Bill Bennett's *Book of Virtues.*

Nor—despite the dire warnings of People for the American Way—will it result in the emotional scarring-for-life of millions of pint-sized atheists, agnostics, and Zoroastrians.

Which is not to say that it isn't worth the effort. The classroom is a major arena in the ongoing clash of values. Secularists have made it so.

Since 1962, when the Supreme Court declared the Supreme Being persona non grata in the schoolhouse, we've seen an escalating attack on all forms of religion in public life.

The Court has been relentless, prohibiting prayer, Bible reading, a moment of silence, and even posting the Ten Commandments on a school bulletin board.

Additionally, judicial oligarchs have pronounced unconstitutional:

1. Graduation invocations by members of the clergy
2. Taxpayer support for the instruction of handicapped Hasidic students
3. Public display of crèches and menorahs unless sanitized by jingle-bell baubles.

The judiciary is ably assisted by battalions of bureaucrats, educrats, and self-appointed guardians of the wall of separation. In Jackson, Mississippi, a principal was fired (later reinstated) for allowing students to read a prayer over the intercom.

In Missouri, a student got detention for praying over his lunch. Assaulting a teacher is probably a lesser infraction.

A second-grader in upstate New York was told the storybook she brought to share with her class was "inappropriate" because it contained the dreaded G-word. A cop in LaGrange, Georgia, was suspended for a day for coming to work with ashes on his forehead on Ash Wednesday.

My all-time favorite example of First Amendment fetishism: In 1991, the Pennsylvania supreme court overturned a death sentence because the prosecutor quoted Leviticus to the jury.

And the beat (as in bashing) goes on. When it comes to ferreting out religious expression, secularism never sleeps. This spring, the Equal Employment Opportunity Commission floated a set of regulations to create a religion-free workplace. Under the rules, a picture of Jesus on a worker's desk could have been considered religious harassment. The regs were withdrawn after a congressional outcry.

Last month the postal service announced it would discontinue issuance of Madonna-and-Child stamps. "We're moving away from being denominational," a postal official explained.

A federal subsidy for a photo of a crucifix suspended in a jar of urine is fine, but religious figures on stamps are offensive. After patrons threatened to staple, fold, and mutilate the service—and with a presidential "request" en route—USPS reversed course.

As traditional values—which once were the core of public education—have been driven from their fortified positions, secular dogmas have occupied those battlements.

If a voluntary, nondenominational prayer is coercive, what would you call the left indoctrination that has become the mainstay of modern pedagogy, from condom distribution to AIDS education to multiculturalism to Earth worship?

The results of decoupling learning from morality are as conspicuous as the first lady's bouffant hairdo. In a recent survey of the nation's top high school students, 27 percent of the females and 49 percent of the males said they'd have sex with a total stranger—if the price were right.

The elite will fight school prayer like cornered bobcats for a simple reason: Religion is a direct refutation of values they are cramming into callow craniums. They don't want competition for the hearts and minds of the future.

Republicans should offer an amendment much broader than school prayer to protect any reasonable, nondenominational government support for faith.

The amendment would say, in effect: Listen, you ACLU meatheads and black-robed dweebs, the First Amendment establishment clause means exactly what it says: No national church—not no Christmas cookies in kindergarten, no menorahs on the courthouse steps, or no vouchers for parochial schools.

Gary Bauer of the Family Research Council believes such an amendment would send an unmistakable signal: "The last thirty-two years were an odd experiment that we have now rejected as a culture."

## Judeo-Christian Ethic Is No Cliché
*December 14, 1992*

Whenever I read *Newsweek*—a torture to which I occasionally subject myself—I play a little game called look-for-the-hidden-agenda. In any article touching on politics or culture, be sure the publication is pushing its party line. An article that appeared in the Religion section of the December 7 issue, which seeks to debunk the "myth" of Judeo-Christian values, is no exception.

The piece begins by noting Mississippi Governor Kirk Fordice's earlier outrage—his reference to America as a Christian nation.

"Wasn't this the sort of divisive rhetoric that cost the party the White House?" the publication argumentatively inquires.

That's it, by golly. The economy was a nonissue in the past campaign. It was Pat-riotism—the convention oratory of Buchanan and Robertson—that lost the election.

But Fordice isn't the quarry here. *Newsweek* has much bigger game in its sights. It reports on a number of eminent authorities who maintain "the idea of a single 'Judeo-Christian tradition' is a made-in-America myth that many of them no longer regard as valid."

Jacob Neusner, a distinguished talmudic scholar, is cited dismissing the tradition as a "secular myth favored by people who are not really believers themselves."

Sociologist John Murray Cuddihy elaborates on the point, declaring: "It's a device created by ecumenist public relations.... The more orthodox a Jew is and the more orthodox a Christian is, the more likely they are to say, 'To hell with the Judeo-Christian tradition.' "

The article deceptively mixes theology and ethics, jumping from one to the other without any warning. It begins by discussing the term *Judeo-Christian* in a theological sense (the context in which Neusner is quoted)—the rather fanciful notion that there is some core religion of which Judaism and Christianity are variants, as if anyone actually believes such pap.

It then subtly switches to an attack on "Judeo-Christian values," the concept of a common spiritual worldview. But as Neusner, who defended Fordice in a recent *Wall Street Journal* column, told me during a subsequent interview: "While the theology of Judaism and Christianity are very different, they agree on nearly all ethical and moral questions."

There's a significant scriptural overlap between the two faiths, namely the value-saturated Five Books of Moses, which Jews call the Torah and Christians the Old Testament.

Beyond that, both religions affirm an omnipotent deity who controls this world and guides history toward its fulfillment. Both believe He has revealed himself to mankind through Scriptures, and that His principal demands are righteousness (honesty, compassion, and sexual restraint) and holiness. Both also hold that He has endowed man with free will and ultimately will judge us.

Each has far more in common with the other than with the modern secularist, with his relativistic, hedonistic, live-for-the-moment, TV talk-show ethics.

In fact, the more orthodox a Jew and the more orthodox a Christian, the more common cultural ground between them, as may be seen in the alliances formed in recent years among Catholics, evangelical Protestants, and traditional Jews to oppose abortion on demand, euthanasia, gay rights, and condom-proselytizing in the public schools.

The covert agenda in the *Newsweek* piece is brought home in the last paragraph, where Jonathan Sarna, a Brandeis University professor, is approvingly quoted observing that we need "a new language of inclusion to encompass American Muslims, Buddhists, and Hindus."

But if the latter two (polytheists) are to be brought under the ethical umbrella, why not include secular humanists, neo-pagans, goddess-worshipers, and nature deifiers in an absolutely meaningless ethical mush?

The war on the Judeo-Christian ethic is a war on transcendent values. Without a common framework, it's impossible to speak of a universal morality, standards against which to measure public policy and social trends, which is precisely what opponents of the ethic want.

Absent a common code that extends beyond denominational boundaries, who's to say that giving condoms to fifteen year olds, or abortion as birth control, or the sexual exploitation of congressional aides, or a powerful jurist sending extortion notes to his ex-lover, or *Heather Has Two Mommies*, or killing the comatose and elderly ill is wrong? Or, as Neusner puts it, "absent such a foundation in faith, humanity can be seen as negotiable—witness 'ethnic cleansing,' 'extermination,' and those who refer to the fetus as a blob of protoplasm."

To hell with the Judeo-Christian tradition? That is precisely where we're headed without it.

## Jewish Liberalism: A Community's Death Wish
*April 24, 1994*

Pat Robertson, James Dobson, and Beverly LaHaye are better Jews than the leadership of the American Jewish Committee.

No, I am not suggesting these luminaries of the religious right keep kosher or celebrate Shavuot, but that they defend Jewish values—the Torah's moral code—far better than the sachems of secular Jewish organizations.

I am prompted to this observation by a just-released AJC study, "The Political Activity of the Religious Right in the 1990s—A Critical Analysis."

Critical it is not. It is superficial, sensational, and dogmatic. The publication begins with an overview of religious right leaders and organizations, delivered in the terrified tones of a beleaguered soldier viewing an oncoming enemy horde.

Robertson (of *The 700 Club* and Christian Coalition) "has created a multimillion-dollar evangelical conglomerate." Dr. Dobson "hosts a daily radio show that airs on an estimated 1,800 religious and general stations," while LaHaye's Concerned Women for America can "mobilize massive numbers of women" to lobby legislators.

And what do these zealots want? (Start digging the trenches, ye defenders of democracy!) Their "long-range goal is to have abortion declared unconstitutional." They favor school prayer and vouchers and "adamantly oppose social acceptance of homosexuality.... They base their arguments on Leviticus"—a Jewish bestseller of a few years back.

Said positions "are in direct conflict with views held by most Jews, who tend to give strong support to… feminism, choice on abortion, increased legal protection for gays and lesbians, a national commitment to the public school system, and the teaching of evolution and sex education," the report advises.

These may well be the views of a majority of American Jews, but they have absolutely nothing to do with historic Judaism, which invariably takes the opposite position on each of the issues cited.

Propagandists of the religious right are everywhere. Consider the following judgmental, nonpluralistic statements: (1) "Homosexual activists' goal is to subvert all of society's laws that protect or promote normal marriage and morality." (2) "Were our societal standards in conformity with divinely mandated norms, the opportunity for individual (AIDS) contagion would simply not arise." (3) "The nuclear family as the basic unit of the social fabric is now under siege." (4) "Fetal life is inviolate unless continuation of pregnancy poses a serious threat to the life of the mother." And (5) "Few American Jews take Judaism seriously because they already have a deep and passionate commitment to another religion—liberalism."

The foregoing frightfully intolerant and blatantly moralistic comments all were made by religious Jews: (1) Rabbis Marc Angel, Hillel Goldberg, and Pinchas Stolper, writing in the magazine *Jewish Action;* (2) Rabbi J. David Bleich, professor of Talmud and ethics at Yeshiva University; (3) Lord Immanuel Jakobovits, former chief rabbi of the United Kingdom; (4) The Orthodox Union, representing over eight hundred synagogues; and (5) Dennis Prager, author of a popular introduction to Judaism, *Nine Questions People Ask About Judaism.*

It's bad enough that the stands of secular Jewish organizations manifest a thorough disregard of Torah and a chronic liberalism. Worse, they consistently undermine the necessary conditions for Jewish survival.

American Jews have three king-size problems—intermarriage, secularism, and assimilation. Because of these trends, we have become the incredible shrinking people. While the overall population increased 22 percent between 1970 and 1990, Jewish demographic growth was an insignificant 1.8 percent.

There is an antidote to these afflictions—Jewish education. Jewish day school graduates have a high level of observance and community involvement. Thanks primarily to the Orthodox and the Lubavitsch Hasidim, there are now five hundred Jewish day schools nationwide. Most struggle to stay afloat.

Rabbi Larry Scheindlin of the Los Angeles Sinai-Akiba Day School discloses: "One of the things that pains me as a Jewish educator is knowing that there are people who never call because they figure they can't afford it. Others call and hang up when they hear the number."

With vouchers, day school enrollment would soar, and we'd have a real chance of reversing the process of disintegration. So who's in the vanguard of the anti-voucher campaign? "We're Voting No on Prop 174" says an ad that appeared during California's school choice campaign by the American Jewish Committee and fifteen other Jewish organizations.

Prager comments, "At a time when Jews were the only group in America to diminish in numbers, Jewish leaders opposed the single best way to stem Jewish assimilation—providing Jewish parents with the means to send their children to a Jewish day school."

These miserable fundamentalists. If they have their way, by enacting choice in education, Jewish learning and commitment will flourish. Against this clear and present danger, the secular Jewish community must man the ramparts.

## In Israel and Here: Devout Under Fire
*January 26, 1995*

The media just doesn't get it—religion, that is. A study by the University of Rochester's theology department faults the way the media covers faith. "The press should recognize that a few buzzwords thrown about with neither explanation nor context do not equal objective, complete reporting," the survey warned.

A case in point is the media's use of the catch phrase "ultra-Orthodox." Take the headline on a story about Jews in Israel that appeared in the *New York Times* on July 19, 1995, that read: "Growing Power of Jerusalem's Ultra-Orthodox Makes Other Jews Uneasy."

"Jews of different religious convictions are locked in a struggle over whose vision of the holy city will prevail," the article reported. In one corner are the "fiercely traditional Orthodox Jews," distinguished by their funny clothes ("black suits and hats and modest dresses"), large families, and blatant religiosity. In the other corner are the nice, normal Jews, who are modern and tolerant and practice family planning.

The ultra-Orthodox were described as the "powerful, single-minded community" which helped elect Jerusalem's conservative mayor and which demands a redirection of funding from parks and culture to shelter for its oversized broods. Much is made of their alleged conquest of whole neighborhoods, which is said to be driving secular Jews out of the city.

While acknowledging that the ultras haven't tried to close down the city's non-kosher restaurants or the discos that remain open on the Sabbath, the *Times* added an ominous "at least not yet."

"Ultra" is not a term of endearment. In domestic politics, the media labels "ultra-conservative" those politicians they consider the most dangerous and depraved, such as Sen. Jesse Helms (R-N.C.).

Journalists see "ultra" only when looking rightward. Leaders of the left such as Sen. Ted Kennedy and the Reverend Jesse Jackson are rarely described as ultra-liberals.

In the Israeli context, those Jews who have the chutzpah to practice traditional Judaism in the Jewish homeland are ultras, but Shulamit Aloni, the leftist education minister who says King David was a homosexual and wants to delete references to God from the prayer for fallen soldiers, is not ultra-secular. Presumably, the media consider her positions both moderate and reasonable.

You will not see an article on the ultra-Orthodox without reference to their reproductive patterns. In an April 6, 1995, piece, the *Christian Science Monitor* claims their "power is born out of sheer demographics," i.e., "a birth rate that is twice the Israeli average."

The media find this quite sinister. Here is a malignant force, growing in numbers, biding its time, and waiting to pounce on Israeli society, destroy democracy, and drag the nation back to *Fiddler on the Roof.*

There are striking parallels between media treatment of Israel's ultra-Orthodox and their abuse of the religious right in America. By and large, reporters and editors are devoutly secular and deeply distrustful of those who act on faith.

The media can almost tolerate people who seek solace in the privacy of a house of worship. It's quite another thing to do it in public. Hence their distress over school-prayer proposals.

They unfailingly portray those who advocate public prayer as militant and aggressive. A December 1, 1994, report on CNN, for example, warned: "Holy war is raging in America, and the battleground is your child's classroom.... In a number of school districts across the country, Christian conservatives are on the march." Praise the Lord, and pass the invective!

What do Israel's ultra-Orthodox want? Well, they would prefer that women in bikinis not march through their neighborhoods on the Sabbath. Beyond that, they'd like a fair allotment of public funding for their educational institutions and housing.

In America, parents who are classified as Christian conservatives would prefer that their children not be showered with condoms or indoctrinated in sexual diversity.

The *Times* article was illustrated with a picture of a young man praying at Jerusalem's Central Bus Station. He's wearing a prayer shawl and *tefillin* (leather boxes containing biblical verses), but is clean shaven and has a short-sleeve shirt. In reality, the fearsome fellow is modern Orthodox.

But the very fact that he's praying in public marks him as a zealot in the *Times*'s estimation. He takes his religion seriously. Perhaps he intends to act on those convictions. If he hasn't thrown stones at cars passing through his neighborhood on the Sabbath or tried to resurrect the theocracy of the Book of Judges, the *Times* would qualify that disclosure with an admonitory "at least not yet."

The message: In dealing with news coverage of those whose values the media disdains, extreme caution is warranted.

## Church Catches Hell in *Priest*
### *March 29, 1995*

If an institution is known by the enemies it makes, the Catholic Church should feel honored by Hollywood's entrenched hostility, manifested in the movie *Priest*.

*Priest* is so warped that it could come only from an entertainment industry at war with traditional religion.

There are five priests in the movie, which is set in Liverpool, England. All are dysfunctional. The central character is a theologically conservative young priest who tells the older priest with whom he shares a parish to get rid of his mistress, then sneaks out to gay bars. There's also an alcoholic priest; a bitter, disillusioned priest; and a bishop who exudes the warmth of a cathedral's stone facade.

Not only are all five of the priests aberrant, but, as William

Donohue of the Catholic League for Religious and Civil Rights pointed out, their problems are "directly attributed to the depraved nature of Catholicism"—particularly the Church's insistence on priestly celibacy and opposition to homosexual conduct.

Hollywood's anti-Catholicism is pervasive. Unlike in the past, today the Bells of St. Mary's are ringing a tocsin for clerical character assassination. *Monsignor* (1982) gave us Christopher Reeve as a priest who's in league with the Mafia and in bed with a nun. *The Godfather Part III* (1990) also fantasized a Vatican–Mafia connection.

*Household Saints* (1993) has a novice nun driven crazy by religious fervor—to the point that she has delusions of playing pinochle with the Trinity. For sheer malice, nothing surpasses 1985's *Agnes of God,* in which a nun murders the child she gave birth to in a convent. In the movie, Jane Fonda (notorious for her real-life attacks on the Vatican) played an atheist psychologist who does battle with the order's mother superior, Anne Bancroft, for the soul of the young sister. The theme is unmistakable when Fonda shouts at Bancroft, "poverty, chastity, and ignorance is what you live by," or when she tells the infanticidal nun that it's "all right to hate God."

*Priest* is equally subtle. Director Antonia Bird told the *Los Angeles Times* that she "seethes with rage" over the pope's opposition to artificial birth control and that the movie's central message is opposition to "a hierarchy adhering to old-fashioned rules without looking at the way the world's changed." Screenwriter Jimmy McGovern railed at the priests of his childhood as "reactionary bastards."

If the five tarnished clerics weren't enough, Bird and McGovern drag in incest in the form of a fourteen-year-old girl who confesses to the gay priest that her father is molesting her. The priest is in agony, being unable to protect the child because of yet another antiquated church doctrine—the sanctity of the confessional.

In a video he narrates (*Hollywood vs. Religion,* distributed by Focus on the Family), movie critic Michael Medved notes: "The Catholic Church is the most visible religious institution in the world so Hollywood views it as a particularly juicy target."

The entertainment community knows where the danger lies to its values: Live for the moment, trust your instincts, and always let your hormones be your guide.

Some religions it will tolerate. Catholics and Amish share a biblical morality. Yet the Amish, who've isolated themselves from society, don't challenge the dominant culture. This affords Hollywood the luxury of viewing them as quaint and charming, à la *Witness.*

The Roman Catholic hierarchy, however, is inclined to activism and unapologetically articulates the Church's teachings on a broad range of issues. Catholics march in front of abortion clinics. Various bishops have come out strongly against homosexual marriage and adoption.

Hence the need to portray churchgoing Catholics as superstitious, priests as fornicating and hypocritical, and the hierarchy as money-grubbing, power-lusting, and fanatical.

Toward the end of *Priest,* the father with the mistress comes to the aid of the recently disgraced father with the male lover, asking his congregation if God really cares what men do with their sexual organs.

If this is indeed a matter of supreme indifference to the Supreme Being, then why should God care what a man does with the same organ to his teenage daughter?

Bird and McGovern would reply that we all know that incest is wrong. But that knowledge is inseparable from the Judeo-Christian ethic whose other applications by the Church *Priest* decries.

Produced by the BBC, *Priest* is being distributed by Disney-owned Miramax. There are fifty-nine million Catholics in this country. If a tiny fraction of them boycott Disney videos, disconnect the Disney Channel, and cancel vacations to Disney World, the message to CEO Michael Eisner would come through as clearly as the message in *Priest*.

## Gallup Catholics Lecture Church
*August 16, 1993*

The media will never be guilty of originality. In preparation for the pope's third visit to the United States, which ended yesterday, it resorted to a timeworn tactic—opinion polls of American Catholics, so-called.

Two days before the pope arrived in Denver for a series of international youth events, a front-page story in *USA Today*, America's comic book newspaper, trumpeted the divergence between John Paul II and his flock.

According to this survey of Catholics ages thirty to forty-nine, one can: use birth control (89 percent), have sex outside marriage (57 percent), divorce without an annulment (71 percent), have an abortion (57 percent), and not go to confession even once a year (71 percent), and still be a "good Catholic."

We're so subtle. The pleading fairly leaps off the page: "See, see, even his own people disagree with him on every controversial issue. How many loyal divisions does the pope have? His views are quaint ecclesiastical anachronisms, representative of nearly no one."

As an accompaniment, we heard from the habitual harping chorus of "disaffected Catholics" the media invariably deploys to preempt papal sojourns—feminist Catholics, homosexual Catholics, those who think the priesthood should be a 9-to-5 job (off with the vestments, back home to the wife and kiddies), trendy theologians, and proponents of cafeteria-style Catholicism.

What qualifies opinion-poll Catholics to have an opinion on a faith from which they are alienated and of which the majority are clearly ignorant?

Now, if *USA Today* had run a survey of adults who had a Catholic education; were steeped in the works of Thomas Aquinas, Cardinal Newman, and Fulton Sheen; attend mass weekly; go to confession; take communion; and are active in Catholic life, their perspective might be significant.

However, for the media's purposes, it is enough to be born into a Catholic family to be counted in these studies. That's far too much deference for a tenuous connection. Opinion-poll Catholics will be found in church only for weddings and baptisms. (The average evangelical has a better understanding of Catholic teaching.)

Their affinity for the ancient faith is essentially nostalgic.

One of the conscientious Catholics quoted in the *USA Today* piece is Fred Ruof of Baltimore, who—while proclaiming his opposition to the Vatican—insists: "It's a church I love." But what precisely does he love—the music, the candles, the stained-glass windows, bingo?

These are to Catholicism what bagels and cream cheese are to Judaism. To love the Catholic Church on this basis is like saying one loves America because July is his favorite month and red, white, and blue his preferred colors.

Say you met a man who said he "loved" America, but couldn't stand the Constitution, representative government, or our history and heritage (besides which, the American Revolution was a tragic mistake). Having rejected the essence of Americanism, his profession of devotion would be a sham.

When we say that someone is a good whatever—Jew, Baptist, Rotarian, Republican—we mean the individual is loyal to a creed, understands and accepts the tenets thereof, is willing to sacrifice for that with which he identifies, and is committed to making his actions conform to certain norms.

But language has become so twisted that words have lost any semblance of meaning. Thus academic liberals can consider themselves champions of free expression while seeking to suppress opposing views. Democrats are paladins of the people while raising taxes. Gay-rights proponents label immoral those who refuse to condone immorality.

Hence the notion of good, anti-papal Catholics. At what are they good? Ignoring the dictates of their faith? Uncritically absorbing the values of their culture?

In the final analysis, even assuming opinion-survey Catholics were knowledgeable and committed, would it really matter? To be a Catholic is, by definition, to submit to authority. Doctrine isn't determined by the temper of the times but is validated by a more venerable source.

The idea of democracy, while fine in its realm, isn't universally applicable. Religions are based on revelations, not plebiscites.

No one elected God. Once dogma is subject to popular opinion, what will be sacred? Perhaps all of the Gallup Catholics should get together and vote on the concept of the Trinity or the Christian doctrine of atonement and redemption.

There's nothing more sobering than listening to the theologically unwashed lecturing a two thousand-year-old church.

## Harvard Divinity School Disses Christianity
*April 4, 1994*

Yesterday, Christians the world over observed their holiest day. Wonder what they were doing at the Harvard Divinity School?

A friend of mine, a closet conservative ("they know I'm a white heterosexual; if they find out I'm a Republican, I'm dead"), enrolled there last fall.

With an indignant air, he presented me with the March 18–25 issue of its student newsletter, *The Nave*. Spell it with a *K*, and you'll have an idea of the content, my friend growled.

Instead of singing hymns, they're sitting in the lotus position, chanting "oom" at America's oldest school of theology. *The Nave's* calendar reminds students that March 20 is Spring Ohigon, "a special time to listen to the Buddha and meditate on the perfection of enlightenment."

Wouldn't miss it for the world. The next day is the Zoroastrian holiday of Naw Ruz. Wonder what the Zoroastrian population of the United States is these days?

There's no mention of Palm Sunday or Passover, reflecting their insignificance at an institution where all is venerated save Western religion.

Even the most fantastic humbug reposes comfortably in the school's New Age bosom. The calendar notes a meeting of the Harvard Theosophical Union with a lecture on "Man's Electro-Magnetic Nature." Theosophy is a witch's brew of Eastern mysticism and pseudo-science, founded by a nineteenth-century quack named Madame Blavatsky, who claimed to have received written communication from dead Tibetan masters.

The publication also lists a peace dance, meditation sessions, a Nigerian tribal drum performance, feminist symposiums, and a showing of *Thelma and Louise.*

A panel discussion with Catholic, Protestant, and Jewish feminists considers the pressing question of whether to attempt to reform male-dominated, misogynistic (blah, blah, blah) religion or leave en masse. Don't let the door hit you on your way out.

At the pinnacle of the school's pantheon are feminism (goddess worship) and liberation theology (Marxism of the miter). Its catalog lists courses in Feminist Biblical Interpretation, Introduction to Feminist Theology and Feminist Critical Theories, and Radical Critiques of Religion.

Almost every course has a healthy dose of estrogen and a revolutionary spin, to wit: The Gospel of Mark ("attention will be paid to... feminist approaches"), New Testament Theology (taught "in conjunction with the hermeneutical questions raised by feminist and liberation theologies"), and New Testament Ethics ("special attention will be given to the contributions of feminist and liberation theological analysis").

These poison-ivy-covered walls harbor a deep-seated contempt for Christianity.

In *The Nave*'s "community forum," a third-year student sniffs: "Christianity—the whole of it—is a sect. With its baptism and Eucharist borrowed from the Greek mystery religions; its cross a transformed Egyptian ankh... its clergy modeled on Roman bureaucracy," and so on.

The author speaks affectionately of Native American religion possessing "none-too-primitive beliefs regarding human immortality and interdependence of humanity and nature."

Get thee to a shaman's teepee! Then again, why bother? The shamans, gurus, witch doctors, and mahatmas have all come to Harvard.

"Here," says my friend, "all religions are equal except Christianity, which is very bad, and Judaism, which loses points where it intersects with Christianity."

Harvard was founded by the Puritans to train Christian clergy. They reverently proclaimed the university was established by colonists who "dreaded to leave an illiterate ministry to the churches, when our present ministers shall lie in the dust."

At the Divinity School, it's Christian orthodoxy that lies a-moldering in the grave. The school is an elite institution, training the next generation of mainline church leadership. Its degrees are passports to power in the Protestant establishment. Its heresies are a reflection of the spiritual sickness of these once-venerable mainline denominations.

Its graduates will go on to propagate their Mork-from-Ork theology in churches where cobwebs outnumber congregants. They will assume leadership of ecclesiastical bodies with dwindling rosters that no one, especially their members, takes seriously. "God is killing mainline Protestantism in America," observes a Methodist theologian at Duke University, "and we goddam well deserve it."

Why go to church when you can get the same message in the pages of *Ms.* magazine or the collected writings of Kim Il Sung?

What's up at the Harvard Divinity School? Mystic crystal emanations and the soul's annihilation.

Will the last graduating Christian please collect the Bibles and turn out the lights?

## Menorah Menace Mobilizes Crèche Cops
*December 9, 1993*

**M**eet the latest threat to the separation of church and state, Rabbi Yossi Geisinsky. In the face of formidable opposition, the thirty-one-year-old, Moscow-born Hasidic rabbi secured permission to erect an eighteen-foot menorah on the town square in Great Neck, New York.

The menorah menace mobilized the crèche cops, an elite corps dedicated, in this season of good will, to crushing any manifestation of the Divine in the public realm. At a heated meeting of the Great Neck Park Commission on November 23, a reform rabbi named Jerome Davidson declared religious displays on municipal property were the first step on the road to perdition and will end in the betrayal of "America and each faith."

Robert Unger, a local lawyer who described himself as a "bagel-and-cream cheese Jew," waved a dollar bill, calling attention to the motto thereon. If the menorah is a breach of the cherished wall of separation, what about the name of God "plastered all over our currency, historical documents, and public properties?" Unger asked.

The controversy divided the mostly Jewish city's modernist rabbis and Orthodox community. The Park Commission was finally swayed by a letter from a Washington lawyer noting the

Supreme Court had upheld an identical display in its 1989 Pittsburgh case.

What dire consequences could result from exhibiting the Hanukkah lights? Will unsuspecting gentiles, confronted by the giant candelabrum, suddenly grow beards, dress in black, and begin studying Talmud?

Worse, says Davidson, who explained to me that once the menorah gains a foothold, Christians will demand the right to set up a nativity scene. Scandalous!

Let us assume the absolute worst, I say: that Catholics, Moslems, Buddhists, and everyone else gets to display their sacred symbols. Then what?

Aha, says the rabbi, next they'll invade the sacred precincts of the public schools, and won't that be an unmitigated disaster? I agree. Christmas carols, nondenominational prayers, and the like could subvert the finely crafted moral climate created by condom distribution and AIDS education.

Of course, this is not what the Founding Fathers had in mind when they drafted the Constitution, and Davidson reluctantly admits as much. He speaks of "evolving" constitutional concepts. Then why can't the First Amendment evolve a bit further—back into something that acknowledges reality?

"Our freedom as American Jews depends upon America remaining a democratic pluralistic society in which the First Amendment to the Constitution [his interpretation] is held sacred," Davidson intones. Really? The nation welcomed my grandparents from the shtetl at a time when our Judeo-Christian roots were regularly celebrated by public institutions.

For over one hundred years, we had prayer, Bible reading, and carols in the schools, and crèches in the parks, without the most minute movement toward the establishment of a national church, pogroms, theocracy, or holy war.

What really concerns the crèche contenders and menorah

opponents is the possibility that public display of religious tokens will signify a governmental endorsement of Bible-based morality. Being ever so comfortable with our secularized society, where candidates are afraid to quote Scripture and only religious concepts are excluded from the political debate, they find that prospect daunting.

Rabbi Geisinsky explains the importance of a public menorah lighting. It reminds Jews of who they are (a people with a mission to proclaim God's sovereignty). "It proves that the state is not—God forbid—against God. We are a God-fearing nation."

The Maccabean revolt that Hanukkah commemorates wasn't just a struggle to end the Syrian Greek occupation of Ancient Israel. It was also a civil war, pitting Jew against Jew.

Like modern secularists, Jewish Hellenists were eager to accommodate the prevailing ethos. They wanted to exercise in Greek gymnasiums and enjoy Aristophanes in the amphitheater. They saw nothing amiss in sacrificing to the deities of the dominant culture, while maintaining Jewish ritual in their homes.

Transported to late twentieth-century America, they would probably pour libations to the gods of liberalism and turn the First Amendment into an object of veneration.

The Greeks didn't ban Judaism outright (though they did prohibit certain distinctive practices). Have your little religion, they seemed to say. But don't take it seriously. Don't practice it openly.

Daniel Lapin, a Seattle-area rabbi and president of Toward Tradition, notes: "The chasm that rips across our cultural landscape divides not black and white, Jew and Christian, but those who welcome God into the public square and those who vigorously reject him."

The menorah that lights the park in Great Neck this evening is a beacon to people of all faiths, a symbol of resolve not to be intimidated by militants. It's also an affirmation that we can be Jews or Christians in the public sphere without endangering democracy, descending to intolerance, or endorsing religious compulsion.

# Me Generation Gets a Me Religion
*December 22, 1994*

H ave baby boomers, like the wise men at the manger, found religion? Don't bet the collection plate on it.

Stories of the spiritual quest of the sixties generation crowd the lifestyle pages of magazines and newspapers. No longer skeptics, boomers are seeking answers to eternal questions, trying to understand their place in the universe, we are told.

Take the cover story in the November 28 *Newsweek* ("In Search of the Sacred"), which sees a great awakening in the Woodstock Nation. In a *Newsweek* poll, 58 percent of Americans say they feel the need to experience spiritual growth.

"Now it's suddenly OK, even chic to use the S words—soul, sacred, spiritual, sin," the magazine noted. An album of Gregorian chants has sold 2.8 million copies; an Internet guru called Doctress Neutopia offers on-line salvation and—the ultimate validation of any cultural trend—Oprah has done shows on spirituality.

What does it all add up to? Less than words can say.

Many boomers never left the faith of their fathers. Others returned after a rocky passage into their middle years.

But what passes for religion among many of my contemporaries is frankly laughable. *Newsweek* mentions Deja Vu Tours in Berkeley, California, which offers mystical excursions to Stonehenge, the "Room of the Spirits" at the Dalai Lama's monastery, and the Inca ruins at Machu Picchu where an authentic shaman will rattle his bones for you.

One of the seekers spotlighted is a fifty-year-old nurse who left the Pentecostal church of her childhood and dabbled in Native American customs, Buddhism, and meditation.

Today, *Newsweek* writes, her home has an eclectic altar displaying "an angel statue, a small bottle of 'sacred water' blessed at a women's vigil, a crystal ball, a pyramid, a small brass image of

Buddha sitting on a brass leaf, a votive candle," and Shirley MacLaine in a pear tree.

Wade Clark Roof, a religion professor at the University of California, has written the definitive study of the inner lives of boomers. According to his data, 60 percent believe it's better to explore various religions than commit to one faith, 70 percent say you should attend religious services only if they "meet your needs," 28 percent believe in reincarnation, and 14 percent practice meditation.

There's no count on the number who've tried to levitate their cats.

Must it be said? This isn't religion, but New Age aerobics performed to choir music—as faddish and hollow as any other yuppie diversion.

Semantics is a dead giveaway. Note the preference for describing the experience as *spirituality* instead of *religion*. Religion is about rules—those oh-so-limiting thou-shalts and thou-shalt-nots. *Spirituality* is free-form, feel-good faith, devotion without demands.

Indicative of this shallowness is the angels craze. Angels, angels everywhere. Books on angels. Angel newsletters. They are seraphim refashioned for a flaccid age.

Gone are the celestial creatures of the Bible, stern messengers of the Lord bearing flaming swords. The nineties models are thoroughly benign and nonjudgmental beings bestowing blessings indiscriminately—Santas of the spirit world.

Just how frivolous, narcissistic, and ego-centered the faith of the boomers is can be seen in one of those metaphysical guides that pop up on bestseller lists, *Hymns to an Unknown God: Awakening the Spirit in Everyday Life*.

The volume lists "six ways to feed your soul": "slow down, listen to your body's wisdom, start your day gently, follow your bliss, tell a story, create a ritual." Whatever happened to prayer, study, and commandments?

Poor, lost souls. For boomers, religion is Me to the *n*th degree. Where do I fit in? What can this experience do for me? Instead of religion, call it psychotherapy with a candle in place of a couch.

Is the essence of religion feeling good about yourself or doing good for others? Is it "following your bliss" or controlling your impulses? Is it worshiping yourself or your Creator?

"Ethics of the Fathers," a book of the Talmud, explains why idol worship—in its multitudinous forms—is so seductively dangerous. Paganism allows the idolater to feel "spiritual" without actually doing anything positive, like practicing self-denial, following rules of ethical conduct, or performing acts of kindness.

Earlier this month, Jews lit Hanukkah candles, whose glow symbolizes the light of God's law illuminating the world. His wisdom, not ours. For Christians, the magi came to the stable not to venerate themselves but to worship the transcendent.

The Me generation has a Me religion. Its self-centered faith is the ultimate idolatry.

## Today God Speaks with a Quiet Voice
*December 25, 1995*

In this holiday season, our thoughts turn naturally to the eternal. Is it dangerous to dwell too deeply on these matters?

Arthur Schlesinger, Jr., eminent historian and recipient of two Pulitzer Prizes, worries about those who seek to fathom the intent of the Almighty.

In a *Wall Street Journal* piece following the assassination of Israeli Prime Minister Yitzhak Rabin, Schlesinger chronicled crimes committed in the name of "executing the will of God," with the admonition that "there will be more outrages to come."

He frets over a Gallup poll which shows that one-third of adult Americans believe God speaks to them. "Am I alone in finding that a scary statistic?" the historian asks. "How does God talk to them? Do they hear voices like Joan of Arc? And what does God say to them?"

For elitists, belief in God is fine as long as no conclusions are drawn therefrom.

But the moment someone says, "I believe God wants me to behave this way or that" (especially if the conviction has implications for the ordering of society), secularists recoil in horror, anticipating another edition of the Spanish Inquisition.

"There is an awful arrogance in claiming access to divine purpose," Schlesinger declares. Has he thought this through?

If God does not proclaim His truth to humanity, how do we know anything in a moral sense? How do we know, for instance, that He wants us to be charitable? How do we know that He wants us to refrain from acts of avarice or aggression?

Western religion rests on the premise that God has communicated with man and continues to do so. Hark, the herald angels sing—*herald*, as in one who comes bearing a message.

For Judaism, there was the revelation at Sinai. For Christians, the logos is manifest in the Gospels.

*O, tidings of comfort and joy.*

Might as well admit it, I'm one of those creepy visionaries—yea, a mad prophet who believes God talks to him.

Not in the ordinary sense of communication. I don't recall ever hearing a voice from heaven commanding me to lead the armies of France to victory and have the dauphin crowned king in Rheims. How could I have, when I look nothing like Ingrid Bergman?

During a recent address to a group of Japanese women, I was asked in what ways I have "experienced God."

The question was awkward. While I frequently write about spiritual concerns, for me, religion is a private matter. To parade one's faith seems ostentatious and to somehow diminish its authenticity.

In answer to the question, I tried to explain that people experience God differently. Some see His handiwork in a sunset, a snow-fall, or a symphony. Others sense His presence in their lover's eyes, in the face of their first born, or in their mother's embrace.

Some hear the voice of God in quiet moments—in the warm glow of doing good for others, in the awe that comes from contemplating the intricate beauty of the natural world, in the serene contentment of knowing that, however arduous, we have done our duty.

Given my penchant to overintellectualize, I believe I can perceive God and discern His purpose in history, especially in the saga of this century, which has been both remarkable and awful—truly one of miracles.

How often in this age has humanity gone to the brink, only to be seemingly yanked back by the hand of God like a parent restraining a toddler who wanders toward a busy intersection?

It's true—religion can lead to fanaticism. So can secular creeds; witness the genocidal furies of communism, fascism, and the feral nationalism at work in the Balkans.

Faith can also prompt amazing acts of charity, kindness, and sacrifice and, in more mundane cases, lead to ordinary, decent living. Mother Teresa believes God talks to her. So do the Salvation Army officers who, living on a pittance themselves, feed the hungry and shelter the homeless.

So too did the four chaplains of World War II fame. When their troop transport, the USS *Dorchester*, was torpedoed in February 1943, a priest, a rabbi, and two ministers gave away their life jackets and were last seen standing on deck with their arms linked. Whose words did they hear as the waves lapped at their feet?

*Hark, the herald angels sing.*

*Hear, O Israel.*

In every season, God speaks to us. Some who think the Almighty talks to them hear only the echoes of their own tormented psyches. Others attend His voice with wonder and humility.

# chapter four

# THE FAMILY UNDER FIRE

## Astrology, Phrenology, and Sex Education

I'm often asked the mostly rhetorical question: "Mr. Feder, do you believe in sex education?" The inquiry usually is made with the same smug self-assurance and contemptuous disregard of opposing views that typified the super-patriot of a generation ago who confronted antiwar protesters with the challenge: Do you love your country?

Do I believe in sex education? Define your terms.

If by sex education you mean instructing students in the mechanics of human reproduction (what goes where, why, and the potential consequences) and providing information on disease prevention, the answer most assuredly is yes.

However, this is not the reality of sex education as it is committed in the public schools. Human reproduction and prophylaxis could be taught in a few hours of class time. Why then the need for semester-long courses—a curriculum frequently stretching over many years?

Answer: It takes time to socialize, to indoctrinate, to alter values. That is the real objective of sex education, not preventing teen pregnancies and certainly not combating the spread of venereal disease.

Consider the following examples of values inculcation which are inflicted upon students and families in the name of contraception or health.

In Fairfax County, Virginia, students are subjected to a twenty-nine-minute filmstrip titled *What If I'm Gay?* which proceeds from the wholly unscientific assumption that homosexuality is genetically determined.

In Atlanta, Georgia, teachers are told to refer to married couples as "partners," rather than "husband and wife," so as not to offend what are designated alternative families.

Children are instructed that only 4.6 percent of the population is "exclusively heterosexual or exclusively homosexual," that the overwhelming majority of Americans in fact are bisexual—a nation of Madonnas, if you will.

In New York City, former Chancellor of Schools Joseph Fernandez distributed over three hundred thousand copies of a booklet informing students of their "right to have sex." One wonders—Is teen copulation a constitutional right? Does it derive from natural law? Who is to bear the cost of the exercise of this inalienable right by liberated thirteen-year-olds?

*Learning About Sex*, a cutting-edge curriculum used across the country, helpfully advises: "Sadomasochism may be very acceptable and safe for sexual partners who know each other's needs."

Another course plan *(I Deserve Love)* contains a series of affirmations endorsing promiscuity, such as: "My lovers now approve of each other." "God approves of my sex life." "Christ intended for me to have abundance." The Gospel according to Hugh Hefner.

Last fall, the Rutgers University Press produced *Learning About Family Life*, the first sex-ed curricula specifically geared toward (now get this) five- to eight-year-olds.

The dogma, currently used in seventy school districts, has lesson plans—with titles like *Uncle Seth has HIV* and *Learning About Our*

*Genital Parts*—that sound as if they were concocted by a lecherous Mister Rogers: "Can you say transsexual? Of course you can!"

In Swampscott, Massachussets, students as young as eleven brought home a dandy little booklet called *Risky Times,* which explained, in graphic detail, how to have anal and oral intercourse—something every eleven-year-old desperately wants to know.

The publication was provided courtesy of the pornographers in the town's school system.

In 1992, one Suzi Landolphi, a self-styled "hot-and-sexy" AIDS educator (who is to pedagogy what Louis Farrakhan is to race relations), brought her sideshow to the Chelmsford, Massachusetts, high school.

At a mandatory ninety-minute assembly, her sensitive approach to a delicate subject included dancing in the aisles with male students, using obscenities for male and female reproductive organs, stretching a condom over a student's head (presumably to prove that one size fits all), pulling students out of the audience at random, and humiliating them on stage and imparting such vital information as the observation that orgasm relieves tension and is "10 times stronger than valium."

For this raunchy routine, the Chelmsford school system paid her $1,000—itself an obscenity. In October 1995, the First U.S. Circuit Court of Appeals upheld the dismissal of a suit by parents and students contending that their civil rights had been violated.

If a teacher or administrator treated a student the way Landolphi behaved toward the individuals she accosted, they could be sued for sexual harassment.

But apparently the courts are willing to condone anything in the sacred name of sex education.

My friend, Boston College Professor Bill Kirkpatrick, in his book *Why Johnny Can't Tell Right from Wrong,* mentions a Bay State high school where tenth-graders were told to masturbate as a homework assignment.

Does this sound like biology, disease control, or lifestyle indoctrination?

The type of input our children desperately need in these matters is deliberately withheld from them because the truth isn't politically correct.

If objectivity and candor were the goals here, we would tell students, as often as possible, that there is only one reliable way to prevent the transmission of AIDS or any other venereal disease—premarital abstinence combined with fidelity in marriage.

However (the pleading of AIDS advocates notwithstanding), unless they engage in anal intercourse, use intravenous drugs, or have a partner who indulges in one of these perilous pursuits, their chances of contracting AIDS are so remote as to be infinitesimal.

We would also tell them that if they're concerned about contracting AIDS or another sexually transmitted disease, or pregnancy prevention, condoms offer little protection.

As a birth control device, condoms have a 15 percent to 18 percent failure rate.

To stop the spread of AIDS, they are even less reliable. A woman is fertile for only a few days each month—AIDS, gonorrhea, genital herpes, and syphilis can be contracted anytime. The HIV virus is 450 times smaller than a human sperm, thus better able to permeate the latex barrier.

Dr. Theresa Crenshaw of the Presidential AIDS Commission did a straw poll at a conference of more than eight hundred sexologists. Crenshaw asked the audience if they had available the partner of their dreams, and knew that person had a venereal disease, would they have sex relying on a condom for protection? Not one answered in the affirmative.

Giving kids condoms is like telling them to put a bullet in a revolver, spin the chamber, put the barrel to their head, and pull the trigger—latex roulette.

Finally, if we really cared about children, we would tell them that—viral contagions aside—adolescent sex is extremely hazardous, that it does physical damage (especially to young girls) as well as psychological harm. It also lessens their chances of having a successful marriage.

But this is not the sort of information you're likely to encounter in the average sex education course.

What is the ideology of sex education?

- That human intercourse is no more than an animal act or biological function, and needn't necessarily have emotional content. In the words of a Planned Parenthood pamphlet: "If, however, you have separated your sex and love needs then you could have a hundred partners and still be a perfect candidate for a good close relationship later on. So having multiple sex partners in itself doesn't mean anything." Believe in the Easter Bunny, believe the moon is made of green cheese, believe that Ed MacMahon and the Publishers Clearing House is at this very moment pulling up to your front door with $10 million for you, before you believe such toxic nonsense.

- That in sexual matters judgments must be avoided at all costs. That a monogamous relationship confined to marriage isn't necessarily better or worse than any of a dozen other forms of sexual expression.

- That premarital abstinence is unnatural, probably unhealthy, and unquestionably beyond the capacity of all but saints.

- That sexual conduct is biologically determined and no one can really control the erotic dictates of fate.

● That our exclusive concerns in addressing these matters must be public health, population control, and
otherwise making people feel as comfortable as possible with their "nature" and/or choices.

What are the consequences of this carnal circus? It's time that sex
education was called to an accounting.

Sex education is hardly a pioneering program, although it does
seem to get progressively more radical, bizarre, and absurd. In most
school systems, this dogma has been taught for the past three decades.

By any objective standard, it must be judged the most spectacular failure in the history of public education, even in light of the
system's other prominent defaults. Drs. Alexandra and Vernon
Mark noted in *Medical World News:* "The mounting evidence
indicting the leaders of the sexual revolution is impressive. They
promised joy, liberation, and good health. They've delivered misery, disease, and even death."

After thirty-plus years of explicit sex education, the results are
staggering. As former Education Secretary William Bennett notes,
since 1960, we've seen a "419 percent increase in illegitimate
births; a quadrupling in divorce rates; a tripling of the percentage
of children in single-parent homes; [and] more than a 200 percent
increase in the teenage suicide rate."

Since 1983, the rate of teenage syphilis has increased fifteen
times. More than half of all young Americans now have intercourse by age seventeen. Each year, over one million teenagers
become pregnant. Almost 40 percent of all twenty-year-old
women were pregnant at least once during their teenage years.

In the March 1989 issue of *Pediatrics Magazine,* Dr. James Stout
published an analysis of the five most recent and comprehensive
studies on the effects of sex education on teen sexuality.

Stout concluded: "The available evidence indicates that there
is little or no effect from school-based sex education on sexual

activity, contraception, or teenage pregnancy." Three strikes and you're out.

Dr. Stout may be too optimistic. A 1986 study by the Alan Guttmacher Institute, formerly associated with Planned Parenthood, found that fourteen-year-old girls who have had comprehensive sex education are 40 percent more likely to have sex than those who were deprived of such enlightenment. Another study disclosed that plying kids with contraceptives increases sexual activity by 50 percent.

Sex educators attribute each failure to not enough of a good thing. The curriculum isn't comprehensive enough, or explicit enough, or it doesn't begin early enough. We have yet to achieve sex education for preschoolers, but I'm confident it's coming.

If simple instruction in contraception doesn't work, distribute condoms. If that doesn't do the trick, how about in-school clinics that monitor and attempt to regulate students' sex lives? What about Norplant, the latest contraceptive panacea?

They will try anything and everything save admitting that their philosophy is bankrupt, morally as well as intellectually; that lifestyles have consequences (physical and psychological); that sex is the most emotion-charged activity two people can engage in; that it is not a plaything for "mature" fifteen-year-olds; that human conduct can be controlled only through moral education; that if human sexuality is treated like an animal function, that's exactly what we'll get—animal behavior; that sexuality can't be divorced from spirituality.

On March 29, 1993, readers of the *New York Times* encountered a front-page story on the middle-class city of Lakewood, California, where a group of high school boys who call themselves the Spur Posse were arrested for crimes ranging from rape to indecent assault on a ten-year-old.

It seems these juvenile delinquents had a competition going to see who could sleep with the most girls. Reportedly, the top scorer was up to seventy. Their conquests were exploited for a few evenings, then discarded like used tissue paper. Some of the girls said they were physically coerced or intimidated.

You may wonder what it takes to produce such monsters. One of the students arrested, but not charged, seventeen-year-old Eric Richardson, made the following true confession about the guidance he had received from concerned educators: "They pass out condoms, teach sex education, and pregnancy-this and pregnancy-that. But they don't teach us any rules." That about sums it up.

There are glimmers of hope on the horizon. Parents are up in arms, organizing, and not about to take it any more. In 1993, something extraordinary happened in New York City. The citywide board of education voted not to renew the contract of controversial chancellor Joe Fernandez, whose coat-of-arms should be condoms crossed above a copy of *Heather Has Two Mommies*.

The man who instituted one of the first condom distribution programs in the nation, who pushed lifestyle brainwashing in the guise of multiculturalism, and who tried to intimidate locally elected school committees, was ousted by a parents' coalition. If this could happen in New York, liberalism's hometown, is anything impossible?

A month later, the New Jersey State Assembly voted, fifty-four to seven, to require that all sex education courses in the state stress abstinence as "the only completely reliable means" of preventing sexually transmitted diseases, including AIDS.

As they used to say when I was in college back in the sixties, you don't have to be a weatherman to see which way the wind is blowing.

Make no mistake, the sex-ed lobby is powerful and implacable. It has the public school establishment (including the teachers unions), the media, the foundations, and a large part of the judiciary in its pocket. All we have are the numbers, old-fashioned common sense (which increasingly is a most uncommon commodity), and the truth.

This is a fight we can win. This is a fight we must win.

If we do our job well, in years to come, what currently goes under the guise of sex education will be considered as scientific and useful as astrology, phrenology, and tea-leaf reading.

## Family Values: Where to Begin
*January 19, 1995*

H ere we go again. The Reverend Andrew Greeley, best-selling author of ecclesiastical bodice-rippers, is the latest to lecture family activists on why they must cease carrying on about homosexuality and concentrate on divorce instead.

"The family-values rhetoric we've been hearing lately reeks of self-righteous hypocrisy," the liberal priest declares. "Most of it involves imposing values on other people." Shocking!

If activists were serious about saving the family, they would stop obsessing about gays, abortion, pornography, and premarital sex, and focus on the real threat to family stability, Greeley declares.

His dictum follows similar instruction by Jonathan Rauch in the *Wall Street Journal* and the Cato Institute's David Boaz in the *New York Times*.

Greeley raises the level of invective by suggesting that the family movement neglects divorce reform because its male leaders are all planning to ditch their wives and children at some unspecified date—presumably when they meet an evangelical temptress at a Bible conference.

The charge that the family movement doesn't care about divorce is a pure canard. Other than a handful of academics, for the past decade family activists were practically the only ones talking about the devastation of family dissolution.

Phyllis Schlafly, foremother of social conservatism, lobbied against a no-fault divorce bill when it was before the Illinois legislature in the 1970s. A monograph by the Family Research Council, the movement's premier think tank, blames divorce on demand for "millions of abandoned spouses, fatherless children, and the resulting harvest of loneliness, lovelessness, and cynicism."

A Colorado-based group called Promise Keepers holds football stadium rallies where men pray for husbands to keep their commitments to their wives, families, and God. The pro-family movement isn't doing enough on divorce? Compared with whom?

How does Greeley intend to reform divorce laws without imposing his values on others? Forcing fathers to pay more support, instituting cooling-off periods, and abolishing no-fault divorce all are based on value judgments.

Given the acknowledged impact of divorce, why the movement's emphasis on gay rights? Because it's easier to stop a revolution in progress than it is to launch a counterrevolution. Divorce on demand is enshrined in the legal system of every state. As yet, only a handful have gay rights laws.

No one is marching with banners proclaiming the merits of divorce. No one is suggesting that schoolchildren be indoctrinated in the positive aspects of family breakup.

The homoerotic movement seeks abolition of age-of-consent laws, acceptance of gay marriage and adoption, and offers homosexuals as role models (in the Boy Scouts, for instance). Should family forces roll over on these demands as well?

Gay rights and easy divorce are based on the same egoistic perspective—that society matters less than individual whims, and all forms of sexual expression, from serial marriage to sodomy, are equally valid.

In their article in *Guide* magazine, homosexual authors Marshall Kirk and Erastes Pill acknowledge the interconnectedness of the two issues and the common morality opposing both.

"We can undermine the moral authority of homophobic churches by portraying them as antiquated backwaters, badly out of step with the times and with the findings of psychology," the authors write. "Such an unholy alliance [science and public opinion] has worked well against the church before, on such topics as divorce and abortion."

The homosexual threat to the family is more subtle than that posed by divorce. The danger is not that millions of young heterosexuals will go gay if homosexuality is sanctioned (though the society that condones it invariably gets more of it). But once this particular vice is accepted, no other can rationally be rejected.

A society that normalizes homosexuality will find it impossible to hold the line against adultery and heterosexual adolescent experimentation, which—by contrast—seem quite mild and inoffensive.

The foundation of the family is exclusivity, the principle that sex confined to marriage alone is legitimate. The acceptance of competing models (cohabitation, multiple marriage, homosexual liaisons) undermines the only functional unit.

Divorcing sexuality from morality promotes both family dissolution and gay liberation. Both are legitimate concerns of family advocates.

## Don't Hit Parents for Kids' Misdeeds
*June 12, 1995*

You're traveling through space and time. Look, up ahead, there's a signpost. Hitler's Reich? Castro's Cuba? No, it's Silverton, Oregon, the town that punishes parents for adolescent misconduct.

Parents of delinquents can be fined up to $1,000 or ordered to attend parenting classes. Citations have been issued to families whose children were caught shoplifting, drinking, smoking cigarettes, or in possession of marijuana. More than eighty communities have expressed an interest in following the town's thumbscrews example.

The danger in the Silverton approach lies in its broad appeal.

Some conservatives will fall panting into the arms of anything that looks like law and order. For liberals, the prospect of state intervention in the family causes an immediate state of arousal.

Writing on the Silverton ordinance, conservative legal analyst Bruce Fein casually observed that "a parent's influence over child behavior is ordinarily decisive." Can we get the coordinates of his home planet? Surely, Fein cannot be a resident of 1990s America.

Most parents try to raise decent children, only to be frustrated at every turn by a society intent on undercutting their authority and undermining their values.

The typical family does its best to instill virtue—parents talk about right and wrong, punish when punishment is necessary, set reasonable limits, and try to keep kids away from bad companions.

Despite their best efforts, children will rebel. One day, a kid from a good home is picked up for vandalism or drugs. On top of parental heartache, should we add fines and social stigma? Is redemption to be found in a childless expert lecturing on parenting techniques?

Raising children today is like running an obstacle course full of sharpened stakes and careening boulders (Indiana Dad in the Temple of Pop Culture).

Desperate parents are driven to extremes to save their kids from the streets. Take the Vietnamese immigrant in Worcester, Massachusetts, who chained his thirteen-year-old son to the bedroom floor to keep the child away from a gang.

"What is a parent's real authority over a child?" asks Hunter Hurst of the National Center for Juvenile Justice. "We've been focusing on enfranchising youth—to choose who to live with, whether to go to drug treatment, whether to have abortions. As those rights progressed, the authority of parents eroded."

When it comes to influence, families struggle to be heard above the cultural din.

Hollywood works its magic to convince your children that you are a malicious idiot—a control freak who gets his kicks out of making their lives miserable.

Simultaneously, it projects the seductive notion that people should live primarily for themselves, that sex is always good, that violence is often the answer to an intolerable situation. Families are badly outmatched. How can Ward and June Cleaver possibly compete with Brad Pitt and Nicole Kidman?

Public schools indoctrinate in the name of ethics education, values clarification, or self-esteem training. The corrosive message is the same: Right and wrong are subjective. Feeling good about yourself is more important than doing good. One grade school classroom, mentioned in a news story, had posted a picture of applauding hands with the caption: "We applaud ourselves."

The victims of this pedagogy are accustomed to thinking of themselves first, to rationalizing selfishness—habits that do not enhance self-control and consideration of others.

The justice system directly assaults parental discipline. Last month, a Canadian court acquitted an American couple on charges of child abuse. The father had spanked his daughter after she slammed the car door on her brother's fingers. Despite the absence of injury to the girl and the obvious reasonableness of the punishment, Canadian authorities insisted on prosecuting the man.

In 1994 a Georgia mother was arrested for slapping her nine-year-old son after he sassed her in a store. In a few years—when the brat matures to teenage thug—the lady will probably be hauled into court and branded a parental failure.

The organization Of The People has a better idea. The Virginia-based group is pushing parental-rights amendments to state constitutions—measures that would give families more control of their children's education, ensuring that the values taught in school don't conflict with those imparted at home.

Empowering parents makes more sense than punishing them for circumstances beyond their control.

## License Parents? What If We Flunk?
*October 13, 1994*

J ack C. Westman, you are one scary dude. A professor of psychiatry at the University of Wisconsin, Westman would be Dr.
Kevorkian for the American family if his prescription for licensing
parents is adopted.

In his new book, *Licensing Parents: Can We Prevent Child Abuse
and Neglect?*, Westman declares what others in the child abuse
industry have only intimated: Parenthood is a privilege, not a
right.

After citing the usual inflated statistics of childhood trauma,
Westman bemoans the fact that today any man and woman can
procreate without demonstrating the "minimal competence"
needed to get a driver's license.

Aside: Why do liberals assume that state certification is a quality control? Over forty thousand highway fatalities and several
million collisions a year demonstrate government's abject failure
to weed out automotive incompetents and motorized maniacs.

Back to Westman's pernicious proposal, implementation of
which "won't compromise the right of each woman and man to
conceive and each woman to give birth," he assures us.

That assurance is contradicted several chapters later when
basic qualifications for parenting are promulgated. These include
an age requirement and a promise to support and care for the
child.

"The third, possibly optional [note how casually this is slipped
in], criterion would be completion of a parenting course or its
equivalent." Here, presumably stupid middle-class parents would
be disabused of their prejudices and indoctrinated in the latest
parenting techniques of academic theorists.

The license could be revoked at any time, not in a criminal but
a civil proceeding. Instead of the state being compelled to prove

abuse or neglect, families would be required to demonstrate a threshold level of "parental fitness."

Just how insidiously this might work can be seen in the Kivi case. Lynn Kivi is a Georgia mother who was arrested after a store clerk reported that she had slapped her bratty nine-year-old in the face. The child confessed he had it coming. Other than a momentary sting, there were no ill effects.

Still, after admitting that she struck her son, the thirty-five-year-old woman was arrested, handcuffed, and charged with a felony (cruelty to children) that could have resulted in a twenty-year prison term. On realizing the absurdity of the situation, the authorities dropped all charges.

Under Westman's parent licensing law, the state would be relieved of the burden of proof beyond a reasonable doubt. After creating a suspicion in the minds of administrators, Kivi would be compelled to demonstrate parental competence.

Her children could be seized and farmed out to foster care. Then again, her family might be subjected to such modest intervention as home visitation—regular supervision by teams of officious social workers over months or years.

Having been bombarded with tales of all-too-real tragedies, the public thinks it knows what the experts mean by "abuse."

For these innocents, Dana Mack's article—"Are Parents Bad for Children?"—in the March 1994 issue of *Commentary* is required reading. Mack points to the ever-expanding definitions of *abuse* and *neglect* in books like *Toxic Parents* and *When Parents Love Too Much.*

Besides life-threatening beatings, according to the experts, child abuse can include: spankings, too many breakfasts at McDonald's, restricting TV viewing, constant scolding, withholding affection, and too much affection (thought to foster dependence).

As for physical punishment as mild as a swat on the behind,

James Garbarino, of the Erickson Institute for Advanced Study in Child Development, insists: "Assault is what it is. Let's not call it discipline." Perhaps Garbarino will be one of the authorities called on to devise the criteria for parental licensing.

Professionals believe most families are sick and in urgent need of therapy. Mack quotes an article in a New York parents' magazine that advises: "If we live in America in 1992, we are more than likely the product of a dysfunctional family system, carrying our pain into our new family."

Interventionists have some powerful allies in the Clinton administration. Attorney General Janet Reno—described by her hometown newspaper as "part crime fighter, part social worker"—says it's up to the federal government to make sure families are "taught parenting skills."

Westman's scheme will find a receptive audience among the legion of social planners, child-protection bureaucrats, and politicians eager to mount a final assault on the ultimate bastion of freedom. G. K. Chesterton observed that the family is "the only check on the state that is bound to renew itself as eternally as the state, and more naturally than the state."

Parent licensing is a mandate for government to regulate, manipulate, and ultimately eradicate our best hope for preserving decency and liberty.

## Domestic Violence Distortions Abound
*July 14, 1994*

B esides preempting soap operas with his personal drama, O. J. Simpson has become the spouse-abuse poster child.

The Cause of the Month Club is having a grand time. Since the case began, domestic violence has been a cover story in all three national news magazines. Health and Human Services Secretary

Donna Shalala—truly, an original thinker—has pronounced wife-battering an "unacknowledged epidemic."

Hardly unacknowledged. The media are in the midst of moral-izing frenzy. The *New York Times* confides that spouse abuse is "an all-too-common crime" that constitutes "the most serious health threat to American women."

It has become an article of faith that four million women are battered in this nation each year.

Advocates would have us believe that (1) battering is pervasive (the coalition claims over 50 percent of wives will experience some form of violence from their husbands in the course of their mar-riage); (2) society is doing next to nothing about the crisis; and (3) wife abuse is another product of Patriarchy, Inc., violence being a tool of male dominance.

The numbers and analysis are equally fallacious. In her book *Who Stole Feminism?* Clark University philosophy professor Christina Hoff Sommers debunks the myth of the four million.

The statistic, Sommers explains, comes from the twenty-five-year research of social scientists Richard Gelles and Murray Straus. Feminists misrepresent these findings by neglecting to mention that the number includes pushing, shoving, and grab-bing, as well as serious acts of violence.

According to Gelles and Straus, "Women assault their partners at the same rate as men." The researchers add, however, that women are far more likely to sustain severe injuries.

A 1986 study, published in the *Journal of Marriage and Family*, found that women cause 54 percent of all severe family violence.

Feminists insist abusers are ordinary men—middle-class hus-bands, corporate executives, football fans. (Recall the Great Super Bowl Hoax of 1993, when the screamers alleged that abuse reports went up 40 percent on the day of the annual gridiron orgy—another manufactured statistic.)

Advocacy collides with reality in Sommers's book. She cites a study financed by the Ford Foundation and conducted by Andrew Klein, chief probation officer of the Quincy, Massachusetts, district court.

Klein told Sommers: "When Massachusetts computerized its civil restraining orders file in 1992, linking them with the state's criminal offender data base, it found that almost 80 percent of the first 8,500 male subjects of restraining orders had prior criminal records in the state."

In other words, the typical man who physically abuses his wife or girlfriend (a girlfriend is five times more likely to be assaulted than a wife) is a sociopath with a history of violence against men as well as women, drug or alcohol abuse, and other criminal conduct.

This is reinforced by an op-ed piece in the *Wall Street Journal* (July 6, 1993) by Shawn Sullivan. Coming from the Bedford-Stuyvesant section of Brooklyn, Sullivan—who says all five of her sisters have been victims of abuse—sees domestic violence as one more inner-city pathology, a byproduct of broken homes, youth raised without appropriate male role models, and a culture where ameliorating institutions (churches, schools, families) are severely weakened or nonexistent.

She mentions a visit to a therapy session for abusers where "three-quarters of the men were black, 15 percent Hispanic, and 10 percent white. Virtually all the men lived in urban neighborhoods."

More than race or ethnicity, socioeconomic conditions seem to be the determining factor. According to the Justice Department, someone in a white household with an annual income of less than $7,500 is five times as likely to be abused as a family member from a household with more than $50,000 in annual income.

Sullivan speaks of young men being taught by fathers ("if they have one") or male companions "to refer to women as 'ho's [whores] who need abuse; where physical violence is a common way of ending verbal disputes; and where women are mistrusted and detested."

She sees this attitude reflected in the most popular music, in rap songs with lyrics that call women "bitches" and ditties by groups like NWA that describe killing women after having sex with them.

Monogamy, faith, and family cohesion are the best insurance against domestic violence. A man from an intact family, who grew up seeing his mother and father in a loving relationship (instead of mom's latest boyfriend mistreating her), is unlikely to become an abuser. And it is just this type of traditional family that feminists have targeted for extinction.

## Restore Sense of Shame in Children
*November 3, 1994*

Thinking about the three Norwegian children who killed a class-mate, I recalled a question I was asked at a speech I gave.

In chilly Norway, cradle of social democracy, little Silje Marie Redergard, a five-year-old girl, was kicked, stoned, and left to freeze to death by three boys, ages five to six. Norway's prime min-ister blamed Silje's death on "free market" violence, specifically those combative capitalists, the Teenage Mutant Ninja Turtles.

Terrible as it is, the Scandinavian tragedy is child's play next to the everyday horrors of America's cities.

The Centers for Disease Control report that while the overall homicide rate remained fairly steady between 1985 and 1991, the murder rate for fifteen- to nineteen-year-olds jumped 154 percent.

The cultural elite has its usual unedifying explanations. On *CBS This Morning*, CDC Director Dr. David Satcher claimed, "Easy access to guns for teenagers is certainly a major factor."

Were guns less prevalent in our society in 1985? Did teens of the mid-1980s not know where to obtain firearms or how to use them? Satcher's analysis confuses cause and effect. A teenager who picks up a gun does so volitionally. The question Satcher ignores is why more teens are grabbing guns today.

Equally predictable was an article on kid killers by Alex Kotlowitz, author of *There Are No Children Here*, which appeared in *USA Today*.

Kotlowitz's solutions? Keep schools open evenings. Attract working people back to inner-city neighborhoods and "get involved yourself: We're all neighbors." Thank you, Mister Rogers.

Why are these kids so violent? Kotlowitz would say it's because they're desensitized by the violence they see around them. Because they're poor. Because they're not getting enough counseling.

But where did the violence that's traumatized kid killers originate? Poverty? Compared with the poor of the Depression, the poor today live like royalty. So why did the crime rate decline during the 1930s?

Depressed neighborhoods? Turn-of-the-century immigrant slums and the shantytowns that dotted the landscape of the South thirty years ago were positively pacific compared to the mean streets of contemporary urban America.

Our poverty—one which makes us particularly susceptible to the crime contagion—is a poverty of values. In this regard, I recall a question I once was asked by a college student at the end of a speech.

I said a moral reversion to the 1940s and 1950s would be an absolute blessing for this nation. In the Q-and-A period came the predictable challenge. Did I really believe people were more moral a generation ago, and if so, why?

That Americans generally were better behaved can't be denied. In the days of Dwight Eisenhower, we didn't need "The Club" to retain possession of our autos. Women could walk city streets at night in relative safety.

Human nature didn't change in four decades. People were just as covetous, lecherous, and violence-prone in 1954 as they are in 1994. Teens were every bit as rebellious and hormone-driven.

The difference? All of society's red lights have turned green. Once we taught sexual restraint through our schools and popular culture. Now we teach indulgence.

Once we taught personal responsibility. Now we teach that if you do something despicable, it's everyone's fault but your own. Were you an abused child? Do you lack an adequate education, a meaningful job, self-esteem?

The results of these lessons are glaringly apparent in the young, who are impressionable and haven't lived long enough to learn by experience. Adults mouth clichés. Children live them.

We tell them they're not responsible for their conduct, that the world owes them everything from material possessions to happiness, to trust their feelings, then wonder that they act on these beliefs with murderous consistency.

In this regard, the Jimmy Stewart movie, *Mr. Smith Goes To Washington,* contains a powerful message.

Jefferson Smith, an idealistic young senator, has been framed by Claude Rains's character (a Dan Rostenkowski prototype) because Smith has threatened to expose the latter's crooked schemes. Smith is filibustering to prevent his expulsion. He's been on his feet for days, pleading his innocence to an indifferent Senate. Finally, he collapses from exhaustion.

Rains leaps up and—after attempting suicide—confesses his guilt in an anguished voice: My cronies and I are thieves, he shouts, but "not that boy!"

Given the moral climate of the times, viewers found this credible. Corrupt as Rains's character was, he still had a sense of shame, instilled by his parents, church, teachers—someone.

That is what too many of our children lack. Give it to them now. Give it to them quickly, or they will seem positively angelic beside the monsters they breed.

## Childless Owe Huge Debt to Parents
*December 11, 1995*

**H**aving failed to torpedo the GOP's $500-per-child credit by damning it as a "tax cut for the rich" (actually, 89 percent of the savings would go to families with incomes below $75,000), the media have a new line of attack—it's so-o-o unfair to taxpayers who won't get it.

"Resentment simmers among those left out," an Associated Press story breathlessly discloses. "They include childless taxpayers, parents of children too old to qualify… and divorced parents without custody." Minions of the welfare state have a genius for fomenting envy and group animosity.

"I do not have a chance to claim any exemptions, being single," snivels Emerald Star of Hendersonville, Tennessee, who admits she's frankly "sick of 'families' receiving aid."

Poor Emerald has somehow missed the last thirty years of fiscal history, wherein singles saw their taxes (as a portion of income) remain fairly stable, while the bassinet set was taken to the IRS dry cleaners.

As if to cinch its case, AP reports that Star and other left-outs are in the majority. "Only 29 million would get the credit, in effect shifting some of the tax burden to the other 86 million households."

That's right; the families of *only* 51 million children would see their taxes lowered. The proposal would direct *only* an additional $22 billion annually to parents barely treading water.

The Heritage Foundation notes that for a family with two children, a $1,000 tax credit is *only* the equivalent of 19.6 months of children's clothing, 14.7 months of family health insurance, or three months of groceries.

Money to finance the credit comes from savings in the Republicans' seven-year budget plan, not—as AP would have it—by raising taxes on the childless.

Have Americans grown so selfish and shortsighted that they'd even reject a tax cut unless there's an immediate, perceptible benefit for them?

Should those who own neither stocks, bonds, nor real-estate investments spurn a reduction in the capital-gains tax? What's in it for them? Only the redirection of funds from tax shelters to more useful investments, with a corresponding rise in gross domestic product and job creation.

Similarly, the childless have a stake in the children someone else takes the pains to rear. The credit isn't the equivalent of giving a seventeen-year-old with three kids and no husband a monthly bonanza for having a fourth—a child who will likely grow up to aggravate our crime and drug problems. This the media consider compassionate.

The credit will help struggling middle-class families raise their children to productive, responsible, tax-paying adulthood.

Who does Star imagine will pay her Social Security benefits when she hits golden agedom?

The government Ponzi scheme is a pay-as-you-go system. Without young workers "contributing" to offset payments to retirees, every bingo parlor in the land would close its doors.

The Family Research Council's William Mattox has a blunt retort for the childless who gripe about family "subsidies": "We don't think it's right for you to live it up today on your own income and live it up tomorrow (when you retire) on the income of someone else's children."

Individuals who burden themselves, financially and emotionally, to raise children in today's culture are making an incalculable contribution to the future.

Years hence, their progeny will operate the industrial and commercial engines that drive our civilization. Some of them will police our streets, grow our food, write our books, and lead us. Those who serve in the armed forces will man the ramparts that defend our nation.

The U.S. Department of Agriculture estimates that it costs approximately $198,060 to raise a child from birth to age eighteen. And that doesn't include the cost of bringing it into the world ($4,700 for a normal delivery) or providing a college education (an estimated $100,000 at a public college, by 2013).

If economic life weren't hard enough for parents, their federal taxes have soared. In 1948, the Cleavers (a family of four) sent 3 percent of their income to that great sinkhole on the Potomac. Today, Washington reaps 24.5 percent of their earnings.

The difference is due in part to the shrinking value of personal and dependent exemptions. For a family with two children, these exclusions sheltered 42 percent of income in 1948 but only 11 percent by 1993.

If there are freeloaders here (besides "nonessential government workers" and the welfare leisure class), they're the DINKs (dual income, no kids), condo-dwelling singles, and other yuppie parasites.

They should thank whatever deity they worship that there are still folks with the sense of responsibility and fortitude to rear the next generation of workers.


## In Search of the Father Figure
*June 19, 1994*

In ten years, the child under eighteen who spends Father's Day with his father will be one of the fortunate few.

The disappearing dad is the gaping wound at the heart of our social trauma. Dr. Wade Horn, director of the National Fatherhood Initiative, observes: "On any given night, four out of every 10 children in America will be sleeping in a house in which their father does not live." More than 40 percent of these children won't see their fathers once a year.

A father's absence is the most accurate predictor of poverty and future failure. Children in fatherless homes are five times more likely to be poor. As teens, these children are more apt to do poorly in school, drop out, turn to crime, use drugs, and go on welfare than kids from intact families.

Society's response to the crisis of the fugitive father is to tell men to be mothers. The essence of fatherhood, so the theory goes, is to roll up one's sleeves, put on an apron, and get to work changing diapers and burping baby—Make Room for Mommy No. 2.

"Men haven't been socialized," wails Marie Wilson of the Ms. Foundation for Women—she means housebroken, trained to shoulder their fair share of the child rearing burden.

Dr. Benjamin Spock, the parenting expert who was never a parent himself, advises: "The father—any father—should be sharing with the mother the day-to-day care of their child from birth onward.... This is the natural way for the father to start the relationship, just as it is for the mother."

Two problems arise here. (1) Men won't do it. In the past twenty years, despite strenuous cultural signals, the amount of time husbands spend on household chores has increased only 6 percent. (2) Men can't do it as well as women. Mothers have a special connection with a newborn (a postpartum umbilical cord), an almost intuitive sense of what an infant needs, that men lack.

While we're trying to get fathers to do what they're ill-equipped for (and most won't do anyway), we completely ignore their natural and indispensable functions.

In family matters, society has come to embrace feminist doctrine. Feminists can't admit that fathers and mothers aren't interchangeable because that would imply that men and women have emotional/psychological differences. For the sisterhood, any challenge to psychic androgyny is heresy.

So we end up telling 1990s fathers: "Stay with your family because they need your income, because two pairs of eyes and hands are better than one. And, if you try very hard, someday you may make an adequate surrogate mother. Please understand, however, that you have no unique role to play." The average man is somewhat less than inspired by this message.

What do dads do? They love differently from mothers—and the difference is significant. David Blankenhorn, author of *Fatherless America,* says a father's affection is more qualified. The mother is worried about the child's survival; the father's focus is on success.

Blankenhorn writes: "Fathers, more than mothers, are haunted by the fear that their children will turn out to be bums, largely because a father understands that his child's character is, in some sense, a measure of his character as well."

The good father is constantly encouraging his children to strive, explore their world, overcome obstacles, and deal with frustrations.

Boys bereft of fathers frequently mature with low self-esteem. They turn to peers for validation and role models. They have difficulty controlling aggressive urges, absent an adult of their sex to show them how to handle dangerous emotions.

The inner city, with its father substitutes (the gang) and misogynistic males who grow up exploiting and/or brutalizing women (they've never known a man committed to one in a loving relationship), is a horror-show preview of a fatherless world.

Girls suffer, too. Without a father in the home, adolescent girls recklessly hunger for the affection missing in their lives. Among white families, daughters raised by their mothers alone are 164 percent more likely to bear a child out of wedlock.

Then there's the not-so-small matter of parental discipline. The average fifteen-year-old boy towers over his mother, not his father. For younger children, a masculine voice has authority that can make them jump. The old man is the heavy artillery rolled out as a last resort.

Just watching dad go to work every day to support his family, seeing him treat his wife lovingly and respectfully, provides a pow-erful example of masculine responsibility.

If we want men to stay with their children and fulfill their obli-gations, we'd better start recognizing and extolling their special contribution to the family. Men have to feel needed. They need assignments, jobs reserved for them alone. Mr. Mom just doesn't fill the bill.

# chapter five

# THE GAY NINETIES

## Bishop Sanctifies Self-Indulgence
*May 31, 1995*

With his announcement that God has given us "promiscuous genes," Anglican Bishop Richard Holloway, "Bishop Bonker" to the cheeky London tabloids, officiates at the marriage of liberal theology and pop science.

God made us horny ("gave us a built-in sex drive to go out and propagate as widely as possible"), the Edinburgh bishop proclaims.

The church shouldn't condemn affairs as wrong and sinful, but "accept that adultery is caused by our genetics and help people control their instincts so they can share loving, caring relationships," the prelate urges.

How people can overcome their instincts or change their genetic code, the bishop did not explain.

Are seminaries now giving degrees in microbiology along with doctorates of divinity? When and where was the Joey Buttafuoco gene isolated?

The bishop has fallen into a common error: the tendency to

attribute all human behavior to the mighty chromosome. If people act a certain way—in defiance of decency and enlightened self-interest—it must be in response to the irresistible pull of nature, modernists reason.

If Holloway had said that man is flawed, that it's easy for us to sin (especially sins of the flesh), he would have been on solid biblical ground.

But there's an unbridgeable chasm between inclination and biological mandate. The former can be overcome by discipline, reason, and prayer. The latter is destiny writ in undulating strands of DNA.

Joey's genes made him do it, rather than his inability to contain urges focused in his Calvin Kleins.

Holloway is traveling a well-trod road. For years, those who engage in homosexual acts have been telling us that this is the way they were born. Something made them homosexual, they insist, in the same way that others were born blue-eyed or left-handed.

A number of studies (most by gay researchers) have attempted to prove a biological basis for homosexuality. In pursuit of the elusive gay gene, the brains of cadavers are dissected and identical twins scrutinized.

There's even speculation about a genetic cause for violent behavior. A research project funded by the United States Department of Justice, no less, is currently studying the brain chemistry of prison inmates.

The purveyors of this modern phrenology—especially in the media—tend to be laymen whose knowledge of genetics is, shall we say, less than comprehensive.

While providing extensive coverage for the scientific equivalent of UFO sightings, the media generally ignore reputable refutations of attempts to link bad behavior to genetics.

Writing in the March 1993 issue of the *Archives of General Psychiatry*, Drs. William Byne and Bruce Parsons examine the claims of gay-gene hunters and conclude "there is no evidence at present to substantiate a biologic theory" of homosexuality.

"Misuses of genetics have found a home in psychology," says Doug Wahlsten, a genetics researcher at the University of Alberta, who suggests: "It would be better if we could stop this [linking genes and conduct] before it gets out of hand." Too late.

Steve Jones, a British geneticist and author of the book *Language of Genes,* calls Holloway's explanation for sexual appetite "bloody stupid."

"Human behavior has long since transcended the genetic code," Jones told *The Guardian,* adding: "For a churchman, whose only expertise is morals, to make callow and half-informed scientific judgments, beggars belief."

Holloway's revelation is a handy explanation for those confounded by the sexual revolution. Divorce, out-of-wedlock births, and sexually transmitted disease on the rise?—blame the great bio-engineer in the sky, who gave us our "promiscuous" nature.

But if DNA is destiny, why was the divorce rate so much lower thirty years ago? Did our genetic code change in the interim, or did we begin making bad choices?

Why is the illegitimacy rate much higher in the inner cities than the suburbs? Do minorities have promiscuous genes that suburbanites lack, or do the latter have a social infrastructure largely demolished in poorer neighborhoods?

If the mainline churches hadn't abandoned the biblical worldview (switched from salvation to social action), Bishop Holloway wouldn't be compelled to resort to pseudoscience to explain why lust is so powerful and prevalent an emotion.

In the nineteenth century, the Church of England was described as the Tory Party at prayer. Today it's trendy theology pronouncing a sly benediction over self-indulgence.

## Morality Counts, Scout's Honor
*October 2, 1995*

"**O**n my honor I will do my best to promote sexual diversity… to keep myself physically strong, mentally awake, and politically correct."

If gay activists have their way, that could become the revised Boy Scout oath. With a compulsive need for affirmation, militants have targeted a national symbol of moral rectitude.

A single member of the Chicago Human Rights Commission recently found the Scouts in violation of the city's antidiscrimination ordinance for refusing to hire a homosexual for an office position. The Boy Scouts of America has appealed the ruling to the full commission.

"There is nothing associated with the hiring of an openly gay man which would require the Scouts to alter anything other than its discriminatory policy," hearing officer Jeffrey Taren blithely proclaimed. Nothing need be changed—other than its fundamental character ("duty to God" and a commitment to be "morally straight," among other trifles).

Harvey Grossman, an ACLU official, gloated over the potential impact of the ruling, noting that 130 cities and 9 states have human-rights codes that include sexual orientation. The Scouts could come under fire in each.

Activists of various stripes want to remake the organization in their image. There are two suits against the Scouts pending in the California Supreme Court. One challenges its policy on homosexuality, the other—brought by atheists—objects to the requirement that Scouts profess a belief in God. Internationalists, who could take issue with the oath's allegiance to country, have yet to be heard from.

Separate appellate courts in the state have ruled that the Boy Scouts (1) most assuredly are and (2) clearly are not a public accommodation for civil-rights purposes. The inherent contradiction aside, only a tortuous reasoning process could equate a Motel 6 with a voluntary organization whose animating purpose is the inculcation of values.

Atheists and homosexuals are free to organize their own youth groups to expound their values. But of course, neither can create, they can only destroy what God-fearing folk have arduously built over decades.

And demolish they will. Few parents will entrust impressionable juveniles to a social organization in which they could be supervised by flagrant homosexuals.

In the schizophrenic universe of gay politics, there's both a compulsive need for the perceived legitimacy that comes from affiliation with respected organizations and an in-your-face drive to reject normalcy.

Writing in the January 31 *Village Voice*, gay author Michael Warner sees something fundamental in the swing back to unprotected sex among homosexuals. "The appeal of queer sex, for many, lies in its ability to violate the responsibilizing frames of good, right-thinking people."

One reason AIDS education fails, Warner muses, is because "most efforts to encourage us to take care of ourselves through safer sex also invite us to pretend that our only desire is to be good and proper."

But, quaint as it may seem to some, that is precisely the function of the Boy Scouts—to promote decency and propriety. It's in its oath; it's in its manual; it is evident throughout its eighty-five-year history. It would be nothing short of criminal to compel the group to condone those who flout its ethos.

Eventually, challenges to the Boy Scouts will be heard by the United States Supreme Court, where—it is hoped—they will encounter the cool, bracing logic of the court's reasoning in the South Boston St. Patrick's Day Parade case (decided last June), where a unanimous bench ruled that organizers of the annual Gaelic festivities could exclude a homosexual contingent.

Despite its use of city streets, the parade isn't a public accommodation, the justices held, but a "form of expression with which government may not interfere." Justice David Souter, no friend of traditional values, explained, "One important manifestation of the principle of free speech is that one who chooses to speak may also decide what not to say."

In other words, organizers had every right to rebuff the message of homosexual marchers ("that people of their sexual orientation have as much claim to unqualified social acceptance as heterosexuals"). If a parade is a form of expression, how much more so an organization that exists to advance an ethical perspective?

That code has served the Scouts and their families well for most of this century. In an age of drugs, gang violence, and social disintegration, the 4.2 million boys who participate in Scouting need it more than ever—but they need it with its principles intact, unsullied, and uncompromised.

## Abby Turns PC on Homosexuality
*November 11, 1993*

D ear Abby may be the ultimate cultural chameleon, blending perfectly with the background of her times. If the culture says the naked emperor is well dressed, Abby admires his elegant ensemble.

Her response to a plea from a homosexual who's anything but gay proved once again that she is a slave to social fashion.

"I'll get right to the point," Unhappy writes. "I am gay, but I don't like being gay.... Abby, adjusting to homosexuality is fine for those who have accepted their homosexuality, but I have not. I know I'd be happier straight. Please help me."

Abby's support consists of skepticism and platitudes.

"Did you choose to be homosexual? If so, you could choose to be straight. But if you have always had erotic feelings for men instead of women, then face it, you are a homosexual.... To thine own self be true. Only then will you find true happiness." Sounds like a Hallmark card from ACT-UP.

The culture decrees that homosexuality is biologic, inborn, immutable. To this, Abby vigorously assents. From the popular media, she has ingested whole the orientation argument.

Three media-touted studies have asserted a genetic basis for homosexuality. All were flawed. All were the work of homosexual researchers eager to prove a point.

The latest, released in July, is the work of Dr. Dean Hamer, a geneticist with the National Institutes of Health. Hamer claims to have found the same genetic markers on the X chromosome of thirty-one of forty pairs of homosexual brothers. "Gay gene," the headlines screamed.

A few problems arise: (1) The sampling was too small. (2) What about the nine sets of gay brothers who didn't have the markers? (3) There was no control group, no way of knowing if heterosexuals also have the markers.

The Hamer study replicated errors in earlier efforts. Neurobiologist Simon LeVay examined the brains of forty-one cadavers. He studied a tiny area of the hypothalamus (INAH-3) believed to influence sexual behavior. Of nineteen homosexuals in the group, sixteen had a smaller than normal INAH-3. Ergo: Little INAH-3 equals homosexual.

Reports on the amazing breakthrough failed to note that this region is smaller than a grain of sand and has no distinct boundaries, making measurements imprecise. Based on medical records, LeVay assumed that twenty-two of his subjects were heterosexual, though all had died of AIDS.

Then there was the Bailey-Pillard study of homosexuals and

their brothers, which found that if one of a pair of identical twins was homosexual, there was a 52 percent chance the other would be. But twins tend to be raised in very similar environments. Is it nature or nurture?

After a thorough examination of the two earlier studies, Drs. William Byne and Bruce Parsons of Columbia University conclude: "There is no evidence at present to substantiate a biologic theory" of homosexuality.

If you've always been attracted to members of your sex, you're a homosexual, now and forevermore, writes Abby. "Most male homosexuals will tell you that their first erotic feelings were for men," says Dr. Joseph Nicolosi, whose knowledge comes not from the popular press but personal experience.

Nicolosi, a clinical psychologist who has treated more than 250 homosexuals in fifteen years of practice, believes homosexuality is "a treatable developmental disorder."

Though his views are disdained by a profession in the throes of political correctness, Nicolosi says the condition arises primarily from a son's failure to identify with his father. If the father is absent, emotionally detached, weak, or brutal, the son responds defensively by withdrawing.

During adolescence, this failure to bond has consequences. "Men remain mysterious, and the young man is sexually attracted to yet fearful of men—bound into a same-sex ambivalence. This same-sex ambivalence has much to do with the characteristic unfaithfulness in male homosexual relationships."

Nicolosi's treatment consists of getting clients to understand the origins of their erotic feelings and includes fostering nonsexual intimacy and trust among men.

Homosexual activists respond that gays who seek treatment have internalized homophobia. Those who claim to be cured have repressed their natures and are living a lie, they charge. Nicolosi replies that his patients "achieve enlightenment. People who go through therapy successfully experience a transformation in their feelings, not a suppression."

Nicolosi's judgment is supported by the testimony of thousands of former homosexuals. One, Alan Medinger, who now heads an outreach ministry, led a homosexual life for seventeen years.

Abby rhetorically asks her reader if he chose to be homosexual. Medinger observes that no one "chooses" to be homosexual—but (and this is crucial) with help, one can choose not to be.

## Glamour-izing the Gay Lifestyle
*December 21, 1994*

O ur troops will soon be entrenched on Capitol Hill. But the culture is still enemy territory. Its fortifications even stud the pages of airhead fashion magazines.

In the November issue of *Glamour*—nestled among sex surveys and articles like "The Secret Life of Models"—is an editorial that could have been lifted from the *Advocate*, or any other gay publication.

*Glamour* (circulation: 2,186,214) offers food for thought for those with modest appetites. As a lady in readers' services explained to me, over the past decade the magazine has become quite "socially conscious."

Its editorial is a sneering attack on family advocates. In the gay-rights debate, the opposition's rallying cry is no special rights, *Glamour* discloses, "yet you won't hear anyone explain what these special rights are, because they don't exist."

Ah, but they do.

Among them is the right to forced association—to compel others to employ you or rent to you on the basis of your sexual habits. Homosexuals are the only "sexual minority" for whom such privileges are claimed.

If someone shows up at your three-family house and announces: "Hi, I'm a promiscuous heterosexual/cross-dresser/pedophile/ sadomasochist," you can ever so gently close the door in his face.

If, however, he says: "Hi, I'm a homosexual," in cities and states with gay-rights laws, reject him—for any reason—at your peril.

*Glamour* portrays family activists as purveyors of "bogus statistics" and bigots who paint a distorted picture of gays as perverts and pedophiles.

It's almost funny, listening to the gay-OK crowd accuse the opposition of manipulating statistics, when they are guilty of hyping the biggest lie in the entire debate—the myth that 10 percent of the adult population is homosexual—for a decade and more.

Despite the refutation of this Kinsey-induced fantasy by the highly respected Alan Guttmacher Institute (whose 1993 report said only 1.1 percent of the population is exclusively homosexual), some in the movement cling to the discredited statistic.

On the pathology of the gay lifestyle, a soon-to-be-published study by Judith Reisman, Ph.D., should create quite a stir.

Reisman compared ten thousand personal ads that ran from 1988 to 1992 in the *Washingtonian* (a mainstream magazine with a mostly straight readership) and the *Advocate* (a gay periodical), which have nearly identical reader age and economic demographics.

She found 98 percent of *Advocate* advertisers were seeking casual sex. Among the *Washingtonian* personals, 87 percent wanted long-term fidelity.

Commonly used abbreviations in the *Washingtonian* included "S" for single, "J" for Jewish, and "NS" for nonsmoking. In the *Advocate*, ISOs (in search of) typically were looking for "B/D" (bondage and discipline) and "S/M" (sadomasochism), or presented themselves as "daddies" in search of "sons."

On the subject of pedophilia, *Glamour* deploys the oft-cited figure that a child is a hundred times more likely to be molested by a heterosexual than a homosexual. Leaving aside the fact that there are fifty to one hundred times more heterosexuals in the adult population, this simply isn't true.

In a letter to the *New York Times* (February 28, 1993) Lynn Hecht Schafran, director of the National Judicial Education Program for the National Organization for Women's Legal Defense Fund—a group not widely renowned for homophobia—cites a study by an Emory University researcher.

Schafran notes that of 377 nonincestuous pedophiles, the study found 224 men who targeted 4,435 girls and 153 men who acknowledged assaulting 22,981 boys. That's about 20 victims per heterosexual pedophile and 150 per homosexual abuser.

How does the movement treat this disturbing phenomenon? A March 26, 1992, editorial in the homosexual San Francisco *Sentinel* trashed a lesbian reader who complained about the inclusion of the North American Man-Boy Love Association in gay-pride parades.

Calling the reader a "homo-homophobe," the publication blandly observed, "NAMBLA's position on sex is not unreasonable, just unpopular.... When a 14-year-old boy approaches a man for sex, it's because he wants sex with a man.... The love between men and boys is the foundation of homosexuality."

Perhaps *Glamour* could enlighten its fashion-conscious—but otherwise unconscious—readers by reprinting this as its next editorial on the subject. It might even shake a few out of their L'Oreal-induced stupor.

The culture will have to be retaken street by street, block by block, house by house.

## AIDS Activists Do a Disservice
*November 13, 1995*

What causes the spread of AIDS? I hope you're not one of those repressed reactionaries who believes the contagion is propagated by promiscuity, anonymous sex, or acts formerly designated unnatural.

An ad ("Does Homophobia Spread AIDS?") in the *New York Times* on November 6 claims the fault lies with—well, people like you and me. Why does "concern about AIDS mean attacking those actually living with the disease?" the screed by the Public Media Center rhetorically inquires.

"Irrational prejudices like homophobia have obstructed public health efforts to prevent the spread of AIDS," the center charges.

The ad ran in the lower right-hand corner of the *Times* op-ed page—liberalism's bulletin board, where elitists meet to spasmodically jerk their knees at each other. The libel is instructive only in demonstrating the paranoia and prejudices of AIDS activists.

If public health efforts to prevent the spread of AIDS are measured in dollars and cents, homophobes have been spectacularly ineffective in attempting to obstruct the same. AIDS is the platinum-plated, diamond-encrusted disease, which gets a wildly disproportionate share of federal funding.

In 1994, AIDS killed about 42,000 Americans. The same year, more than 730,000 died of heart disease and cancer claimed around 520,000.

Not counting entitlement spending on Medicare and Medicaid, under the president's proposed budget for the current fiscal year, Washington will allocate $1,134 per heart-disease death, $4,808 for every cancer victim, and $71,429 for each individual who died of AIDS last year. Homophobia is not among the factors driving AIDS policy.

AIDS is our first politicized disease—a tribute to the power of the homosexual lobby. How many activists against a killer like heart disease are out there beating their fists and feet on the floor over "inadequate funding" for their ailment?

At the Academy Awards ceremonies, celebrities don't wear

miniature insulin bottles to express solidarity with diabetics (even though, each year, diabetes kills more than AIDS). There are no elderly demonstrators lying down in front of traffic to protest the lack of a cure for Alzheimer's disease.

Activists are intent on safeguarding AIDS funding because much of it goes toward promoting the whole homosexual agenda. According to an April 6, 1994, article in the *Trentonian,* a $100,000 federal AIDS grant was used to sponsor a "drag-queens' ball" in Newark, New Jersey.

We homophobes reckon that AIDS is a lifestyle disease. By and large, you get it from doing certain things that everyone knows are highly hazardous. Trouble is, certain people just keep doing them anyway.

In a 1992 feature on gays, *Newsweek* profiled Wally Hansen, who works for a San Francisco gay newspaper and is HIV-positive. Hansen believes pushing condoms in the schools is crucial to stopping the spread of AIDS.

But, says *Newsweek,* personally, "Hansen is reckless," despite the risk of acquiring other strains of AIDS and giving his disease to partners. "I can only think positively," Wally explains. "I do anything I want. I feel like I'm doing more damage to myself by stressing my system out of worry."

Last December, the *City Paper,* a Washington, D.C., weekly, reported on the doings at an establishment called Men's Massage Parties (less than a mile from the White House) where more than a therapeutic rubdown is available. A journalist who checked it out saw group sex ("three-, four-, or more-some"), often unprotected.

The *Washington Blade,* a gay paper, urges its readers to practice "safer sex," while carrying display ads for these orgies. Since the publication clearly is not homophobic, it couldn't possibly be facilitating the spread of AIDS.

We know what works in combating a sexually transmitted disease—testing and contact tracing. Before penicillin, that's how syphilis was checked. The average AIDS activist will marry the girl next door before dropping his opposition to either approach.

In July, the U.S. Senate rejected an amendment to reauthorize the Ryan White Act, which would have required HIV testing for all mothers and newborns. True to form, AIDS activists opposed the amendment as an intolerable intrusion on privacy, never mind that children born with the virus won't get the care they need. For the AIDS lobby, mom's privacy trumps baby's health.

Here another dastardly effort of vile homophobes to spread AIDS through ignorance and prejudice was stopped dead in its tracks by heroic activists. Hurrah, hurrah.

## Gays in the Military: Clinton Plants a Land Mine
### July 22, 1993

In his strategic retreat on lifting the ban on homosexuals in the military, our gay-rights president has planted a number of land mines that, if not immediately defused, are destined to explode in the faces of defense advocates and family activists.

Forget the for-the-record whining of gay groups. Instead, heed the enthusiasm of U.S. Rep. Gerry Studds, (D–Mass.), one of three openly homosexual members of Congress. "I really have to hand it to him [Clinton], he's shed political blood on this issue," beamed the legislator whose lifestyle formerly included seducing a minor with liquor. "I really think it's important to keep a perspective here," the congressman cautioned his allies.

So let's put the proposal in focus. Military recruiters will no longer be able to inquire into applicants' sexual histories. On the one hand, homosexual conduct is still "incompatible" with military service. On the other, the services don't officially care how much of it a recruit engaged in before he enlisted, thus creating a Twilight Zone of privacy.

Homosexual conduct—consisting of erotic acts, public declarations of orientation, and same-sex marriages—is still proscribed. But merely frequenting a leather bar, reading a homosexual newspaper, or marching with the North American Man-Boy Love Association will be insufficient grounds for conjecture.

Even an open affirmation of homosexuality only creates a "rebuttable presumption" of conduct. Presumably, personnel will be permitted to speciously argue that this says nothing about behavior, that their homosexuality is purely theoretical.

The policy is erroneously designated "don't ask/don't tell." Turn-a-blind-eye/ignore-the-obvious would be a better description.

Investigations are actively discouraged. The charge by a service member that the guy in the next bunk is a homosexual isn't enough to cause an inquiry. Only officers above the rank of major can initiate the same, but are urged to "exercise sound discretion regarding when credible information exists to launch an investigation."

In other words, anything short of a serviceman screaming "I love Roger Clinton" on the parade ground, while the battalion passes in review, is safe.

As Elaine Donnelly of the Center for Military Readiness points out, "The policy's contradictory statements and vague definitions [will] make it relatively easy for attorneys for homosexual groups to achieve their objectives through the courts."

Lt. Col. William Gregor, formerly a professor of military science at the University of Michigan, demonstrates how the inherent inconsistencies will be employed to overturn the modified ban. "If a recruit is not asked about the 'private matter' of his homosexuality upon entry, his attorney would argue that since his sexual conduct prior to induction was not important to the military, his sexual behavior after induction ought not be important either."

The Lambda Legal Defense and Education Fund and ACLU are planning challenges to the new policy, preparing to exploit the opening Clinton has given them.

The courts will be their eager allies here. The day the new policy was announced, Colorado's Supreme Court delivered a fatal blow to the state's constitutional prohibition on gay-rights laws, enacted by voters last year. The court projected a right to sodomy into the state's constitution, which must be overcome by a "compelling state interest" for the anti–gay-rights measure to stand.

The president's most fantastic statement at Fort McNair, a measure of Willie's lubricity, was his thesis that there was no reason to believe that homosexuals "could not serve effectively and with distinction."

How naive of 96.9 percent of generals and admirals who— according to a survey undertaken by the House Republican Research Committee—agree that open homosexuals in the military are "prejudicial to good order and discipline."

What was the Army's surgeon general thinking of when he issued a detailed report, in April, on the health hazards of rescinding the ban? Gen. Alcide Lanoue observed this would compromise the "walking blood supply" and lead to the enlistment of individuals twenty-three times more likely to contract a venereal disease.

How about the homophobic 74 percent of enlisted personnel who favor keeping the prohibition exactly as it is or the 10 percent (two hundred thousand) who said they'd resign immediately if the ban is abolished?

According to the latest Associated Press poll, 58 percent of the American people think the president has broken his promises too often. To families with children, middle-class taxpayers, those who want to clean up the mess in Washington—sure. With homosexuals, he has kept faith. His advance disguised as a retreat will give them everything their hearts desire, if only they have the patience to wait.

# Gay Parenting, Little Experiments Will Suffer in Silence
*September 27, 1995*

R egarding his colleagues' support for gay adoption/custody, psychologist Joe Nicolosi observes: "One of the beautiful things about a democracy is that social scientists can ruin a generation, and then come back twenty years later with our objective measures to validate what common sense should have told us."

Social science is far from the only transgressor here. Last week, a juvenile court commissioner in Whatcom County, Washington, ordered a three-year-old boy placed with two male homosexuals as the first step toward adoption.

The child is the center of a raging controversy. His mother, who had placed him for adoption, changed her mind when she learned of the arrangement. "I don't want my child raised like that," says Megan Lucas. But that is precisely the way her son will be raised, if Washington State has its way.

In this matter courts are anything but consistent. Earlier this month, a Virginia judge took a child away from his mother and her lesbian lover, awarding custody to the maternal grandmother.

In a few states, when homosexuality is an aspect of divorce, courts invariably grant custody to the heterosexual parent. In others, it's a factor but by no means decisive. New York, New Jersey, Vermont, Minnesota, and California allow gay adoption, usually by the partner of a biological parent.

Psychologists have added their voices to the trendy chorus. The American Psychological Association complains that courts "often have assumed that... children are likely to be emotionally harmed, subject to molestation, impaired in gender role development or themselves homosexual. None of these assumptions is supported by extant research data."

There was a time when psychologists insisted there were no long-term effects of divorce on children. Then researchers like

Judith Wallerstein discovered that the children of divorce are far more likely to be withdrawn and afraid of commitment.

Twenty years ago, Jay Belsky, a Pennsylvania State University psychologist, was running around telling anyone who would listen that there was nothing wrong with putting infants in day care. Today, he's one of the most outspoken critics of collective child-rearing, contending that children placed in day care at an early age suffer from weak parental attachment and have emotional problems later in life.

When it comes to child welfare, the claims of social scientists must be viewed with extreme skepticism.

Most researchers, who are biased in favor of homosexuals, ignore their own data. Paul Cameron, Ph.D., of the Family Research Institute, has surveyed the admittedly scant findings of his profession on children raised in households with at least one homosexual.

In these studies, between 8 percent and 33 percent of adult respondents said they considered themselves homosexual or bisexual, far above the national norm of 1 percent to 2 percent of the adult male population.

How surprising is this? In almost every area, parental behavior has a profound, at times predominant, impact on children. The children of smokers frequently become smokers. Kids from abusive homes often become abusers. Children from broken homes are more likely to divorce. Only in the case of homosexuality are we asked to believe that what happens in the home is irrelevant to emotional development.

Jaki Edwards of Milpitas, California, who runs a support and recovery program for those coming out of the homosexual lifestyle and their families, has knowledge beyond questionnaires and graphs. From age ten to sixteen, she and a younger brother lived with their lesbian mother and a succession of her companions.

"I realize that homosexuals feel they can give a child love and support that even many straight families can't provide," Edwards admits. "But I've been there. I know the finger-pointing and the shame one carries.

"For years, you struggle with the thought that you might be a homosexual. People say 'like mother like daughter.' Most of us become promiscuous to prove we're straight."

The absence of role models presents it own problems. "How will a man raised by two men know how to relate to a woman? A woman brought up like this doesn't know how to emotionally connect with men. I had to struggle for years to believe a man could really love me."

How many lives will be broken, how many little experiments will suffer in silence (unobserved by omniscient researchers) before courts and social scientists learn you can't fool nature? Children were meant to be nurtured by a man and woman together. Absent that, at least they shouldn't be placed in a situation where a distorted version of human sexuality is presented as the norm, to satisfy the latest demands for equality.

# chapter six

# ABORTING THE AMERICAN DREAM

## Abortion in the Context of Western Values

In the wake of the Oklahoma City bombing, the worst terrorist incident in our history, we learned that many Americans on the right and left believe in conspiracies—the notion that shadowy, sinister forces are at work to deprive us of our liberty.

Though lamentable, this is completely understandable. We look around us at a disintegrating social order—an epidemic of violence (drive-by shootings, children who murder their parents, parents who kill their children), drug abuse, teen alcoholism, nudity on cable television, a divorce rate of 50 percent, an illegitimacy rate approaching 80 percent in the inner cities, and one and one-half million abortions a year in this country—and ask how it all came about.

It's easy to survey the social landscape and think: This did not happen accidentally. It is not all a coincidence but the work of a grand conspiracy. Powerful forces are deliberately trying to destroy our nation.

Those who fail to understand the impact of ideas (the ways in which they shape public policy and drive a culture) are particularly susceptible to such theories.

In reality, it isn't conspiracies but concepts that change the course of history. Ideas are the lever that turns the world. Certain doctrines promote the well-being of a society, others act like a cancer—consuming healthy tissue and leading to a lingering death. This is what we confront today.

The abortion debate (the most hotly contested values conflict of our time) is an integral part of a much wider struggle called the *culture war*. Met on a political battlefield are two opposing forces with irreconcilable worldviews.

The conflict has been going on for a very long time. If you were asked to name the individual most responsible for legalized abortion in America, you might say Supreme Court Justice Harry Blackmun or feminist theorist Betty Freidan or sexual visionary Hugh Hefner. But what about philosophers Jean Jacques Rousseau and Friedrich Nietzsche?

To the best of my knowledge, neither of them ever addressed the issue of abortion. But one hundred and two hundred years before *Roe v. Wade*, they set the stage for the moral revolution that made legalized abortion possible.

The other side understands the interconnectedness of ideas far better than we. Question: Do homosexuals have to worry about unplanned pregnancies? Silly question, right? But then what are all of those gay activists doing at pro–abortion demonstrations?

Answer: They know very well what's at stake. Abortion advocacy and gay rights share the same premises. Both are about breaking down societal restraints and advancing the concept of absolute autonomy in the sexual realm. Both want a Cole Porter society in which, in a moral sense, "anything goes." The two movements have a synergistic effect; they simultaneously enhance and advance each other.

I'd like to offer a grisly example of this interconnectedness of ideas: the Clinton administration. Bill Clinton's first executive act after his inauguration was to rescind those Reagan-Bush era presidential orders restricting federal funding of abortion. His second was to try to lift the ban on homosexuals in the military.

The media would have us believe the president is a power-driven pragmatist bereft of guiding principles. In reality, he is a child of the sixties who may at times trim his sails but whose ideological compass consistently points in one direction. Aptly did House Speaker Newt Gingrich call the president and first lady "counter-culture McGoverniks."

Who but Bill Clinton could have assembled a cabinet that includes Janet Reno (attorney general cum social worker), Donna Shalala (known as the queen of political correctness during her academic career), Mr. Industrial Policy—Robert Reich, and Warren Christopher, impresario of the New World Order?

Who but a flower child in jogging shorts could have gone from Surgeon General Joycelyn Elders—who wants to legalize drugs, give condoms to third-graders, promote gay adoption, and have public schools teach masturbation—to defeated Surgeon General-nominee Henry Foster, a part-time abortionist, safe-sex proselytizer, and Planned Parenthood activist?

Bill Clinton promotes gay rights for the same reason he supports public funding of abortion, for the same reason he tried to nationalize health care, for the same reason he wants to confiscate firearms.

All of these positions are linked by an underlying ethos, the rejection of the Judeo-Christian ethic for a secular/utopian worldview.

Western civilization is in critical condition, afflicted by a virulent contagion. The virus can't be understood by considering its symptoms in isolation but only by studying the origins of the ailment and its effects, both individually and in terms of their interaction.

Let us begin with a familiar argument, what is euphemistically termed the pro-choice position. Cut through the cliché-ridden verbiage and it's clear that this doctrine is based on two premises. First, that life is not God-given, hence expendable. Second, radical autonomy—the notion that a person's primary responsibility (a factor of such overriding magnitude that it dwarfs every other consideration) is to him- or herself, that the sole purpose of existence is to secure the individual's happiness, prosperity, and freedom of action.

The pro-abortion position is closely aligned with a panoply of political causes advanced by the left—that collection of liberals, Marxists, feminists, gay activists, environmentalists, New Agers, and other adherents of secular isms who are united by far more than divides them.

Consider some of these related issues, with the understanding that, in the final analysis, all issues are related.

Euthanasia is the abortion movement of the 1990s. Like its counterpart on the other end of the life continuum, it holds that people are disposable, for their own good or the accommodation of others. What is important, we are told, is not life per se, but a highly subjective "quality of life."

The practical applications of this fatal advocacy include living wills, judicial rulings that allow relatives to kill comatose patients by starvation or dehydration, and right-to-die legislation, which would legalize medically assisted suicide.

There are even those like Daniel Callahan, director of the prestigious Hastings Center, who maintain that beyond a certain age society should withhold life-extending care, regardless of the individual's wishes or physical condition. Had the Clintons' health care scheme been enacted, this might have become a reality all too soon.

Gay rights is a societal death-wish of a different sort. It disavows the ethical norms of Christianity and Judaism and seeks social sanction for a deadly perversion.

Proponents of homosexual rights boldly proclaim what other champions of the secularist ethic only intimate: that sensory indulgence is life's ultimate purpose, that religious injunctions, family stability, and the very survival of the human race all take a backseat to hedonism.

The effort to legitimize perversion and give homosexuals the status of an oppressed minority is gaining on every front.

It is affirmed by my colleagues in the media, who refer to the "gay community" as if they were speaking of a race or religion, instead of individuals whose group identity is defined exclusively by sexual practices condemned by thirty-three hundred years of Western morality.

It's celebrated by Hollywood, in movies like *Philadelphia* and the critically acclaimed *The Crying Game*.

It is propagated in the schools through sex education, AIDS education, and lifestyle advocacy.

It is afforded legal protection by court rulings affirming the "right" of open homosexuals to serve in the military and striking down democratic attempts to forestall gay-rights legislation, like Colorado's Proposition 2.

The secularist agenda includes other attacks on the family. This offensive comes in a number of familiar guises, among them: gender sameness (the dogma that the sexes are psychologically identical), state usurpation of the family's child-rearing function, efforts to eliminate the role of homemaker and force women into the workplace, and sexual liberation—the removal of societal sanctions against premarital sex, promiscuity, perversion, and infidelity.

The political enactment of this agenda includes subsidized day care, comparable-worth legislation, public-school indoctrination, no-fault divorce, and a welfare system that encourages family dissolution.

The foregoing may seem obvious. But the same insidious principles are also at work in areas seemingly far removed from social concerns. For instance, our criminal justice system is increasingly influenced by the following theories: that individuals aren't responsible for their actions, that personal conduct is dictated by genetics or environment, that the role of our courts and prisons is to reform rather than to punish criminals.

The deadly fruit of this dogma is the current atmosphere of permissiveness: judicial leniency, furloughs for killers, work release, and other aspects of a Club Med penal system.

A few years ago, a Massachusetts judge sentenced a young man who had raped a teenage girl to probation. If you come before me again, the judge sternly intoned, I'm going to "burn you." In other words, you have been a very bad boy. If you rape another sixteen-year-old, I shall be seriously annoyed.

With justice thus perverted, is it any wonder that our city streets have come to resemble jungle clearings?

The idea that people aren't responsible for their actions is carried over to the economic realm. Because the average person is inherently incapable of providing or caring for himself, we are told, government must assure his prosperity, protect him from his own improvidence, and dispose of the greater portion of his income to promote the common good.

The application of these doctrines includes confiscatory taxation, government spending approaching 40 percent of national income, the most minute regulation of our business affairs by hordes of officious bureaucrats, handouts for all classes of society and every sector of the economy, and programs designed to counter every ill, real or imagined.

Ideas do not exist in a vacuum. All of the theories I've touched on, and their political ramifications, derive from a very cohesive, well-integrated worldview.

There are essentially two philosophies competing for the hearts and minds of mankind. Each can be given any of a number of designations. For our purposes we'll refer to them as the secular (or neopagan) and the sacred (or supernatural) perspectives.

The metaphysical foundations of secularism are as follows:

1. God does not exist or—if He does—He is unknowable, uninvolved, completely detached from his creation.

2. Therefore, man is no longer imbued with holiness, sanctified

by having been made in His image. Humanity becomes merely another species of the animal kingdom, clever creatures to be sure (able to construct skyscrapers and compose symphonies) but animals nonetheless, which may be used and disposed of like any other denizen of field or forest.

3. Thus, morality is relative. Recall that in the Decalogue the statement "I am the Lord your God" precedes all of the other commandments. Laws against murder, rape, and theft have force only when premised on the understanding that they are immutable injunctions given mankind by its Maker. As the Declaration of Independence so eloquently puts it, man has inalienable rights because he is endowed with the same "by his Creator."

The flip side of this coin was expressed by the Russian novelist Dostoyevsky who wrote in *The Brothers Karamazov* that without God all is permitted.

4. Moral relativism leads to situational ethics, determined by time and circumstance—a morality of popularity and convenience. Hence, the Eskimo custom of leaving the elderly to die on an ice floe is moral, given the values of Eskimo society. During the French Revolution, cutting off the heads of aristocrats was commendable in that it conformed to the desires of a majority of the population.

The crematoria at Auschwitz and Dachau may be justified by prevailing opinion in Berlin and Nuremberg. It's no coincidence that legalized abortion followed in the wake of the 1960s, the flood tide of moral relativism in this country.

5. Since existence holds no higher purpose (nothing beyond the grave), life becomes an end in itself. Pleasure—sensory indulgence—becomes the great goal, fun the holy grail, endlessly pursued at dining tables and in bedrooms, sports arenas, casinos, concerts halls, and movie theaters.

6. Two seemingly contradictory positions are simultaneously advanced and neatly reconciled: First, radical autonomy—the notion that man has no responsibility to society or to past or future

generations. Each person does indeed become an island unto himself, unconnected to the mainland, responsible for his own well-being and contentment and nothing else.

But this misguided individualism in turn inevitably leads to ant-hill collectivism. Man can not bear the existential loneliness of separation from life's source. Having dispensed with God, secularists must infuse life with ersatz meaning by creating a new deity.

This golden calf takes the form of the collective, which is endlessly worshiped in the name of race, gender, class, equality, fatherland, or simply "the people." The good, we are told, lies in sacrificing to this idol—offering up our property, our values, our families, and, when demanded, our very lives. The dead end of this philosophy is the isms mentioned earlier.

DETERMINISM—There is no God, hence no free will, therefore no individual responsibility. Timothy McVeigh (charged with the Oklahoma City bombing) and Mother Teresa are assigned the same moral status, each having been genetically programmed or conditioned by their environment to act as they have.

HEDONISM—The here and now is all there is. Live for the moment, or as the kids used to say when I was in college, "If it feels good, do it." The consequences of this exaltation of the senses include promiscuity, drug abuse, and a consumer culture that measures the value of life in terms of VCRs, compact disc players, and time-sharing condominiums accumulated.

ECONOMIC EGALITARIANISM (or SOCIALISM)— determinism in the economic realm. Individuals aren't responsible for their material circumstances. Property, including the ability to accumulate the same, is an accident of birth. Justice, then, requires radical redistributionism to rectify the whims of fate.

A FALSE LIBERTARIANISM or the promulgation of nonrights—the right to dispose of inconvenient life (fetal, elderly or infirm), the right not to be held accountable for one's actions, the right to offend the deepest sensibilities of the overwhelming majority of the American people in the name of culture and to force them to pay for it, the right to that which has not been earned.

Opposed to the secularist worldview, as it challenged the original paganism which preceded it, is the sacred or supernaturalist outlook, based on the following concepts:

1. The existence of God—beneficent, all-powerful, and intimately involved with His creation. He shapes human destiny and, in the stirring words of "My Country 'Tis of Thee," is "the author of liberty."

2. The reality of God's communication with humanity. He has given us a blueprint for successful living, a guide which only He in His infinite wisdom could devise, as it fully accords with the nature He gave us.

While there is disagreement on the specific content of the divine communication and the nature of salvation, all of the great Western religions agree on what God requires of us in terms of how we treat others: morality, charity, and justice.

3. The sanctity of the individual, because we were created by God and shaped in His spiritual likeness. We do not weigh human life in terms of dollars and cents or personal preference.

4. Objective ethics—eternal and unchangeable—for all people, at all times, in all places. Values that do not alter with the seasons nor adapt themselves to technological change but remain as constant as the source from which they emanate. The same ethical code for Eskimos, French revolutionaries, German soldiers, Hollywood celebrities, and American career women.

5. Free will, endowed by our Creator. This validates individual responsibility, with rewards and punishments based on the way our acts conform to eternal law.

6. The free market, which is simply free will extended to the economic realm. "As ye sow, so shall ye reap."

The philosophy we adhere to determines the values we embrace and the policies we espouse.

Here then are the forces—in diametrical opposition—engaged in a momentous struggle. It's a conflict as old as humanity, but never have the stakes been higher.

The war is waged on many fronts: in the courts, in the legislatures, at the polls, in the media, in our educational and religious institutions.

Ultimately, one side or the other must prevail. The outcome of this conflict will determine, perhaps for millennia to come, whether mankind will fulfill its mission of repairing the world under the rule of God (of reaching for the stars within each of us) or if we will spiritually descend into the primordial slime.

The key to resolving the struggle in our favor lies in understanding what it is we oppose and, of equal significance, what we are for, and then communicating that knowledge to our countrymen.

We are pro-life because we are pro-morality—because we understand that to survive a society must have a coherent moral vision, that a nation can be multiracial, multiethnic, and multidenominational (as America has been since its inception), and prosper. But a nation without a moral consensus—in other words, a nation that is multi-values—is doomed.

We are pro-life because we care about the lives of unborn children. But we also care about families under attack (from the rampant expansion of government, militant perversion, and attempts to undermine parental authority). And we're pro-life because we care about the victims of violent crime and absolutely repudiate the judicial/sociological drivel that facilitates their victimization.

In other words, we are pro-life in the deepest, most profound sense of the word.

I invite you to join me in an open conspiracy to advance these values and this vision.

# Week One of Casey: The Sky Hasn't Fallen
*March 28, 1995*

I t has been a week since Pennsylvania's new abortion law went into effect. Strange to say, the sky is still firmly in place.

"Abortion law unleashed" screamed a headline in the *Pittsburgh Post-Gazette* chronicling the dire event. Unleashed? As in Genghis Khan unleashed his Mongol horde on the unsuspecting inhabitants of thirteenth-century Europe?

Actually, the new measure is far from fearsome. It mandates a twenty-four-hour waiting period before an abortion is performed. Clinics are required to notify a woman of the age of the fetus and advise her that material is available describing the stages of fetal development and listing agencies that provide alternatives.

According to a 1992 Gallup poll, such an informed consent requirement is favored by 86 percent of the American people.

Among the 14 percent who oppose it are a well-heeled abortion industry and an increasingly desperate pro-choice movement. They fought Pennsylvania's Casey law (named for Democratic Governor Robert Casey, who filed it) all the way up to the Supreme Court and, even after losing there, still managed to delay its implementation for two years.

Women have to wait all of twenty-four hours before taking a step that could permanently alter their lives, not to mention ending the life blossoming in their bodies. Clinics must offer material on gestation. Seems pretty mild, not the sort of stuff to inspire the legal equivalent of Meade's defense of Cemetery Ridge.

But for pro-abortion forces, the stakes really are sky high. The abortion philosophy is based on a denial of reality. Essential to their strategy is misrepresenting the nature of fetal life. Reality avoidance defines their jargon—"reproductive rights," "products of conception," "woman's center."

In Michigan, where a similar law is on hold until a federal court

hearing, abortion advocates are furious over a disclosure requirement. The provision "treats all women in Michigan as if they were
thoughtless children," charges the state's ACLU director.

From a movement dedicated to keeping women in the dark, this
is really rich. Countless women who've had abortions over the past
twenty-one years were never told the truth or were deliberately
deceived.

In congressional testimony and comments solicited by the
General Accounting Office in 1988, women who've had abortions
said they were told their unborn children were a "clump of cells"
(at twelve weeks), a "blob of tissue" (at nine weeks), comparable
to a "wad of wet toilet paper," and a "ring of cells." Scientific?
Accurate?

Next to the abortion industry, your average used-car salesman
is the soul of candor and a wellspring of helpful information.

While we're learning more each day, prenatal life is hardly
veiled in clouds of mystery. The following comes not from the
National Right to Life Committee, Operation Rescue, or another
partisan source but a 1992 pamphlet of the March of Dimes Birth
Defects Foundation.

During the first month of fetal development, the publication
notes, "tiny limb buds, which will grow into arms and legs,
appear." "By the 25th day, the heart starts to beat." Imagine, a blob
of tissue with a heartbeat.

During the second month, "all major body organs and systems
are formed but not completely developed," while "fingers and toes
are developed." By the tenth to twelfth week, "you can hear your
baby's heartbeat for the first time... using a special instrument
called a 'doptone.'" Between the twelfth and sixteenth weeks, "the
fetus moves, kicks, swallows, and can hear your voice."

Julie Engel, a clinic victim who was told by a counselor that her
unborn child was "just a lump of cells," recalls looking at pictures
of fetal development years later. "When I saw that a 3-month-old

'clump of cells' had fingers and toes and was a tiny, perfectly formed baby, I became really hysterical. I had been lied to and misled."

During a 1990 panel discussion, Monte Liebman, M.D., a pro-life activist, offered to provide the director of Planned Parenthood of Wisconsin with models depicting stages of gestation for use in the group's clinics. She refused, saying they would "frighten" clients. Once again, who treats women like "thoughtless children"?

Even without adequate input, a 1989 *Los Angeles Times* poll disclosed that 56 percent of women who have had abortions feel a sense of guilt and 26 percent say they "mostly regret the abortions." The probability of conscience pangs, postabortion stress, and the risk of complications are among the other minor details clinics thoughtfully withhold from their patients.

For abortion clinics, disclosure is bad for business. For a movement that thrives on ignorance, even the mellow light of Casey is anathema. Instead of those coat hangers, it should adopt window shades, blinders, or white canes as its symbol.

## Title X Keeps 'Em Barefoot and Pregnant
*August 9, 1995*

While there is much to applaud in the Labor, Health, and Education appropriations bill passed in 1995 by the Republican-dominated U.S. House of Representatives, the survival of Title X is a tragedy. Pro-family advocates lost a big one here.

Reverently referred to as the "cornerstone of the government's family-planning effort," Title X of the Public Health Service Act has for a quarter of a century lavished billions of dollars on clinics that shower condoms, IUDs, and birth-control pills on adolescents.

To hear its proponents talk, you'd think Title X was as successful as the space program, as efficient as the March of Dimes, and as noble as our Cold War defense of democracy.

"When you prevent unplanned babies, you prevent abortions," explained Rep. Jim Greenwood (R-Pa.), who led the fight to save the contraceptive boondoggle. "And when you prevent unwanted babies, you prevent welfare dependency." All for a measly $193 million a year.

Greenwood didn't cite any evidence to bolster his lofty claims for a simple reason—none exists.

The rationale for Title X is another of the illogical deductions that abound in national politics. To wit: Some crimes are committed with guns. Ergo, fewer guns, less crime. Contraceptives sometimes work. Therefore, more condoms, less abortion and illegitimacy.

That dubious assumption is demolished with two words: Planned Parenthood. The Planned Parenthood Federation of America is the nation's chief abortion provider. From 1985 through 1993, its clinics performed more than one million abortions.

PPFA is also the chief beneficiary of Title X. This year, its affiliates will collect $34 million in Title X subsidies.

A provision of the law sternly provides that "None of the funds appropriated under this title shall be used in programs where abortion is a method of family planning."

Those canny folks at the Planned Parenthood clinics have a number of stratagems to circumvent this prohibition. Some perform abortions on odd-numbered days of the week and counsel on even days. Others maintain the fiction of separate entities through creative accounting—this page for family planning, that page for pregnancy termination.

Would you be shocked to learn that many family-planning clients soon become consumers of abortion services—especially the kids?

Title X is supposed to provide family planning for poor women. Except there's an odd means test. You could have the combination to the vault of the Bank of England, but if your fifteen-year-old strolls into a Planned Parenthood facility and asks for contraceptives, it looks at her income, not yours.

Don't expect them to tell you that they're supplying your darling with what she (in her juvenile innocence) believes to be the means of risk-free sex. Her privacy comes first.

Bill Clinton couldn't have a found a more fitting head for the Office of Population Affairs, which oversees Title X, than Dr. Felicia Hance Stewart. Stewart established the first outpatient abortion clinic in Sacramento, California (1973), and worked with Planned Parenthood, whose own clinic there advertises "early or late abortions."

The statistics are telling. Since Title X was enacted in 1970, the out-of-wedlock birthrate for teens nearly doubled (from 22.4 per 1,000 to 44.6 per 1,000). The abortion rate for women ages fifteen to nineteen more than doubled, climbing from 19.1 per 1,000 in the early seventies to 40.6 per 1,000 in 1990.

Sexually active thirteen-year-olds, welfare as a family business, sexually transmitted diseases with tongue-twister Latin names? We've got 'em. In 1970, 35 percent of girls and 56 percent of boys had intercourse before age eighteen. Today, the figures are 55 percent and 73 percent, respectively.

All of those babies that weren't prevented are crowding the welfare rolls. Many have had their own unprevented progeny. The number receiving Aid to Families with Dependent Children grew from fewer than 2 million in 1970 to 4.6 million in 1990. The population increased 18 percent in the same period.

Doesn't it make sense?

Birth control isn't foolproof, particularly in the hands of a teenager. (One-third of teenage pregnancies occur while a contraceptive is being used.) With Title X, more contraception has meant more intercourse and more conception, leading in turn to more abortion, illegitimacy, and welfare dependency.

We've put the government's seal of approval on adolescent fornication. We give kids the technical information and devices that provide the illusion of safety—everything they need except the maturity and morality to make the right choices.

## Feminists Squirm at Men's Advocate
*January 10, 1996*

Feminists must hate Mel Feit. The head of the National Center for Men puts abortion advocates in the painful position of being forced to admit a logical extension of *Roe v. Wade* or open themselves to charges of hypocrisy.

The New York-based organization is currently plaintiff-shopping—looking for a "compelling set of circumstances" to challenge court-ordered child support from dads who didn't choose paternity.

Feit claims it's a matter of fairness. Women aren't the only ones confronted by "unwanted pregnancies," he says. If a man has sex with a woman and she conceives (without his prior consent) and decides to keep the child, why should he be burdened with support payments?

"Once contraception has failed, the woman has all the rights," Feit complains. She can get an abortion. If she decides to have the child, she can make the father pay support, whether or not he wanted it.

"Reproductive freedom for men is an essential component of *Roe* that's currently missing," the self-styled men's activist argues.

But how can it reasonably be maintained that being forced to pay support violates a man's right to privacy—the basis of *Roe*?

Feit replies that this may have been the original rationale, but *Roe* has evolved far beyond the privacy doctrine.

"For women, *Roe* means more than having control over their bodies," he notes. "It allows a woman to plan her life. If there's a contraceptive failure, the law protects her, permits her to decide whether or not to become a parent."

Ridiculous, feminists snort! Men don't have reproductive

systems in the sense that women do. A woman has to carry a child for nine months, then deliver it. If she doesn't place the child for adoption, she has to raise it to maturity. The man's obligation begins and ends in his wallet.

True, but money facilitates existence. The quality of life is measured in dollars and cents. Inarguably, the man who is required to pay support for eighteen years will have his standard of living diminished (severely so, if his circumstances are modest). Certain career, education, and family options will be foreclosed.

If maximizing personal freedom is the primary goal of our legal system, why should men be held to their traditional obligations (supporting the children they've fathered) while women are liberated from theirs?

Feit—who has debated feminists on the talk-TV circuit (*Oprah, Donahue, Sally Jessy,* etc.)—says that at some point in the discussion he always turns to his opponent and asks: "Do you believe the government should be able to force someone to become a parent?" Sensing the trap, they dodge the question. But their silence is telling.

Equally revealing is the feminist response to Feit's basic contention. Says Cheryl Garriety, president of the Massachusetts chapter of the National Organization for Women: "Men do have a number of options. They could use contraceptives or they could abstain from having sex at all…. They have to face the consequences of their actions."

Sounds familiar, doesn't it? Obviously, women have exactly the same options (plus adoption), as pro-lifers have argued ad infinitum.

Feit is absolutely right and positively wrong. No, men should not be free to desert their offspring. And yes, his pleading follows logically from *Roe*'s demented reasoning.

This is a freedom that neither men nor women should have— she to destroy the child she has conceived (intentionally or accidentally), he to abandon the family he has created (deliberately or inadvertently).

Both have to take responsibility for the natural results of their actions. Wish or plan (take precautions) as you will, men and women in bed make babies. If you're not prepared to deal with potentialities, alter your behavior, but don't demand the freedom to make others suffer for your folly.

But, of course, today people want to have it all—rights without obligations, freedom without consequences. Feit would like a man to be able to cohabit with a woman for months or years, then, when she gets in the family way (unless there's been an explicit agreement to the contrary), walk away from the mess.

Some women want to surrender their bodies to the passions of the moment, then have complete control of their bodies when it suits them, including control over a body that is not their own, but happens to temporarily occupy their womb.

It's doubtful there's a federal court that will go along with the Men's Center; the judiciary isn't big on consistency. But it's nice to see Mel Feit out there, making feminists squirm.


## Pro-Life Movement Assassinated
*January 5, 1995*

Scenario No. 1: It's the late 1960s, and America's cities are in flames. The death toll mounts. A die-hard segregationist points an accusatory finger at the Southern Christian Leadership Conference: "If you hadn't stirred up these people, this never would have happened. When you tell them they're oppressed, this is how they react."

Scenario No. 2: Same time. Our campuses are in turmoil. Facilities doing war-related research are bombed. An official of the Johnson administration indicts the antiwar movement. "Words like 'genocide' and 'baby-killer' provoke violence," he charges.

Objective? Fair? Hardly. Now, listen to pro-choicers—heirs to those sixties reactionaries—as they exploit the slayings at two Brookline, Massachusetts, abortion clinics.

"The unstable people hear [pro-life] leaders talk about killing and talk about murder, and they act on what they consider the logic of that," observed Planned Parenthood Federation of America President Pamela Maraldo.

"The anti-abortion movement has created a climate that it's OK to kill," added Susan Newsom of the group's Massachusetts affiliate.

Thus the deranged act of a lone gunman is used to assassinate an entire movement dedicated to peaceful protest, and to further limit its already circumscribed speech.

With the federal Freedom of Clinic Access law, protest-free zones have been created around abortion clinics. Quietly trying to reason with women going inside is deemed to be blocking access, hence a criminal offense.

Under the RICO Act, intended to deal with the Gambino and Patriarca families, the Supreme Court has given a green light to the conspiracy prosecution of grandmothers, priests, and school-girls engaged in civil disobedience.

In the wake of the Brookline shootings, Health and Human Services Secretary Donna Shalala called for strengthening FOCA, though it's hard to imagine a more draconian measure.

Still, Eleanor Smeal of the Feminist Majority Foundation declared: "We've got to do better pro-actively before the shooting occurs." Meaning what—FBI sting operations, wiretaps, and property searches? I know, let's convene a House Anti-Choice Activities Committee and get to the bottom of this pro-life conspiracy.

After twenty-one years of activism on a hotly emotional issue, right-to-lifers probably have the best record of nonviolence of any political movement in history. Would that other protest groups disavowed the carnage committed in their name with the alacrity and fervor of those opposing abortion.

How is the movement supposed to tone down its rhetoric? How

do you say something is evil without calling it evil? If you believe the unborn child is human, how can you describe its destruction other than in terms of absolute abhorrence?

We were all appalled by what happened in the waiting rooms of those two abortion clinics. We saw the bodies being carried out on stretchers on the evening news. We read about the victims and their families in our newspapers.

Most of us don't want to know what goes on inside these clinics on a daily basis. Those victims are unknown and unmourned.

Dr. Mildred Jefferson, a right-to-life leader and assistant clinical professor of surgery at the Boston University School of Medicine, described the most common method of aborting a child in the sixth to tenth weeks of development:

"It's called suction-aspiration. A catheter, which acts like a vacuum cleaner, is inserted in the uterus. It turns the tiny body and its amniotic sac into mush."

With older objects of choice (ten to fourteen weeks), the cartilage of the skull and chest doesn't break up so easily. "So the abortionist resorts to cold steel surgical instruments to remove fragments of the fetus. A nurse practitioner has to reassemble the body parts to be sure nothing is left behind."

At the two clinics where the murders occurred, more than ten thousand such procedures are performed each year under the benevolent gaze of a government instituted to protect life and liberty.

In the face of this reality, what are pro-lifers supposed to do? What the Pamela Maraldos want is no secret. They want them to shut up—to end peaceful pickets and sidewalk vigils, to stop using "inflammatory rhetoric" (the suggestion that abortion is other than a benign and morally neutral act).

Presumably, pro-lifers would be permitted to sit quietly in their homes and think anti-abortion thoughts—for now.

Isn't Planned Parenthood and Company accusing defenders of the unborn of incitement to murder, of being accomplices before the fact? If a nut case on their side takes this invective to heart with a .22-caliber semi-automatic, will they be liable? By their fractured logic, yes.

## Death Stalks the Oregon Ballot Box
*October 27, 1995*

I f patriotism is the last refuge of a scoundrel, Catholic-bashing is the first resort of the secular left. Well, actually the second—after attacks on evangelical Christians.

With Oregon's assisted suicide initiative in trouble, proponents have developed a serious Vatican complex. "They [Catholics] want to impose their own unique theological perspective on the entire state," complains Barbara Coombs, chief petitioner for Measure 16 on that state's November ballot.

Now where do you suppose those crazy Catholics got their unique theological perspective anyway? Probably the same place traditional Protestants, Orthodox Jews, Muslims, and Mormons got their take on medical murder.

Opponents of Oregon's "death with dignity" question include the Lutheran Church—Missouri Synod, African Episcopal Methodist Church, the rabbi of Portland's largest synagogue, and the Quakers, as well as state associations of the elderly, retarded citizens, and pharmacists.

The once-robust initiative is slipping into a coma. In early September, a KPTV-Portland poll showed the measure passing with 65 percent of the vote. By last week, support had dropped to 53 percent.

This follows the pattern in Washington State and California, where similar measures did well in the polls until opponents began explaining the hazards. Ultimately, an informed electorate rejected the proposals.

The Hemlock Society, instigator of the mortuary move, thought it had learned from these defeats. It noted that voters worried about the slippery slope and an overly enthusiastic medic with a syringe at the bottom of the incline.

To allay these fears, backers of Measure 16 included so-called safeguards. Doctors can assist, but the lethal dose must be administered by the "patient."

Only the incurably ill with less than six months to live qualify for assisted suicide. A consulting physician must concur with the diagnosis. The voluntary victim must request aid-in-dying three times, twice orally at least fifteen days apart, and once in writing forty-eight hours before the coup de grace.

On examination, these protections resemble Swiss cheese. Shelly Olsen, a woman in her forties, appears in a commercial for 16's opponents. She was diagnosed as having gastric cancer and told she had a 3 percent chance of surviving three to six months. That was almost two years ago. Wouldn't it be funny if Shelly outlived her doctor?

Consulting physicians rarely disagree with the conclusion they're asked to endorse, a fact Hemlock acknowledges. After the deed is done, we'll have to take the doctor's word that two oral appeals were made.

Perhaps potential suicides will be able to call a toll-free number. "Hello, you've reached the offices of Dr. Doom. If you have cancer, please dial 1 for a recorded message. Be sure to leave your request at the end."

If the patient appears to have psychiatric problems causing impaired judgment, either physician may refer him for counseling, but entirely at the doctor's discretion. As a New York State task force on euthanasia pointed out, most doctors are notoriously ill-equipped to assess mental disorders.

The drugs will be self-administered—for the time being. But proponents admit this is a first step (in Hemlock's words) to get society "comfortable" with the idea. The task force appointed by Gov. Mario Cuomo notes euthanasia policies that "hinge on notions of pain and suffering would be uncontainable" once the genie is out of the vial.

Advocates are playing on the horror of a slow, painful death. "Those fears are purely myths and need to be changed by education," says Dr. Kathleen Foley, chief of Pain Service at New York's Memorial Sloan-Kettering Cancer Center, who maintains that most pain associated with dying can be alleviated.

Opposed to this imaginary fear is the very real concern that America will end up going Dutch. The Netherlands has had active euthanasia for over twenty years. It started with many of the same safeguards as the Oregon initiative—which are routinely ignored.

According to a government study, in 1990, 1,040 patients were killed without their knowledge or consent. The murder of mentally or physically handicapped infants is now so common that the Dutch Pediatric Association is drafting guidelines for its practice. And there's at least one case of a psychiatrist who helped a physically healthy but depressed patient end his life.

It's not just the Catholic Church the Kevorkian crowd fears but religion per se. According to Hemlock's founder, Derek Humphry, Oregon was chosen as the latest battlefield because the state has "more nonreligious people [measured by church attendance] than any state in the country."

Hemlock doesn't want voters whose conscience is pricked by spiritual teachings, who will recall that ultimately their life is not their own, that life and death rests in the hands of a higher authority than a man with a medical degree.

---

Postscript: Measure 16 was narrowly adopted (51 percent to 49 percent, a margin of thirty-two thousand votes) in November of 1994. Federal District Court Judge Michael Hogan declared the measure unconstitutional as a violation of the "equal protection of laws." His ruling has been appealed.

# chapter seven

# THE CULTURE WAR

## It's the Culture, Stupid
*November 10, 1994*

The 1994 election was a primal scream from an anguished public. It will be analyzed, pondered, pontificated upon, and ultimately understood by very few.

Tuesday morning, Democrats held the Senate by 56 to 44 seats and the House by 256 to 178. When the polls closed, Republicans had total control of Congress for the first time in forty years, with a net gain of more than fifty seats in the House. A majority of governors' mansions also fell to the GOP.

James Sasser, slated to be the Senate majority leader, was trounced. Liberal icons Mario Cuomo, Ann Richards, Tom Foley, and Dan Rostenkowski lie fallen in the dust.

The 1994 class of freshmen Republican senators leans decidedly to the right—John Kyl, Spencer Abraham, Rod Grams, Mike DeWine, James Inhofe, Bill Frist, and Rich Santorum, six of them replacing liberal Democrats.

A shell-shocked establishment is staggering from the rubble, desperately casting about for explanations for the carnage.

Was it the economy, stupid? Not this time. Though Clinton did his level best to abort an economic recovery well under way when he took office, GNP growth is stable if weak.

An October 18 *New York Times* headline lamented, "Democrats Get No Bounce from a Healthy Economy." Only Marxists, liberals, and other determinists believe economics is the axis on which the world turns.

Was the election an anti-incumbent spasm—yet another chorus of throw the bums out? Then why was every incumbent Republican governor reelected, most by sizable margins?

Bill Clinton's unprecedented unpopularity doubtless played a part, but only to the extent that the president, in the words of Washington consultant Peter Roff, "provides a window on the soul of the Democratic party."

Clinton and company were singing "Happy Days Are Here Again" in November 1992. For the first time in a dozen years, and only the second time in a quarter century, the Democrats had the whole enchilada—Congress and the presidency.

Americans, who had forgotten the nature of the liberal contagion during the cozy Reagan years, got an ice-cold shower without a towel over the past twenty-one months.

They took a long, hard look at the Clinton administration and gagged. Elected as a New Democrat, Clinton's cabinet came to resemble the San Francisco white pages.

The administration's most notable achievements include easing the ban on homosexuals in the military, a surgeon general who pushes condoms and muses about drug legalization, a Justice Department that tried to weaken child pornography laws, court appointees who are dogmatically anti-death penalty, welfare-state crime control (light on punishment, heavy on midnight basketball), and an international abortion crusade at the Cairo Population conference, where Jane Fonda and Bella Abzug set the tone for the U.S. delegation.

Sure Clinton looks increasingly sleazy as sordid details bubble up through the turbulent Whitewater. Sure the public rejects political royalty—witness the triumph of congressional term limit measures in seven more states and the District of Columbia and the defeat of the Speaker of the House largely on the basis of that issue.

And yes, Americans are fed up with taxes, outraged over crime, and alienated by illegal immigration, as can be seen in the landslide victory of California's Proposition 187. All of these issues had an impact in this watershed election.

But more than anything else, 1994 was a values referendum. Some 69 percent of the American people tell pollsters the nation is heading in the wrong direction.

They look at their streets, schools, homes, and culture and see massive moral erosion—metal detectors in high schools, one-in-three children born out of wedlock, an entertainment industry with the fetid aroma of an open sewer, and four-star generals ordered to sit through indoctrination films like *On Being Gay* during the Defense Department's Diversity Day on September 9.

They hunger for normative values and emphatically reject relativism, victimology, and the retreat from personal responsibility. It's no coincidence that this Sunday, the pope's book will jump to No. 1 on the *New York Times* best-seller list, while Bill Bennett's *Book of Virtues* (on the list for forty-five weeks) has sold more than 1.6 million copies.

Vice President Al Gore cried foul when soon-to-be House Speaker Newt Gingrich pointed to the murder of two toddlers in South Carolina as symptomatic of our moral decline for which the powers that be must bear responsibility. But such horrors weren't our daily fare a generation ago, before McGovern liberals got their hands on America.

"The future of our children and our country are at stake," Clinton told the nation in his radio address last weekend. Voters agreed.

## Mister Rogers: There Goes the Neighborhood
*October 17, 1994*

Given my interest in moral philosophy, it's natural that I would be drawn to the deep thoughts of a man who spends a significant amount of time with a Stepford Wives grin on his face, conversing with hand puppets.

In a bookstore the other day, I picked up Mister Rogers's volume of meditations, *You Are Special.* The jacket informed me it would have "great appeal… to anyone seeking wise, humane advice on how to get the most out of life."

Opening the book at random, I came across the following on page 75: " 'Sometimes People Are Good' and 'Good People Sometimes Do Bad Things' are songs I sing to let children know that everyone does things that are naughty once in a while, but that doing something bad doesn't make you a bad person."

For over twenty-five years on his PBS series, Fred Rogers has been filling the innocent heads of children with this pap. Now he's instructing adults from the lofty heights of his tower of psychobabble. Can basically good people do bad things? Absolutely. It happens all the time.

Is the sinner evil beyond redemption? Excepting the architects of genocide and the creatures who murder children, in most cases, no.

But the malefactor is—dare I say it?—bad, to the same extent that his actions are bad. If conduct is no reflection on character, why strive to improve?

The neighborly man in a cardigan would reply that this judgmentalism will cripple a child's self-esteem. And we all know that lack of self-esteem lies at the heart of our most vexing problems. How often have we been told that if you don't love yourself, you can't love others?

In an appearance on *The Arsenio Hall Show*, Rogers was asked his prescription for the nation's ailments. He replied: "Let every-body know that they have value in this life."

But the Bosnian Serbs who've been busily raping, torturing, and killing for the past several years believe they have value in this life. They fail to appreciate the value of those they're raping, tor-turing, and killing. Self-regard does not automatically lead to a regard for others. Often, the opposite.

The cult of self-esteem dominates education. As psychology professor Harold Stevenson remarked in the *New York Times:* "Educators eager to encourage lagging students have developed a dangerous myth: that raising children's self-esteem is a sure means of improving their achievement and solving many of the nation's social ills."

As an example of self-esteem indoctrination, he cites grade school children mindlessly mouthing slogans like: "You brighten my day," "I'm lucky to know you," and "You're a good buddy."

In consequence, American students tend to feel good about themselves and do poorly on aptitude tests. Japanese students have lower self-esteem and much higher test scores. Under a self-esteem regimen, America is becoming a nation of feel-good mediocrities.

Is self-esteem a panacea? Did Hitler and Stalin feel good about themselves? You bet they did. As psychologists Abraham Maslow and Carl Rogers would say, they were self-actualizing individuals who took control of their destiny.

Does Mother Teresa have low self-esteem? Given her religious outlook—which teaches that we are all flawed—probably. Some of the nicest people I know have low self-esteem. They're driven to do good precisely because they're unsure of themselves.

And then there are those who spend years in therapy to develop a sense of self-worth (to get in touch with their emotions). In the process, they become self-centered and self-absorbed.

At the dead end of our journey to self-esteem stands a bearded little man with a swastika carved on his forehead. On November 11

Charlie Manson turns sixty. In an interview a few months before reaching this milestone, Manson complained: "Everybody in the world wants to get mad at me because I won't show remorse because somebody dies. Somebody dies every day." Note the detached perspective, as if the Tate/La Bianca murders were something he merely heard about.

But he won't allow the judgment of others to affect his self-image. "I am not a bad person. I am a good person." Having done bad things (making wrong choices) doesn't make Charlie a bad man. It's a wonderful day in the neighborhood.

Our parents and grandparents were raised without the ethical guidance of People's Television. They believed that if you wanted to feel good, you should do good; that if you did rotten things, you deserved to feel rotten.

They didn't have high self-esteem. They also lacked our soaring indices of social pathology.

If you want to be my neighbor, Fred, you'll have to start teaching virtue and stop singing siren songs about "good people" who do naughty things.

## What's Between Us and Morality? Just Our Calvins
*May 9, 1994*

N othing comes between American society and decency—except Calvin Klein and a thousand other hucksters who use sex to sell their schlock.

Readers will smirk over the just-published biography of the man who has dominated the fashion industry for the past quarter-century *(Obsession: The Lives and Times of Calvin Klein)*.

Bisexuality, bowls of cocaine and Quaaludes on one side of his bed and porno videos on the other, a stint at a drug rehab center in 1988—such carrying on by a skinny Jewish kid from the Bronx.

Titillated by the details, we are apt to miss a salient point: There's a symmetry between Klein's private life and his marketing techniques—using flesh and fantasies to sell jeans, underwear, and fragrances.

"Calvin Klein didn't just become a famous sportswear designer," says Steven Gaines, the book's co-author. "He changed the face of American advertising; he influenced American morals." Believe it.

From the day in 1979 when then-thirteen-year-old Brooke Shields cooed into a camera, "Nothing comes between me and my Calvins," Klein has reigned as the uncrowned king of sexual exploitation.

A kaleidoscope of erotic images flashes before us. A well-muscled young man in a shower, nude except for a strategically positioned hand holding blue jeans. A hunky dude reclining, clad only in underpants. A woman's torso, left breast exposed, pelvis wrapped in a towel, being embraced by a man with wet hair, his eyes closed in ecstasy as he kisses her rib cage.

Rapper Marky Mark grabbing his crotch in one ad, in another posing with a bare-chested Kate Moss (Klein's wunder waif) pressed against him. In the latest ad for Obsession perfume, Moss lies on her belly, naked, the barest hint of her bottom in view, a dumb-hither expression on her vacant face.

Klein started a stampede. We've come a long way, baby, since the days when saying a toothpaste has "sex appeal" shocked the nation. Today, sex sells everything from exercise equipment ("A hard man is good to find") to beer (look, it's the Swedish bikini team parachuting in with your Old Milwaukee), from sheets to table napkins.

Ads for Georges Marciano's Guess jeans upped the ante on Klein. One showed two pubescent girls embracing in a field, with obvious lesbian overtones. Another displays a tousled woman who seems to be struggling, slung over a man's shoulder as she's carried away, suggesting rape.

One theme dominates salacious advertising. Women are always young and attractive, partially clad, and totally hot. Whether giddy or sulky, the message is their availability. Date rape, anyone?

"Advertising doesn't lead society, it follows," declared the creative director for the Young & Rubicam ad agency in the mid-eighties. Here is the standard exculpatory plea of Hollywood and other cultural polluters: "We merely reflect trends; we don't create them." As if the images that inundate us daily (it's estimated children see 750,000 ads by age eighteen) couldn't conceivably move us, influence attitudes, shape perceptions, motivate, and activate.

We are asked to believe that motivational devices powerful enough to get the impressionable to spend $49 for 3/4 fluid ounces of perfume and $60 for a pair of blue jeans have no ability to sway us in other areas, can't entice, deceive, and seduce.

Advertising doesn't just sell things. It also sells ideas, attitudes, and conduct.

Increasingly, the ideas it propagates are subversive of the social order—a casual attitude toward sex, the exaltation of emotions, passions as the arbiter of behavior, mindless materialism, and a live-for-the-moment ethos.

It detests discipline, denial, and reflection. As Vincent Ryan Ruggiero noted in his book, *Warning: Nonsense Is Destroying America:* "Because advertisements are designed to sell goods and services, irrespective of the consumer's needs for them or ability to afford them, the most commonly used appeals are to self-indulgence—'You deserve this'; impulsiveness—'Don't delay; act now'; and instant gratification—'You'll feel so good.'"

That the behavior assiduously cultivated carries over to other areas of life is undeniable. That the way Madison Avenue debases and trivializes sex has a profound impact on our culture is equally obvious.

Advertising isn't alone in this regard, but another pulverizer of values. To movies, television, and music, it adds its daily dose of social solvent. And it's even more ubiquitous than other media toxins.

"Everybody copies him. He's one of the few people in New York with genuinely good taste," says a colleague of Calvin Klein—a judgment nearly as ironic as Bill Clinton's reputed sensitivity toward the opposite sex.

## What Ever Happened to the Idea of Community?
*November 25, 1993*

Thanksgiving is about togetherness, sharing, basking in the warmth of kith and kin. This column is about isolation, solitary lives that end in obscurity, neighbors who aren't neighborly, and a fast-fading sense of community.

There is an uninvited guest at this year's festivities. If she's looking a bit lean, it's not surprising. Adele Gaboury has been dead for four years.

It is exactly one month to the day that the seventy-three-year-old Gaboury's skeletal remains were removed from the Worcester, Massachusetts house she'd occupied for almost forty years. According to the coroner, Gaboury died in her kitchen sometime in 1989. And there her body remained, buried under mounds of rubbish, decomposing in silent neglect.

Postal workers continued delivering the mail for two years after her demise. Neighbors, more concerned about property values than humanity, arranged for her lawn to be mowed. They took care of everything—except Gaboury herself.

Admittedly, Adele never read Dale Carnegie's book on securing the esteem of acquaintances. She was the neighborhood gargoyle who yelled at kids playing in the street and rebuffed all gestures of friendship.

Still, that no one asked questions, no one put forth the modest effort to determine the fate of this lonely lady, says something about the decline of community in America.

"Community" has become one of the most overused, trivialized words in the English language. We prattle about the black community, the Hispanic community, the disabled community, the gay community—as if those who compose these collectives have more in common than a single characteristic, often an accident of birth.

Yet, the more we carry on about community, the less of it we have.

Increasingly, we exist in near isolation. Extended families have experienced a nuclear meltdown. Over the river and through the woods to grandmother's retirement condominium we go?

How many of us live in the town in which we grew up? The state? Is this your third or fourth house? You probably know your next-door neighbor. How about the folks one house over from you? We change jobs the way my father's generation changed cars.

Women park their preschoolers in day care. Where once neighborhoods bustled with activity and echoed with children's laughter, today—from early morning to late afternoon—they are deserted as ghost towns.

Blame it on the internal combustion engine, bedroom communities, shopping malls, and electronic entertainment.

For commuters, home is a place to eat and sleep. Says social critic Allan Carlson of the Rockford Institute: "Today, a house isn't a place to stay. It isn't even shelter any more. It's an investment. You can't build community around an investment strategy."

For the Pilgrims and other settlers, community came easy. You had to rely on your neighbors for security and sustenance in bad times. Out there, beyond the clearing, lurked ravening beasts and hostile natives. Your neighbors were life insurance of the most tangible type.

But the Pilgrims also were united by a religious vision. They were a fellowship that came to these shores to establish a new Jerusalem, in the words of the Mayflower Compact, "a city upon a hill."

As for the holiday at hand, its origins are both communal and spiritual. The Pilgrims' feast was a reenactment of the "thanksgiving" ordered in Leviticus, where the Children of Israel were commanded to bring the first fruits of their harvest as an offering.

Today, the most close-knit communities—those that have achieved the elusive quality of solidarity in the midst of a cultural centrifuge—share a salient feature with the Plymouth colony. Whether Baptists in the South, black congregations in the inner cities or Hasidic Jews in their urban neighborhoods, all are communities of faith revolving around houses of worship.

One thing never fails to impress the outsider: These people care for each other. They do things together. They socialize and support, celebrate and commiserate. They care for the sick, aid the needy, and bury their dead.

The good neighbor is itself a biblical concept. We recall the injunction: "Love your neighbor as yourself," but forget its source. ("I am the Lord your God.")

Your neighbor may be distinctly unlovable—a crotchety, eccentric old lady who lets her house fill with trash, harasses kids at play, and rebuffs friendly overtures. It doesn't matter. If you take the requirements of faith seriously, you are compelled to care for her. Without a sense of responsibility, there can be no true community.

"People have their own lives," said a lifelong resident of the street on which Gaboury's ended unnoticed until four years after the fact. "They go their own ways. Neighbors don't want to get involved with neighbors." A fitting epitaph for both Adele Gaboury and our society.

## The Left Is No Stranger to Hate
*November 28, 1993*

According to the media, political hatred has reached epidemic proportions. And conservatives are the exclusive source of the contagion. The Jesse Helms contretemps (his joking, if tasteless, comment that the president should bring bodyguards if he visits military installations in North Carolina) will be exploited to reinforce this perception.

Rage on the right was a media theme throughout the 1994 campaign.

The day before the election, the *Washington Post* ran a Style section piece entitled "The Politics of Hate."

"With people headed to the voting booths tomorrow... hate seems to be drifting through the air like smoke from autumn bonfires," the *Post* ominously intoned.

Among the examples cited was a poll showing 25 percent of the American people actually hate Bill Clinton. Imagine that, people hating the president. Why that hasn't happened since... Ronald Reagan.

Those injecting raw venom into the main artery of the body politic, the *Post* disclosed, include Rush Limbaugh, Operation Rescue head Randall Terry, gun owners, and protesters who heckled Hillary Clinton during her health care road show.

Without comment, the article quotes Arnold Bennett, whose Families USA organized Hillary's health caravan, comparing Newt Gingrich and Bob Dole to Depression-era fascist Father Coughlin and David Duke. That's what I like about liberals, their sense of balance.

We must try to be tolerant of liberals and understand their compulsion to see themselves as creatures of light and conservatives as a band of troglodytes, sitting in our dank dwellings, gnawing the bones of malice.

Search as it might, in more than five thousand words the *Post* couldn't come up with a single instance of liberal hysteria.

Admittedly, there are some unstable elements on the right. But to suggest that conservatives have a monopoly on hate is an ideological mugging of reality.

From racist urban anarchy and labor thuggery to campus Jacobins and ACT-UP (the Waffen SS of the gay-rights movement), organized political violence in America comes primarily from the left.

Damian Williams, doing his touchdown victory dance over a bleeding Reginald Denny, wasn't a member of the conservative Opportunity Society.

It isn't the Young Republicans who've turned our campuses into the academic equivalent of Stalinist Russia, with PC mobs harassing speakers and burning alternative newspapers.

The indignant voices calling on Senate Majority Leader Dole to block Helms's chairmanship of the Foreign Relations Committee were conspicuously silent when Surgeon General Joycelyn Elders (Clinton's Queen of Mean) charged the religious right is "un-Christian," the Catholic Church is an institution dominated by "a celibate male hierarchy," and right-to-lifers have a "love affair with the fetus."

For sheer malice, nothing on the right can compare with the terror tactics of homosexual militants. When the Reverend Lou Sheldon of the Traditional Values Coalition tried to speak at a San Francisco church last year, all hell broke loose.

Parishioners, including handicapped children, were assaulted. Threats and obscenities filled the air. Church property was destroyed. Demonstrators pounded on the doors so loudly Sheldon couldn't be heard above the tumult.

When the media analyze political hatred, such incidents are shoved down the memory hole.

Why do liberals persist in demonizing the other side? Because the left sees itself animated by the purest of motives—compassion, generosity, and tolerance—and the right driven by fear and hate.

Leftists can only conceive of opposition to their worldview as the product of enmity. Thus opponents of affirmative action hate minorities and welfare reformers hate the poor. As New York's Democratic Congressman Charles Rangel put it, "It's not 'spic' and 'nigger' anymore. Now racists say, 'Let's cut taxes.'"

During the 1930s, Franklin Roosevelt forged an electoral coalition that lasted more than half a century based on envy—next of kin to hatred.

The American political debate really got vicious in the 1960s, under the tutelage of the new left. It wasn't enough for antiwar activists to disagree with the architects of American policy in Vietnam, those leaders had to be portrayed as pure evil. The pro-life movement didn't coin the term "baby killer," which demonstrators hurled at President Johnson.

For as long as I've been politically aware, the left has incited resentment and rancor, pitting the poor against the affluent, blacks against whites, women against men. And then it has the chutzpah to whine about the politics of hate.

## Defense of NEA: A Vicious Whine by Show-off Snobs
*August 7, 1995*

The cover essay in the August 7 *Time* magazine ("Why America Shouldn't Kill Cultural Funding" by Robert Hughes) is too vicious to be called a diatribe, too devious for mere dishonesty, and would have to rise several levels in objectivity to qualify as propaganda.

Hughes blasts House members who voted to eliminate National Endowment for the Arts funding by 1997 as "Jurassic" conservatives with "limbic forebrains" capable of containing only "one sound bite at a time."

"By what meanness, through what smug philistinism—and, above all, on what actual evidence—do our Jacks-in-office decree that arts and humanities are beneath the interest of the American people and unworthy of their collective support?" Hughes thunders.

With our blather about cultural elites, we'd probably hate Thomas Jefferson, if he were resurrected to preach his concept of democracy fostering a natural aristocracy, the critic charges.

Would that be the same Thomas Jefferson who observed "To compel a man to furnish contributions of money for the propagation of opinions which he disbelieves is sinful and tyrannical"?

Hughes is oblivious to the speciousness of his polemic, arguing that Lilliputian European states spend a higher portion of their national budgets on culture than we do without a peep of protest.

How easily liberals slip into the whiny-kid mode. "Mom, why don't we have socialized medicine? The Europeans have it! Why don't we spend more on the arts?"

Over the NEA's thirty-year history, at most a dozen projects have "excited serious controversy," Hughes asserts. Nobody talked about abolishing the Navy after Tailhook, the writer pouts—as if paying for "Piss Christ" was comparable to the defense of our shores.

Perhaps we could combine the two. In our next war, we could beam Robert Mapplethorpe's proctological photos at enemy forces. While they're retching, we'll overrun them.

The latest in a long line of outrages is an NEA grant of $15,000 to Highways, a California performance-arts center, for its "Ecco Lesbo-Ecco Homo" festival.

The aesthetic orgy includes "Boys 'R' Us," billed as "hot summer nights with hot fags," and comedienne Marga Gomez fantasizing about sex with House Speaker Newt Gingrich's mother.

NEA Chairmouth Jane Alexander defended this grant as fulfilling the agency's "mandated mission of fostering mutual respect for the diverse beliefs of all persons and groups"—everyone, that is, except Republicans, Christians, and the majority of citizens whose confiscated wealth pays for this tendentious crud.

A dozen controversial grants did he say? How about in any six-month period? How about a grant for a painting that portrays Jesus as a junkie, Karen Finley turning herself into a human Hershey bar, HIV-positive performance artist Ron Athey's ritual bloodletting, an exhibit called Abject Art (the joys of excrement), Mapplethorpe's picture of a sad-faced little girl exposing her genitals (so graphic that *Time* said the photographer could have been prosecuted for child pornography), and the distribution of $10 bills to illegal aliens, intended to make an artistic statement about something or other? That's the short list.

I used to think that the NEA existed solely to give the left the perverse pleasure of forcing Mormons in Salt Lake City to subsidize Annie Sprinkle's *Sluts and Goddesses Video Workshop*.

I was wrong. A society glorifies its highest values. For members of the so-called arts community, voyeurism, perversion, nihilism, victimology, and infantile obsession with human waste *are* their highest values.

The mistake NEA opponents make is calling these partisans of the prurient "cultural elitists." Elitism implies discernment and a striving for excellence.

They are snobs and exhibitionists intent on stuffing their values down our throats, with our money, and sneering at us as lowbrows when we protest. Culture? The NEA is to culture what Bosnian Serb commander Radovan Karadzic is to diplomacy.

Granted, not everything the NEA does is contemptible. So what? If I choose to support a theatrical production, I'll buy a ticket. If I want to patronize a museum, I'll pay for admission. I don't need Lady Bountiful Alexander making these decisions for me.

Jurassic conservatives, huh? I seem to recall the *t. rex* in *Jurassic Park* eating one of the more odious characters. What beverage should we serve with the NEA? Given that its fans are white-wine-and-cheese liberals, a crisp Chardonnay, I should think.

# Hiroshima and the War for America's Past
*August 2, 1995*

B y Sunday, the fiftieth anniversary of the Hiroshima bombing, the whining chorus should reach ear-shattering decibels.

From the pages of newly published histories to TV specials, we will again be subjected to the tedious litany of revisionist verdicts on the bombing that ended World War II: America the racist relished the incineration of 140,000 Japanese. Harry Truman used the bomb to scare the Soviets.

Hindsight is wonderful. Truman and his generals were confronting an implacable foe that we had fought all over the Pacific for the better part of four years.

After Pearl Harbor, the Bataan Death March, and a grisly photo of a Japanese soldier beheading a blindfolded Allied airman (widely published in this country), can the American people be blamed for distrusting Japan and insisting on the same unconditional surrender we demanded of Germany?

Nippon's warlords were planning their own götterdämmerung— an "honorable death for 100 million" (the entire population). Fourteen divisions (735,000 men) and five thousand kamikaze planes were in place to defend the southernmost island of Kyushu.

The casualties America would have sustained in the Battle of Japan are a matter of conjecture. The following is indisputable.

Fact: On Iwo Jima, the Japanese garrison of twenty thousand fought almost to the last man.

Fact: On Okinawa, more than two hundred thousand soldiers and civilians died. Of the latter, thousands committed suicide. Truman believed the invasion of the home islands, scheduled for November 1945, would be "Okinawa from one end of Japan to the other."

Fact: The Philadelphia Quartermaster Depot had ordered 370,000 Purple Hearts, anticipating that they would be awarded to the wounded and families of GIs who died in the Kyushu invasion.

Revisionists cite a 1946 War Department report that claimed we could have defeated Japan without the A-bomb or an invasion. They neglect to mention the proposed alternative—a continuation of strategic bombing.

In ten days in March 1945, the 20th Air Force leveled Japan's four largest cities, killing 150,000. Would the annihilation of hundreds of thousands from conventional bombing have been more humane than the deaths of 200,000 in Hiroshima and Nagasaki?

Was Japan ready to surrender in August 1945? After two mushroom clouds sprouted in the summer sky, half of the war cabinet wanted to fight on. After Emperor Hirohito decided to capitulate, an abortive coup attempted to reverse his judgment.

Second-guessing a decision made half a century ago, at the end of the bloodiest conflict in history, is one more offensive in the war for the past.

The left can't bear to admit that America was ever right. Thus our great crusade against fascism becomes a prime target for debunking.

The Smithsonian's original Enola Gay exhibit had a script containing eighty-four pages on the devastation of Japan and exactly one on Japanese war crimes in China, Korea, the Philippines, etc.

"For most Americans, it was a war of vengeance. For most Japanese, it was a war to defend their unique culture against Western imperialism," the script advised.

Presumably, all of the Korean women raped and Chinese murdered in medical experiments and poison-gas attacks appreciate the contribution their suffering made to the preservation of Japanese culture.

If Americans of the 1940s were so racist and vengeful that Truman used nuclear weapons for kicks, then during our occupation of Japan, why didn't we treat the Japanese the way Nazi Germany treated the Poles—as a race of slaves slated for extinction? Instead, we rebuilt Japan's economy and gave it democracy.

Hiroshima is an integral part of the left's victimology, a bridge between our slaughter of the Indians and enslavement of blacks, and our "genocidal war" in Southeast Asia.

The National History Standards—paid for with your tax dollars and appearing soon in classrooms across the country—is another platform to trash America. The Ku Klux Klan gets seventeen mentions while Thomas Edison, Alexander Graham Bell, and Albert Einstein are ignored.

In this exercise in self-loathing, there's even a suggestion that America provoked the sneak attack on Pearl Harbor. No fantasy is too absurd or obscene for the hate-America crowd.

Why apologize for Hiroshima? Ghastly as it was, in the balance, the bombing saved lives. August 6, 1945, recedes into the mists of memory. The war to shape America's vision of its past continues.

## Remembering Woodstock in Horror
*June 23, 1994*

In about six weeks, transcendental tourists will hit the nostalgia trail. Destination—the Woodstock nation. August 15 to 17 marks the twenty-fifth anniversary of the happening in Max Yasgur's alfalfa field, the pretentiously misnamed Woodstock Music and Art Fair—three days of mud and music, rainstorms and raunch, dope (the kind that's smoked), and dope (the kind that smokes it). Two separate musical reunions will mark the milestoned occasion.

Like an acid trip, images flash before us: brain-burned hippies selling $5 lids, a dude and his lady getting naked in a field, adolescents dancing in a downpour, the reality-challenged staggering into the Hog Farm's freak-out tent, five hundred thousand voices screaming the F-word along with Country Joe and the Fish.

If you listen to Woodstock's apostles, it was seventy-two hours of peace, love, and freedom, tied with a pretty psychedelic bow. "The festival represented an ideal," said David Fricke of *Rolling*

*Stone.* "It was a demonstration... of unity and cooperation that suggested there was another, better way to take care of business out there."

In his book *Woodstock: The Oral History*, Aquarian apologist Joel Makower described the bacchanal as "the culmination of all the ideals and sensibilities that were the 1960s... like peace and love and sharing and brotherhood."

Perhaps the Woodstock ethos was best captured by a young man shown in the Warner Bros. documentary of the same name, who insightfully observed: "It's like, people that are nowhere are coming here 'cause there's people that they think are somewhere, so everybody is, like, really looking for, you know, some kind of answer." Oh, wow!

Woodstock was about idealism—the type induced by chemicals; Dorothy, the little girl from Kansas who was carried off to Oz in a cyclone, learned there's no place like home. The Woodstock generation, psychically displaced persons, decided there's no place like dope.

Drugs were Woodstock's essence—a symbol of newfound freedom, a way to get loose and funky, and a vehicle for spiritual discovery. Crackups were common. Of the twenty-seven acts that played there, Janis Joplin, Jimi Hendrix, Tim Hardin, Keith Moon, and Paul Butterfield all subsequently died of overdoses. Bob Hite of Canned Heat died of a drug-related heart attack. Richard Manuel (The Band) and Abbie Hoffmann were suicides.

Freedom? Individualism? Love? Peace? Please. The freedom they wanted was from reality—the need to work, strive, and endure. Theirs was the freedom of the grubby mendicant whose leisure is bought by charity. Had it not been for food donated by the locals and medicine rushed in by the genocidal military, the scene would have been ugly.

They found their individuality in conformity. Each was a cookie-cutter replica of the rest—lanky long hair or frizzy 'fros, love beads, granny glasses, tie–dyes, and bell–bottoms. From dress to music to sex, their originality was depressingly uniform.

Peace? Well, only two people died (one OD'd, the other was run over by a tractor). On the other hand, how much violence is there in a hospital ward of heavily sedated patients? If Woodstock had lasted another seventy-two hours, and the narcotics had run out, it would have been anything but harmonious.

Love is a four-letter word that the kids mistook for one with three. Reminiscing on the twentieth anniversary, columnist Pete Hamill wrote of his friends at Woodstock bathing in the nude and sharing food, joints, and girlfriends (rather dehumanizing demeanor for idealists).

In the quarter-century since Woodstock enlightened us on the higher meaning of sexuality, we've seen galloping rates of divorce, out-of-wedlock births, and venereal disease.

The back-to-nature crowd showed their appreciation for the environment by leaving behind enough garbage to fill several city dumps.

In one area, at least, words and deeds aligned. Property is theft, they said, and proved they meant it by liberating the crops of hard-working farmers. It was Marxist redistributionism turned upside-down, as wealth passed from those with callused hands to a bunch of bourgeois brats.

The year of the Aquarian Exposition, almost the same number of kids, of approximately the same age, served in Vietnam. While the Woodstockians danced in the mud, GIs slogged through rice paddies.

When in trouble, the young soldiers couldn't call home for help. (In Bethel, New York, the sixty pay phones had one hundred–foot lines of kids waiting to exercise their independence by panhandling their parents.) While the children chanted for peace, their khaki counterparts fought for it, by opposing the most malignant force of our era.

After three days, the revelers went home—some with a bad case of sunburn, others with a genital contagion. Many of the 'Nam generation stayed behind, or returned to lie in other fields. If it's all the same to you, I'd rather celebrate their sacrifice and heroism than get misty-eyed over a pretentious drugged-out freak show.

# chapter eight

# OY VEY FOR HOLLYWOOD

## Pocahontas on PC Trail
*June 21, 1995*

Seventeenth-century Native Americans were environmentally conscious, harmonious, altruistic, and gender-correct.

English settlers (You remember them? The folks if not for whom we wouldn't be here) were a cross between Genghis Khan and the Exxon Valdez. That is the message of *Pocahontas*, Disney's thirty-third animated feature.

In *Pocahontas* (Dances with Mouse), bigotry and greed are overcome by communalism and compassion. "Mine, mine, mine!" sings Ratcliffe, the fictional governor of Jamestown, as his underlings despoil the virgin landscape in search of gold.

The shaman of Pocahontas's tribe sums up Disney's perspective on the Europeans who settled our shores: "They prowl the earth like ravenous wolves consuming everything in their path."

"I'm counting on you to make sure these filthy savages don't disrupt our mission," Ratcliffe booms at Capt. John Smith, the expedition's military muscle. But Smith (with a surfer's bod and the voice of Mel Gibson) falls for Pocahontas, alluring in her Frederick's of Chippewa outfit.

She civilizes him, teaching the big lug to love nature "without ever asking what it's worth."

The liberties Disney has taken with history leave one breathless. The real Pocahontas, a child of ten or eleven when she intervened to save Smith's life, becomes a nubile lass of twenty. The first Christian convert in Virginia, Pocahontas is transformed into a pagan priestess who gets advice from trees and weaves white magic.

Not only does the film bend over backward to ensure that Native Americans won't be offended, it panders to feminists in its portrayal of Pocahontas as a liberated squaw who dives off waterfalls and marches to the beat of her own tom-tom.

For the voice of Chief Powhatan, PC-hontas's father, the Magic Kingdom recruited American Indian Movement militant Russell Means, who calls Columbus "a role model for Hitler" and boasts of once urinating on the head of George Washington carved on Mount Rushmore.

Which is more or less what Disney has done to the Jamestown colonists. If they weren't saints, our earliest settlers were hardly the swine depicted in *Pocahontas.*

The 149 men of the Virginia Company who landed on Cape Henry on April 29, 1607, were looking for more than gold. Their first act was to set up a wooden cross brought from England. Their chaplain, the Reverend Robert Hunt, led the company in daily prayer.

They marveled at "fair meadows ablaze with wildflowers" where grew wild strawberries "four times bigger and better than ours in England."

The wealth they dreamed of was farms and towns. Their vision was paid for in blood. Short of rations, they were ravaged by disease. By mid-September, half the company was dead.

If *Pocahontas* caricatures the settlers, it idolizes the Indians. Chief Powhatan may indeed have been brave and sagacious. He was also a tyrant who conquered twenty other tribes, laid ruinous taxes on them, and amassed vast stores of wealth.

Other original inhabitants of this continent despoiled the land to the best of their primitive ability, kept slaves, practiced cruelty in war, and engaged in human sacrifice. Their treatment of women wasn't the equivalent of Phil Donahue in a headdress.

Possibly the most outrageous aspect of *Pocahontas* is Disney's sheer hypocrisy. "With all ya got in ya, boys / Dig up Virginia, boys," sings the avaricious Ratcliffe.

The fictional Jamestown leader isn't the only one who wanted to excavate the Old Dominion. In its lust for tourist gold, Disney planned to ruin a pristine corner of Prince William County, Virginia, to construct its $650-million Disney's America theme park.

Pasture land in a scenic area just miles from the Manassas battlefield would have gone under the backhoe so porcine tourists in Day-Glo shorts could take the Underground Railroad ride and visit the Paul Revere restroom.

Faced with concerted opposition from environmentalists and those outraged by the envisioned assault on American history, Disney gave up its plans last year.

But not before the company's arrogance was graphically illustrated. When questioned about the authenticity and taste of Disney's plan to put Mickey Mouse ears on Abe Lincoln, Chairman Michael Eisner quipped, "The First Amendment gives you the right to be plastic."

It also gives Disney the right to commit cartoon revisionism. Confronted with this travesty, the public should exercise its right to boycott an animated lynching of dead white European males.

## Soulless Hollywood Sells Out Society
*June 7, 1995*

If Bob Dole weren't the leading contender for the GOP presidential nomination, his indictment of Hollywood would be dismissed along with all of the other rebukes.

As it is, his speech last week has ignited the controversy anew. Bearding the MGM lion in its den at a Hollywood fund-raiser, Dole decried movies, music, and television that create "nightmares of depravity" and contribute to "popular culture that threatens to undermine our character as a nation."

Having recently sampled the summer's cinematic crop, I know just what he means.

With its graphic decapitations, throat slittings, and impalements, Mel Gibson's *Braveheart* is the *Gone with the Wind* of gore. Limbs are hacked off, heads smashed, and blood spurts in geysers. When Gibson is tortured in the grand finale, it's a fitting metaphor for the film's effect on audiences who aren't completely brain dead.

After enduring Mel in the thirteenth century, I next subjected myself to Keanu Reeves in the twenty-first. The sadism of *Johnny Mnemonic* is more creative than the action in *Braveheart*—a doctor crucified with scalpels, a woman shot in the mouth with a steel arrow, and a man dissected by a laser. Every other word has four letters. All that's missing is the sterile sex.

The impresarios of offal reacted to Dole's slap as if they were Michelangelo responding to rude remarks about the Sistine Chapel. Marxist moviemaker Oliver Stone found latent McCarthyism in the senator's charges.

Producer Rob Reiner insisted that Hollywood's contribution to crime and moral decay was minimal, "maybe even possibly nonexistent." The real culprits, says Reiner, are assault weapons and handguns.

This is the perfect inversion. Guns are things. They have no message. They neither argue, entice, nor persuade. Electronic entertainment indoctrinates and incites with mass-market allure.

Reiner thus proclaims that while a values-laden medium has no impact on human conduct, inanimate objects do.

Other responses to Dole's comments are even less convincing. Apologists maintain that gangsta rap and movies like *Natural Born Killers* are only a small part of the industry's output and it's unfair to focus on controversial offerings that are leavened by *The Lion King* and *Casper.*

That's like a crack dealer who sells health food on the side, arguing that the wholesome fare absolves him of responsibility for pushing poison.

Former Education Secretary William Bennett was loaded with lame excuses in his meeting with Time Warner executives last month. Bennett has teamed up with C. DeLores Tucker of the National Political Congress of Black Women to convince the conglomerate to stop marketing music that glorifies slaughter and sexual brutality.

Bennett and Tucker presented the executives with a sheet of lyrics from songs distributed under their label. "Big Man with a Gun," by Nine Inch Nails, describes putting a pistol to a woman's head and forcing her to perform oral sex. "Mind of a Lunatic," by the Geto Boys, is an ode to rape and murder ("I slit her throat and watch her shake like on TV").

When asked how they can justify facilitating this spiritual pollution, the media moguls waxed philosophical: "Art is hard to interpret." "Who's to decide what is pornography and what isn't?" "No, these lyrics are not necessarily bad for children to listen to."

If they're serious about the last comment, here's a challenge for Time Warner executives with teenage children: Would you be willing to have your kids tied to chairs in front of a widescreen TV and stereo for eight hours a day and subjected to your more licentious and sanguinary products (that which you sanctify as art and defend as expression)?

If the mental toxins you market are as benign as you maintain, there should be no objection to the experiment.

The First Amendment, artistic integrity, concerns that entertainment is being scapegoated to avoid dealing with "real" problems—Hollywood's rationales would have a hollow ring if the sound weren't muffled by a mound of corpses.

Its ears crammed with cash, the entertainment industry is stone deaf. The lives of children, the safety of women, the survival of our society mean nothing next to the profits of movie studios and record companies.

Dole and Bennett disavow censorship; moral persuasion is the name of their game. But how do you reason with those mesmerized by mammon? How do you appeal to the consciences of the soulless?

## Hollywood Sneers at Seventies Innocence
### March 6, 1995

In his book *The Abolition of Man*, British philosopher C. S. Lewis wrote a requiem for our age:

> We make men without chests and expect of them virtue and enterprise. We laugh at honor and are shocked to find traitors in our midst.

We sneer at modesty and wonder why voyeurism has become our national pastime.

In *The Brady Bunch Movie*—which has been the top-grossing film for at least two consecutive weekends—Hollywood has a grand time lampooning the innocence of the seventies TV family. The gag here is that the Bradys were plucked out of their era and set down in ours—with their polyester fashions, "groovy-chicks" slang, and musty morality intact.

The oldest daughter has a lesbian girlfriend who's constantly coming on to her, but poor, naive Marcia doesn't get it.

The love-starved next-door neighbor invites the two oldest Brady boys over to help her "make a sandwich." They think she means ham and cheese on rye.

The big man on campus picks up Marcia for a date. She takes her shawl in case it rains. Mrs. Brady asks him if he has protection (against the elements). "In assorted colors and textures," he leers at her.

Movie critic Michael Medved says it's all so senseless, that the innuendo adds nothing to the plot. Quite the contrary. The sexual references serve an important purpose. The entertainment industry is driven to ridicule what it calls prudery, to sneer at those with sexual scruples.

The early seventies (the television series ran from 1969 through 1974) was hardly the age of innocence. It was just less degenerate than the nineties.

As the book *Growing Up Brady*—the reminiscences of the actor who played the oldest son—discloses, cast members (who all seemed to have had the hots for someone else on the show) did not exemplify family values. Robert Reed, who played the father, died of AIDS.

So, life didn't reflect art. So, big deal. What matters is the image *The Brady Bunch* beamed into millions of American homes—the wholesomeness of an intact family with loving, involved parents, loyal children, and solidarity in the face of adolescent trauma.

Here we are in the uninhibited (what's the polar opposite of repressed?) 1990s. Television fare is so much more realistic. Take *Real Sex*, HBO's ode to the perverse. The late-night series makes the average R-rated movie look as benign and quaintly charming as a Victorian valentine.

Fighting insomnia, I caught episode No. 11 the other evening. And a rare treat it was. In magazine format, the show consists of a series of reports that sweep the cesspool with microphone and camera.

There's *Love Radio* with Dr. Susie ("I'm a sex addict") Block. Susie does her show from a brass bed, dressed in the boudoir attire of a nineteenth-century Parisian prostitute. She presides over the syndicated circus like a kinky ringmaster. "They will call while they're in bed having sex and put me on the speaker phone." Charming.

Another segment covers a workshop in which men are taught "how to satisfy a woman every time" ("The Ultimate Orgasm with Dr. Bob Schwartz").

My personal favorite was "Debbie Does Dungeons," about a lady who photographs dominatrixes at work. A naked man lies on the floor while a woman in high heels, wearing more leather than you'd ordinarily find at a Harley-Davidson convention, walks on his back.

*Pajama Party Live,* on Southern California's Adam and Eve Channel, bills itself as a "live and interactive pay-for-view show." The next generation of phone sex, viewers call in and tell the ladies what they want them to do, then watch them do it.

"I think America is far too uptight," says one performer. "And if this can bring us to a new level of sexuality, I want to be part of it."

Onward and upward—or do I have the directions reversed?

One in five Americans now has a sexually transmitted disease—excruciating ailments with names like chlamydia, herpes, and genital warts. Each day, another thirty-three thousand casualties of the sexual revolution litter the erotic battlefield.

In 1970, when *The Brady Bunch* was in its second season, the illegitimacy rate was 10.7 percent. In 1991, 29.5 percent of all births were out of wedlock.

The people who entertain us are spiritually sick. In order to convince themselves that their sickness is normal, they must deride normalcy.

We train our children to be sluts and lechers and lament lost innocence. We laugh at decency and wonder why there's an epidemic of child molestation, date rape, infidelity, and broken families. The laugh—as they say—is on us.

## Hollywood Offers More Heroic Kids
*March 15, 1993*

Hollywood holds that teens know best—that with a wave of their callow hands they can sweep away the mountainous debris of adult hypocrisy and injustice.

The entertainment industry is forever lecturing about juvenile virtue. Kids—shouting, singing, shaking various appendages to loud, discordant sounds—will save the universe with their music.

That was the theme of a score of rhythmic offerings over the past decade, including the insufferably sanctimonious *Footloose*, the earnestly tedious *Light of Day*, and the excruciatingly pretentious *Pump Up the Volume*.

The latest entry in the genre, *Swing Kids*, follows the formula, but with a twist. Here, instead of rock, it's the music of Benny Goodman and Count Basie (music I love, by the way) that fuels youthful rebellion.

The movie is set in Hamburg in 1939. A group of alienated adolescents holds covert concerts where they dance to the sounds of American jazz musicians, "Swing heil" their high sign.

How clever to set this tale of musical insurrection in the Third Reich. Nazis are ideal villains. The Swing Kids wear their hair long, dress eccentrically, jive to exhilarating music (one even plays the guitar), and reject the values of their repressive culture. Any parallels come to mind?

Subliminal message—he who opposes the music of youth is a baby Brownshirt. Recall Frank Zappa tarring Tipper Gore with the swastika smear when her Parents Music Resource Center came up with the totally repressive idea of labeling record albums for explicit lyrics.

In Hollywood's eye, music is always liberating. Our cultural elite can't conceive of the reverse, that music can corrupt as well as exalt, that it can subjugate as well as liberate.

One need look no further for verification of this principle than the Germany of *Swing Kids*. As much as any other factor, Hitler's worldview was shaped by the music of Wagner, with its pagan mythology and paeans to chaos—the destruction of the status quo to make way for the new order.

Der Fuhrer sat through Wagner's Ring Cycle (a fifteen-hour ordeal) seventeen or eighteen times. A crucial point in his life came on a November evening in 1906, when the teenage Hitler heard Wagner's *Rienzi* in Vienna. His boyhood friend, August Kubizek, said the future architect of genocide was "in a state of complete ecstasy and rapture." Years later, Hitler ordered that huge Nazi rallies open with the overture from this opera.

Richard Wagner was the original artistic rebel. Given his lifestyle and ethos, if Wagner were alive today, he'd probably be the lead guitarist in a heavy metal band. The composer joined the unsuccessful revolution of 1849 in Dresden, but soon decided that culture, not politics, was a more congenial tool for establishment smashing.

"I shall destroy the order of things that makes millions the slaves of a few and those few the slaves of their own power," Wagner wrote in 1848. "True art is revolutionary, because its very existence is opposed to the ruling spirit of the community," the self-styled Byronic hero proclaimed.

Wagner led a life Madonna would have envied—using and discarding intimates, creating scandals across the continent, impregnating his best friend's wife while living in the family's home, eventually absconding with her.

Many of rock music's favorite themes are foreshadowed in Wagnerian opera—deviant sexuality (Siegmund's incest), violence, nihilistic destruction, misogyny, the juxtaposition of sex and death, and the rejection of Judeo-Christian values.

Wagner's virulent anti-Semitism (which found its fruition in the death camps of Europe) was quite natural, in a pagan sense. The Jews symbolized everything Wagner was revolting against— order and objective morality.

In Germany today, another group of heroic, young rebels is challenging the status quo with their music. Like the *Swing Kids*, they dress differently (leather jackets) and favor an odd tonsorial style (shaved heads). Their music expresses their alienation from society.

And, wouldn't you just know it, uptight adults are once again trying to stamp out musical free expression. Earlier this month, German police began a sweeping crackdown on skinhead record companies. In raids in nine of the German states, police confiscated thirty thousand records (extolling Nazism and inciting xenophobic action), as well as several hundred rounds of ammunition and explosives. Prosecutors maintain the music is one element in fomenting the violence that resulted in the murder of seventeen foreigners last year.

Just a bunch of wild and crazy teens, out to save the universe with their music. Hey kids, let's put on a Nuremberg rally!

## In Hollywood It's a PC Life
*December 20, 1993*

In its holiday releases, Hollywood is once again assaulting viewers with the usual barrage of political pleading, mangled history, and victimology.

The oh-so politically correct presents under tinseltown's tree this Christmas include *Geronimo: An American Legend; Philadelphia,* with Tom Hanks as an AIDS-stricken lawyer fighting job discrimination; *Heaven and Earth,* the last (God be praised) installment of Oliver Stone's Vietnam trilogy; and—to be opened in February—*On Deadly Ground,* starring Steven Seagal as an eco-Rambo battling a slick oil company executive.

Which got me thinking: Given its outlook and obsessions, how would Hollywood remake *It's a Wonderful Life* (the charming 1946 Capra classic) in keeping with the pessimistic/politicized quality of nineties cinema?

What grotesque mutation would it resemble, once Hollywood finished making it relevant, eroticized, and sensitive to minority concerns?

Of course, the film would be renamed *It's a Meaningless Life.* To set the mood, anti-hero George Bailey would be a sexually abused child—Mr. Gower, the seemingly kindly pharmacist George worked for as a boy, having taken a somewhat personal interest in his young assistant.

As a banker, the adult George would be a cross between Charles Keating (head of the defunct Lincoln Savings and Loan) and Ebenezer Scrooge, redlining parts of Bedford Falls to prevent minorities from getting mortgages, perhaps laundering mob money.

I mean, he runs an S&L for crying out loud!

Given Hollywood's anti-business mindset, for the film to be "realistic," he'd have to be scamming both the government and townfolks. Neil Bush or George Bush, Jr., would have a bit part as an officer of the Bailey Building and Loan.

The charming scene where George and Mary take a stroll after being dunked in the high school swimming pool, Mary attired only in a bathrobe that she loses, fleeing to a convenient bush, would be made more socially relevant. In the updated version, George would jump in after her. Sexual harassment? Date rape?

The married George would have an affair (doesn't everyone?) with Violet, the town's hot ticket. This would provide an opportunity for gratuitous nudity and explicit sex scenes.

Mary Bailey—a battered wife à la *Sleeping with the Enemy*—would discover she's a latent lesbian and run off with Annie, the Baileys' African American cook (who has a Ph.D. in sociology but was reduced to working as a menial by entrenched institutional racism), giving the film a chance to explore the timely topics of domestic violence and gay biracial romance.

Uncle Billy, the lovable, befuddled character whose forgetfulness provokes the crisis in the original version, would also be transformed. In the remake, he would suffer a breakdown brought on by the misplaced bank deposit and agonizing memories of the atrocities his platoon committed during World War I (Verdun Stress Syndrome).

Following a flashback triggered by the wafting aroma of baking French bread, Uncle Billy (played by Jean Claude Van Damme) wipes out half of Bedford Falls with an assault rifle before being shot by Bert the cop, who leaves the force to become a vigilante.

Ernie the cabby is a crossdresser (who wears a skirt not visible below the dashboard) driven to suicide by a judgmental society. The foregoing would give the feature an R rating for both sex and violence, assuring sizable teenage audiences.

In our remake, Clarence will be no angel. After all, a religious figure is fair game. This time, Clarence is a radio evangelist who stages phony faith healings, bilks his listeners out of millions, and has an affair with Tammy Faye Bakker.

Old Man Potter, the malevolent wheelchair-bound plotter in the original, would be the only good guy in the remake. To present him in an unfavorable light would constitute both age discrimination and stigmatizing the handicapped.

The new Senior Citizen Potter will be a lone crusader, valiantly fighting to save the masses from the predatory business practices of the Bailey Building and Loan and exposing a power plant whose chemical dumping pollutes the community's water supply causing a rise in the cancer rate and extinction of several endangered species.

After his encounter with Clarence the pseudo-angel, George will understand that his life really wasn't worth living and that existence is unbearable (especially for movie audiences).

At the end of the film, he either (1) finds a higher bridge to jump from or (2) moves to Hollywood and becomes a script-writer.

## Prez, Hollywood Make a Killing
*March 20, 1995*

Just call him Billy Hollywood.

When Clinton steps onto the stage of his April 8 Beverly Hills fund-raiser, the glitz capital of the universe will salute a president whose flashy style and hollow values mirror its own.

All of the millions Hollywood can muster will be marshaled in the defense of a fast-fading administration. Tickets for the gala are expected to cost between $25,000 and $100,000—approaching the price of a Barbra Streisand concert.

With Newt Gingrich in the House Speaker's chair, there's a special urgency to show-biz philanthropy. "Newt's a great poster child for the Hollywood money crowd," observes an aide to Sen. Barbara Boxer (D-Calif.).

Hollywood hysteria is reaching a fevered pitch.

"The far right is waging a war for the soul of America," Streisand warned the trendies in her speech at Harvard's Kennedy School last month.

Like the president she so admires (Babs was an overnight guest at the White House in 1993), the chanteuse of show tunes aspires to be a thinker—and more. Her address was titled "The Artist as Citizen." Artist? Imagine a resurrected Beethoven calling his first album "Color Me Ludwig."

The never-funnier girl spurned the notion that entertainers are self-absorbed "bubbleheads" who are too "insulated, free-thinking, and subversive" to contribute to the political process.

Why are members of the so-called creative community such inveterate leftists? To that perennial question, Babs modestly replied: "Most artists turn up on the humanist, compassionate side of public debate because we have to walk in other people's shoes.... This does tend to make us more sympathetic to politics that are tolerant."

And you thought it was because they live in a dream world, lead lives of dissipation, lean toward moral anarchy, and have conscience pangs over their undeserved wealth.

Committed, thoughtful, authentic—that's the Hollywood left. Among the high-dollar donors to Clinton's last campaign is Alec Baldwin, who told an interviewer in 1990 that he fantasized about joining a terrorist group, like the Black Panthers or IRA.

Kevin Costner, another Friend of Bill, made a fortune celebrating the Lakota Sioux in *Dances with Wolves* and now is in the process of taking some of their tribal land, stolen by the federal government, to build a casino.

Politically, Hollywood speaks with excellent credentials. Consider its contributions to our culture. In 1992, Ted Field was the fifth-largest donor to the Democratic party. Field lives in fear that someday his record company, Interscope, will produce an album with socially redeeming value.

His fears are unfounded. Last week, Interscope released Tupac Shakur's latest lyrical atrocity. The rapper is serving a sentence of 1.5 to 4.5 years for sexual abuse. His music perfectly complements his lifestyle.

Whether it's cop-killer songs, ditties about degrading sex, or odes to gang violence, Interscope makes music to destroy civilization by. Do the Democrats have any qualms over sharing its blood money?

While Clinton cries hooray for Hollywood, tinseltown continues to serve up heaping portions of sex, savagery, and assaults on virtue. *Pulp Fiction* received seven Academy Award nominations, the industry's ultimate acclaim.

Quentin Tarantino's film delivers blood and brain matter by the barrel. It dwells lovingly on sadistic torture.

Still, it's not the most violent movie in recent times—not by a long shot.

That distinction goes to Oliver Stone's *Natural Born Killers*, last year's cinematic slaughterhouse scripted by Tarantino, the Vivaldi of violence. Only Hollywood could come up with a love story about serial killers.

Life copycats art. Earlier this month, fifteen-year-old Jason Lewis of Senoia, Georgia, grabbed his father's twelve-gauge and killed both of his parents after talking to a friend about his favorite inspirational film, *Natural Born Killers*. Lewis wanted to follow its fictional heroes, whose homicidal odyssey started with the murder of the female lead's family.

Truly, there's no business like show business—except, perhaps, for the business of the Cali cartel.

Hollywood knows where its interests lie, knows which party promotes the dissolution of standards and values that creates a ready market for its increasingly sick product.

There is indeed a "war for the soul of America." The cultural polluters, who daily dump tons of psychic toxins into the public consciousness, have found their natural ally in the party of spiritual decline.

# chapter nine

# DIVERSITY DOGMA

## Many Faces of PC at Dear Wellesley
*May 26, 1994*

In less than a fortnight, Wellesley College will welcome its most celebrated alumna for her twentieth class reunion. Hillary Rodham Clinton came to Wellesley a Goldwater girl in 1965 and left a roaring radical four years later. The school's mind-bending propensities have only increased in the interim.

Once a sedate women's college, today Wellesley is a hotbed of all things trendy in academia. At Wellesley, the Three Horsemen (horse-persons?) of Correctness—multiculturalism, feminism, and lesbianism—cut a savage swath of indoctrination and intimidation.

Intellectual homogenization begins during orientation week with a mandatory ICAN (Inter-Cultural Awareness Now) reeducation session. This occurs in small groups, where Pyongyang-style students are required to read aloud from *Unpacking the White Privileged Backpack,* by Peggy McIntosh.

"When I got here, I didn't think I was a racist," says sophomore Kristie Bachna. "At Wellesley, you have to 'find the racist part of you,' or invent it."

Multiculturalism pervades the curricula and social life. In her Psych 101 class, Bachna was assigned Maya Angelou's *I Know Why the Caged Bird Sings.* "We never discussed the book in relation to psychology. It was all a black/white thing—twenty minutes of boohoo, white people are so terrible."

Another student told me a classmate objected when she asked for a "plain, white bagel" in the lunch line one day.

When Bachna criticized the Angelou book, her instructor suggested a course in the Africana Studies Department to instill sensitivity.

Good idea. Perhaps she could take a class from Professor Tony (the-Jews-are-out-to-get-me) Martin, the department's resident hatemonger who assigns to his students a Nation of Islam book on the slave trade alleging Simon Legree's real name was Seymour Saperstein.

Wellesley feminism has reached its fruition in the dingbat theories of the aforesaid McIntosh, associate director of the Wellesley Center for Research on Women. McIntosh believes education is dominated by white, Western, male, heterosexual reasoning ("vertical thinking"), consisting of conceptualization, goal attainment, and logic.

Much to be preferred is feminine "horizontal thinking," with its emphasis on sensitivity, emotion, and intuition. (McIntosh would like to see a science course titled "A Feeling for the Organism: Science Without Mastery.") If she didn't sound like a medieval misogynist (women don't think like men), McIntosh would actually be amusing.

Wellesley feminism also comes in an X-rated version. On January 29, there was a masturbation orientation for dormitory resident assistants. A vibrator was demonstrated and its benefits touted in helping students overcome "sexual repression." If parents wanted their daughters to receive autoerotic instruction, you'd think they could get it for less than $24,700 a year.

Lesbianism is very much in vogue. The school celebrates both National Coming Out Day (October 3) and Lesbian, Bisexual, and Gay Week (February 18–26). The former includes a "womyn's" dance and "kiss and hug-in" on the chapel steps. Bachna: "I'm a good little Catholic girl; that bothers me. Couldn't they do it somewhere else?"

The campus is festooned in pink triangles and plastered with slogans ("Lesbian love is the best"). There's a film series which includes *Last Call at Maud's*, "a delightful look at the 1950s lesbian bar scene," lectures, and a Lesbigay—get it?—ball.

There's even an accredited course in "queer theory," that examines "queerness in its various manifestations and practices, butch-femme, transgendering, cross-dressing, bisexuality, and third gender."

But even at Wellesley, some things are beyond the pale. Last year, a housemother set up a Christmas tree outside her apartment. The president of the college herself forced the miscreant to remove it.

On most campuses, PC dogmatism is opposed by a beleaguered band of conservative iconoclasts, usually grouped around an alternative newspaper. Here, at least, the Wellesley scene offers a glimmer of hope.

A year ago, Larisa Vanov (Wellesley '82), a Houston professional, organized Women for Freedom, a coalition of students, parents, and alumnae to fight Big Sister. It now has four hundred members and a thirty-member student chapter, to which Bachna belongs.

WFF recently sponsored a campus lecture by Christina Hoff Sommers, a philosophy professor at Clark University and author of the book *Who Stole Feminism?* Sommers charges: "A Wellesley education today is a complete betrayal of what a liberal arts education should be. The administration has a radical agenda which is just as vigorously denied to parents as it is promoted to students."

Should Vanov ever tap the power of the purse—get alumni to

withhold financial support until the coercion stops—she would indeed become the Wellesley establishment's worse nightmare.

## Corporate America Goes for Diversity
### *February 3, 1995*

**"W**hite, Male, and Worried" is the cover story in the current issue of *Business Week*. Given corporate America's latest obsession, there is cause for concern.

Quota hiring and promotion apparently aren't enough. The execrable white male must be hectored, humiliated, and reeducated. "Managing diversity," they call it.

More than half the work force now consists of women, non-whites, and the foreign-born, diversity mavens repeat mantra-fashion. To derive maximum benefit from these workers, businesses must learn to "value" differences among their employees.

Mobil, Apple Computer, Xerox, Digital Equipment, and Procter and Gamble all are major players in the diversity game. AT&T celebrates everything from Asian Pacific American Heritage Month to Gay Pride Week.

Diversity training (an estimated 40 percent of businesses have it in some form) is based on the premise that blacks, women, Hispanics, and Asians have group identities. Each has certain cultural attitudes at variance with those of the "white, male ethic." "You don't manage everyone the same, you manage everyone fairly," says Apple's Santiago Rodriguez.

Enter diversity trainers, ready to fight entrenched biases for fat fees. A contract with one consulting firm costs $500,000 for the first year of a three- to five-year commitment.

Diversity dogma would have it both ways. While insisting that we not make assumptions, it makes assumptions. Demanding that we reject stereotypes, it posits its own.

Thus Hispanics "humanize" a business environment. Asians defer to authority and so avoid saying "no" outright. Women are more intuitive and empathic. And so on.

Sensitivity to minority concerns includes an examination of past injustices, which—naturally—necessitates consideration of how the system worked to the advantage of white males (treated as a fungible commodity).

Ken Richardson, a WM who was made to endure a week of diversity defamation in 1992, told *Business Week* he was blamed "for everything from slavery to the glass ceiling." The white female and black male instructors seemed to "feed into the white-male-bashing." Richardson confesses: "I became bitter and remain so."

Diversity doyenne Judith Katz, quoted in Washington's *City Paper*, insists, "Whites need to be reeducated." The problem, Katz comments, is that "White people do not see themselves as White [outrageous!]. This is a way of perpetuating the racist system and being part of the problem."

Another consultant uses a handout that lists right and wrong attitudes for trainees. Wrong: "I deny being White and do not see my whiteness supporting racism." Right: "I own the positive parts of being White and accept the reality of parts of my whiteness supporting racism."

One imagines a group of corporate executives, in Brooks Brothers suits instead of Mao jackets, sitting in a circle, chanting: "I confess my corrupt role in oppressing the minority masses and only wish I could die for the revolution to atone for my sins."

The most daring dimension of diversity indoctrination is instruction in the appreciation of homosexuality. In this regard, AT&T is the leader. "Gay rights is the issue of the nineties, just as civil rights was the issue of the sixties and women's rights the issue of the seventies," said an AT&T spokesman.

The communications conglomerate conducts "Homophobia in

the Workplace" training sessions, designed to expose "examples of homophobic behaviors which effect productivity" and present "accurate information" on the lifestyle.

The "accurate information" comes directly from the canon of the gay-rights movement. Workshops are taught by homosexual consultant Brian McNaught. A reader whose husband was subjected to the Pavlovian procedure told me McNaught spent much of the eight-hour session describing how he had suffered at the hand of the Roman Catholic Church in childhood.

Be assured that the Catholic Church, the Orthodox rabbinate, and the pro-family movement aren't invited in to present their perspective, even though the public, by sizable majorities, agrees with them.

Similarly, when the AT&T facility in North Andover, Massachusetts celebrates Women's Awareness Month, it's with the National Organization for Women and Planned Parenthood, not Concerned Women for America.

It may not have dawned on business leaders that employees didn't go to work for them with the expectation of being scapegoated and having their psyches probed and their values derided.

Regarding inherent differences, the sole concern of managers should be enforcing civility (which could be accomplished by a simple memo annotating behavior that will not be tolerated). Attempts at indoctrination invariably provoke backlashes.

Political correctness is no longer confined to the college campus. Corporate America has joined the ranks of the nation's thought police, wielding a nightstick called diversity training. If you work for a corporation and haven't as yet felt its bone-crushing blows on your cranium, you soon will.

# Gender Insanity: L Street to The Citadel
*June 14, 1995*

It was such a little thing—a tempest in a teapot (a brouhaha over barbells?)—but so symbolic of an age where sexual correctness trumps every other consideration.

"This is 1995, and gender segregation is being done," huffed Debra DiCenso, a weight lifter at South Boston's L Street Bathhouse. "It's [gasp, oh no!] very sexist."

DiCenso's tank top was in a bunch because the city-owned gym maintained separate weight rooms for men and women.

The men's side is twice as large as the women's, the lady lamented. Never mind that the club has three times as many male as female members. The heaviest weight on the women's side is only thirty pounds, DiCenso protested, even though women are far less susceptible to Schwarzenegger-envy.

To protest this gross injustice, DiCenso stormed the bastion of male biceps and got arrested. The outcome was equally predictable: The city caved in, and the weight rooms are now open to both sexes.

Other women complain that men will probably monopolize the equipment, as they did before the separate facilities were established.

But DiCenso has what she wants. No one polled the club's members to ascertain their desires. Do they matter? Majorities are nothing next to placating rampaging feminists and furthering the culturally sanctioned myth that—except for the plumbing—the sexes are identical.

Next we have The Citadel in South Carolina. The military academy's all-male cadet corps of nineteen hundred wants to keep the school's 153-year-old tradition.

One woman, Shannon Faulkner, insists on forcing herself on them.

If she succeeds, she will destroy the school's unique atmosphere, where leaders are created by a frankly brutal—albeit highly success-ful—brother-rat system of discipline and obedience.

A federal district court ordered Faulkner housed in the bar-racks, if she's ultimately admitted to The Citadel. The school wanted her to sleep in the infirmary, to spare Faulkner the harsher aspects of hazing.

Discriminatory! Judge C. Weston Houck intoned. At the same time, the Carter appointee ordered the school to spell out its pol-icy on sexual harassment, noting that in the disciplinary process, cadets routinely use terms "derogatory to women."

Treat her like one of the boys, but guard her sensibilities, the judge ruled, as if the two were somehow compatible.

If The Citadel falls, all single-sex institutions will be imperiled, including the nation's eighty-two women's liberal-arts colleges, their proven worth notwithstanding.

These colleges account for only 4.5 percent of female graduates nationwide, yet their alumni represent fully one-quarter of all women on the boards of Fortune 500 firms.

Males thrive in The Citadel's unabashedly masculine environ-ment. After four years, the graduation rate for black students is 67 percent, double the national average.

Young men and women learn differently. Men like an atmo-sphere where competition and subordination are stressed. Women prefer cooperation and support. Will the obvious benefits of single-sex education soon be lost in the mad rush to annihilate anything that smacks of segregation?

Even if The Citadel and Virginia Military Institute survive intact, our armed forces have unconditionally surrendered to the most mindless form of gender equality, one that blithely refuses to recognize nature.

In February, the fleet set sail for Utopia, when Navy Secretary John Dalton rejected a proposal to give women pregnancy tests before sending them to sea for months on combat ships.

"The Department of the Navy recognizes that pregnancy is a natural event... and is not a presumption of medical incapacity," Dalton inanely declared.

Old age, infirmity, and death are also natural events. One eagerly awaits the day when Clinton's PC Navy recognizes that mortality is a natural occurrence and henceforth sailors won't be checked for vital signs before being sent to sea.

There are times when men and women want to be alone, in the gym or at school. There is a wisdom in voluntary separation beyond the dogma of gender radicals. (After all, DiCenso could have joined a gym where the sexes sweat together, and Faulkner certainly has other educational options.)

As for the reductio ad absurdum of sexual equality—pregnant women on combat ships—pray that in our next war the other side is also an equal opportunity employer.

---

Postscript: Shannon Faulkner was admitted to The Citadel on August 19, 1995. She subsequently quit without spending even a full day as a student. Feminists were crushed by Faulkner's move.

## Navy Women Rocking the Boat
*May 12, 1994*

P at Schroeder, Admiral of the Ocean Seas—doesn't it sound grand? Since she has the power, why not the title, too?

Within days of assuming his post as chief of naval operations, Adm. Jeremy Boorda snapped to, saluted sharply, and stood at attention awaiting orders.

Emerging from a meeting with Rep. Patricia Schroeder (D-Colo.)—powerful member of the House Armed Services Committee and Tailhook grand inquisitor—Boorda announced that yesterday wouldn't be a moment too soon to launch Schroeder's version of Operation Petticoat.

Boorda's predecessor, Adm. Frank Kelso, almost lost two of his stars and a hefty chunk of his retirement pay for insubordination. Tailhook was the excuse, but the vote to demote Kelso prior to retirement was actually an object lesson. (Feminists in Congress wanted to show the brass who was really in charge.) And that was after poor Kelso reversed course on his 1991 opposition to women on war ships.

Boorda's taking no chances of getting on the wrong side of Schroeder. Women on combat ships? Yes ma'am! Will three air-craft carriers be enough for starters? Submarines, too? That may take some time, but we'll get to work on it!

As a face-saving device, Boorda pleaded pragmatism. We're having recruiting problems, the admiral argued. "It doesn't make sense to exclude half the population [from combat branches], does it?"

What doesn't make sense is his reasoning. The combat arms have always had special appeal for male recruits. This has to do with danger and camaraderie—guy stuff. Put women in combat, and its appeal for men drops dramatically.

It will also hurt female recruitment. In a 1992 Pentagon survey, 11 percent of young women said they'd be more likely to enlist if the ban on women in combat were lifted, but 25 percent said they'd be less inclined. Another survey showed only 12 percent of enlisted women and 14 percent of female officers would volunteer for combat posting. Now, many will have no choice.

Women on combat ships will really rock the boat. If national defense were the determining factor, instead of equal employment opportunity, it wouldn't be considered for a moment.

Servicewomen are three to four times as nondeployable as men. Their rates of voluntary and involuntary discharge, due to pregnancy and other family matters, are also significantly higher.

Elaine Donnelly of the Center for Military Readiness notes the loss of skilled personnel on a combat vessel can be catastrophic. It takes eleven months to train a reactor operator on a nuclear submarine. Since the sub is submerged for extended periods, evacuating and replacing a pregnant sailor will create a logistical nightmare.

If women take over a nine-man berthing area, a sub with a crew of 138 would lose one-quarter of its toilet facilities. Close quarters will make physical contact unavoidable, creating opportunities for both intimacy and harassment charges.

Has Boorda noticed the physical differences between the sexes? Sailors don't march with a full pack, but the dollies used to load torpedoes into firing position weigh seventy-five to eighty pounds and require a great deal of strength to maneuver quickly.

A 1985 study undertaken for the Navy revealed "significant male/female differences in emergency shipboard task performance" where grip and upper-torso strength are involved. While substantial majorities of women fell short of physical standards for eight critical shipboard tasks, virtually all of the men passed.

Exciting differences will also come into play. Boorda will turn his Navy into a fleet of floating Tailhook conventions.

The day the sea-dog-turned-lap-dog reported to Admiral Schroeder for his orders, the Navy announced the punishment of eight male and female crew members of the destroyer-tender *Puget Sound* for offenses including sexual harassment, fraternization, adultery, and intimidation. Imagine the possibilities on a combat craft six months at sea.

Dennis Franklin, formerly Commander Franklin, a promising graduate of Annapolis, discovered the hazards here the hard way. Assigned to the destroyer-tender USS *Yellowstone* as executive officer last year, he found himself doing a tour on the Love Boat.

Male superiors protected their girlfriends from discipline. (Franklin couldn't even reprimand a female assistant navigator who almost ran the ship aground.) Sexual harassment of male and female personnel was commonplace. When Franklin blew the whistle, he found himself charged with harassment. Cleared by a court martial, he was nevertheless forced to resign. During Desert Storm, 64 percent of soldiers surveyed said they were aware of sexual activity between male and female troops.

Putting women on combat craft will devastate discipline, morale, and preparedness. Unless we sail into battle against the *Yellow Submarine* or the *Good Ship Lollipop*, we are cruisin' for a bruisin'.

chapter ten

# CRYING SHAME

## We Just Can't Stop Growing Victims
*August 14, 1995*

Apropos the debate over reforming America's illegitimacy engine (which pays adolescents to procreate out of wedlock), there's new research purporting to show that most teenage mothers were sexually abused children who grew up to be exploited by older men.

The study by Judith Musick is a vintage victim lament. In a survey of 445 unwed teen moms, Musick discovered that more than 60 percent were abused earlier in their lives.

According to determinist doctrine, as they matured, the abuse left them vulnerable to exploitation by more worldly men. The scenario conjures up images of hordes of cads (as suave as headwaiters, as slick as olive oil), seducing and abandoning from coast to coast.

The point being? Says Musick, "Punishment [denying them welfare benefits] is an irrelevant way to stop teen mothers." Childhood abuse programmed them to surrender to every man who entered their lives.

For defenders of the status quo, this is most convenient. They want desperately to believe that welfare queens aren't responsible for their lives of indolence—that some compulsion forces them to breed for bucks.

Several problems arise here. There's no uniform definition of sexual abuse, which could span the spectrum from forced intercourse to necking. Like its kissin' cousin—sexual harassment—defined broadly enough, almost everyone could claim victim status.

Musick's study is based on allegations that are impossible to verify. What exactly is a pregnant sixteen-year-old supposed to say to explain her condition? Q: "Were you molested as a child?" A: "Well, no. Actually, I'm just promiscuous." Or: "They told me in school if I used a condom I'd be cool." Of course they're all products of rape and incest.

If sexual abuse made them susceptible to seducers, did it also prevent them from using contraceptives correctly?

There's just no end to psychological exculpation. I recently heard a radio shrink say actor Hugh Grant was "acting out" when he picked up hooker Divine Brown for oral sex. Horny? Heck, no. Grant was "manifesting in observable ways deep-seated anger or resentment."

Susan Smith is the mother lode of the devil made me do it. The South Carolina woman sent her toddlers to a watery grave not because she wanted to marry her rich boyfriend and they were in the way. Shame on you for even thinking such a thing!

She was driven to it (put the Mazda in park, Susan) by her father's suicide, an incestuous stepfather, an unhappy marriage, and a series of disastrous relationships.

Susan was "abused" by her stepdad, Beverly Russell. The abuse began one evening, when then sixteen-year-old Smith decided to sit in Russell's lap. We're not exactly talking candy bars and schoolyards here.

Smith was so traumatized by the experience that she continued having sex with Russell into adulthood and up until a few months before the murders.

Her attorney claimed Smith was distraught when she strapped the kids into their car seats and let her Mazda slide into John D. Long Lake—so agitated that she concocted a story about a black carjacker, which she repeated for nine days.

The jury bought the abuse excuse to the extent of giving Smith thirty years in prison instead of the death she so richly deserves.

New York Lt. Gov. Betsy McCaughey was right when she remarked that Smith's crime "cries out for the death penalty, just as little Alex and Michael cried out for help as they sank in the icy cold water."

Bottom line. With the possible exception of tobacco company executives, no one is responsible for anything. Murderers aren't responsible for their savage acts. Celebrities aren't responsible for their sluttish behavior. Unwed teens aren't to blame for their wanton irresponsibility.

Earlier this month, teenagers Devon Watts and Kelly Heemstra were arrested for the murder of seventy-three-year-old Leonard Hughey in White Cloud, Michigan. Police believe the girls pulled the trigger together, then threw a party for their friends over the corpse of the man who had befriended them.

A sign of things to come is the comment of Heemstra's grandmother that the poor child had a "lifetime" of problems and was shifted from one foster home to another. By the time of the trial Devon and Kelly will have become tragic heroines and the real victim will be all but forgotten.

It's a big, blameless world out there, with 5.4 billion genetically determined, environmentally programmed pawns tugged this way and that by hands invisible to all but sociologists and defense psychiatrists.

## Character Isn't Mass Produced
*October 3, 1994*

The Josephson Institute of Ethics may be incompetent at values education but it certainly knows how to spread the old soft soap.

Its letter of September 19 addressed me as a "respected columnist," who has "written and thought" about "the nation's character crisis." Communicator and philosopher that I am, I'll certainly want to help publicize National Character Counts Week. And why not? We could all use a good laugh.

October 16–22 has been officially designated National Character Counts Week by Congress and the president. Given the stature of the Whitewater surfer and one of the most discredited institutions in the Western Hemisphere, their imprimatur on a morality project is less than impressive.

After noting that violent crime rose 50 percent between 1985 and 1992 and the birthrate among unmarried teens went up 60 percent in the past decade, the institute offers its antidote to moral decay—virtue through clichés.

Character Counts Week will advance its ethical agenda with youth assemblies, school curricula, and "Si, Si, Si" awards—prizes for essays, posters, poems, and songs about good conduct. Socrates meets Sesame Street.

According to the institute, character is based on "six core values—trustworthiness, respect, responsibility, fairness, caring, and citizenship." What happened to bravery, cleanliness, and reverence?

These "six pillars of character" in turn lead to "ten basic rules of conduct"—"be honest, keep promises, be loyal, be kind and caring, pursue excellence," etc.

Some who've endorsed this fluff, like former Education Secretary Bill Bennett, should know better. Others shouldn't be mentioned in the same breath as the word *ethics*.

One of the "qualified interviewees" to whom I'm asked to apply for more information on character development is U.S. Sen. Barbara Mikulski (D-Md.).

Mikulski favors domestic partners legislation (raising same-sex couples to the status of marrieds), supported eliminating funding for abstinence-based education, and opposed an amendment to end federal subsidies for obscene art. What she can teach us about values is the consequences of their absence.

You don't get character by turning on a tap. You don't foster virtue by distributing lists of dos and don'ts. Few intend to do evil. Even Hitler didn't look in the mirror in the morning and muse: "I believe I'll be really vile and vicious today." In a July interview, Charles Manson said he thought of himself as a good person.

People have an incredible capacity to rationalize their actions. "I didn't steal. He cheated me. I was getting back what's mine." "She enjoyed it too, even though she struggled." "I'm just giving the public what it wants."

If you asked a member of Los Angeles's notorious Crips why he's dealing drugs and killing the competition, he might say he is "keeping promises" (to his customers), being "loyal" (to fellow gang members), and pursuing "excellence" in his chosen profession.

Former UN Ambassador Alan Keyes, who ran against Mikulski in 1992, observes: "Values aren't enough. In the end, you need a standard by which values can be judged. How do you get people not just to know what's right but to do what's right?" Said the Bard, "If to do were as easy as to know what were good to do, chapels had been churches, and poor men's cottages princes' palaces."

How did the Josephson Institute come up with its six pillars and ten rules? Sharon Darrow, co-director of the Character Counts project, told me both came out of a July 22–25, 1992, conference in Aspen, Colorado (home of hot-tub psychology), attended by representatives of organizations like the Girls Clubs, YMCA, and Children's Television Workshop.

So you tell your average hormone-driven seventeen-year-old:

"Look, here are six core values you should affirm and ten rules of behavior you should follow." And he says: "Says who?" And you say: "Oh, the professional staff of prominent organizations who met in a playground of the overprivileged two years ago and drew up a list of values that, in their opinion, 'form the core of a democratic society.' "

And he says: "See ya!"

Or you tell him: "Here's a code that comes from God (acknowledged as the ruler of the universe by 90 percent of the adult population). It has been time-tested over the course of three thousand years. It worked for your parents, grandparents, and great-grandparents. It'll work for you, too."

Which approach will have a greater impact? Which will make it easier to overcome temptation? Which is more likely to instill the discipline needed to do the right thing?

It's easier to make a computer out of cornflakes than to teach values without religion. In this regard, National Character Counts Week won't count for much.

## Liberals Discover It's a Cryin' Shame
*February 9, 1995*

B ehold, the liberals discovered shame—and lo, it was very good (First Media, Chapter 3, Verse 19).

The cover story in the February 6 issue of *Newsweek* ("The Return of Shame") represents a milestone in liberal rethinking of ethics. Having told us for decades not to be judgmental and that guilt is neurotic, suddenly, an establishment organ has determined that a sense of shame is appropriate, practical, and socially beneficial.

"Just when shame seemed as dead as Cotton Mather, red faces have begun to shove themselves back into our late-20th-century consciousness," *Newsweek* asserts.

Among the examples of shame inducement, the magazine cites a Chattanooga judge who paddled a juvenile thug; the city of La Mesa, California, which publishes the names and pictures of men who patronize prostitutes; and a Maryland program that requires sex offenders to get down on their knees and apologize to victims.

Overall, "the goal here is not mere retribution," *Newsweek* confides, "but conformity—good conformity, the kind that makes it easier for people to form communities."

This is heady stuff. Where will it lead? Imagine a somber Mister Rogers admonishing children: "People who do bad things are bad." Dare to be judgmental!

Liberals have been the Frank Lloyd Wrights of our guilt-free society. They rejected sin as a superstitious relic of a barbaric past. They psychologized guilt out of existence—cured it with conscience-killing doses of self-esteem instruction.

They even altered our language for maximum blame avoidance. Black-and-white expressions were transmuted to soft, nonoffensive pastels. Thus "illegitimate" became "out of wedlock," "fornication" became "cohabitation," "unnatural acts" became "alternative lifestyles," and "sick" evolved to "dysfunctional."

And now, many on the left regard their creation with horror. Even liberals are beginning to put two and two together and come out with 25,000 murders annually, 1.6 million teens treated for drug or alcohol abuse each year, and an illegitimacy rate of 89 percent in Harlem.

The left has always believed in the virtue of penitence for select groups. They have encouraged corporate executives to feel guilty about the environment, men to agonize over date rape and glass ceilings, the middle class to feel guilty over homelessness, and Caucasians to don sackcloth over just about everything that's happened here in the past 371 years.

At the same time, they've found it impossible to assign blame to designated victim groups: the homeless (even those who've chosen al fresco existence to the buzz of an alarm clock), the AIDS-afflicted (even those whose indulgence courted the contagion), and blacks.

Regarding the latter, recall the media's performance after the 1992 Los Angeles riots, when looting and racist assaults were rationalized as understandable expressions of frustration over police brutality and institutional racism.

A sense of shame and personal responsibility go hand in hand. Unlike their nineteenth-century forebears, modern liberals are determinists at heart.

If you tell people they're not accountable for their conduct (that heredity, an abusive family, or the angst of oppression made them do it), how can you expect them to feel remorse, even over the most loathsome behavior?

The hung jury in the Menendez case, where two greedy young savages got away with parricide by raising the specter of childhood abuse, is literally determinism's dead end.

How did we lose our sense of shame? Misplaced it, perhaps? Negligently left it lying around for any passerby to pick up?

Shame fell by the wayside when religion became irrelevant for many Americans. It happened when we chose the god of psychology (of redemption through self-assertiveness training) over the God of thou-shalts and thou-shalt-nots.

The most reliable source of shame is the knowledge that we are the creations of a compassionate Being who has given us so much, while asking so little in return (not sainthood but decency), and that we have failed to live up to even these minimal standards.

This presents yet another dilemma for liberals, who hold that religion should be a purely private affair and never intrude in the formulation of public policy.

Look at the way they're fighting a thirty second, nondenominational prayer, as if the affirmation of God by schoolchildren will lead to the end of civilization.

Thus neutered, how can faith be expected to shape sensibilities?

Liberals are in a moral muddle. They want a sense of shame without accountability, while fighting for a religion-free public square. Mission impossible.

## Fatty Rights Tip Scales of Justice
*April 3, 1995*

E verybody wants to be a victim. With victimhood comes blame avoidance, the nobility of suffering, and a chance to wallow in self-pity secure in the knowledge that—whatever your condition or conduct—it isn't your fault.

From Boston, Massachusetts, the capital of lobotomized liberalism, here's the latest development on the rights-mania front: large liberation. Two weeks ago, legislative hearings were held on a bill to ban bias against the overweight in employment and public accommodations.

If it passes, Massachusetts will join Michigan as the only states to make size a protected class for civil-rights purposes.

Witnesses at the hearing decried "fat oppression," which apparently includes humor. "We still laugh about fat people," complained state Rep. Byron Rushing, sponsor of the bill. Damn that Dom DeLuise.

The overweight are on the march. In New Hampshire, Mary Needer, a teacher at Rivier College, whose contract isn't being renewed, is suing for discrimination.

The school says it's discontinuing the course she taught. But Needer detects the miasma of group hatred.

Supervisors commented on her size on several occasions. The man who hired her once told the 375-pound Needer, "Now remember, work on your weight." Persecution delusions are the mark of a minority that's "movin' on up," as the Reverend Jesse Jackson is fond of saying.

Irwin Seating, the nation's leading manufacturer of theater seats, now produces chairs to accommodate plentiful posteriors. The new seats are thirty-three to thirty-nine inches, compared with the twenty-one inches of today's standard seats.

Hoping to avoid discrimination suits, theater chains are snapping up the jumbo seats. Terrified pandering is another sign that one more interest group is abornin'.

Under the Americans with Disabilities Act, the Equal Employment Opportunity Commission defines the morbidly overweight (twice the appropriate weight for one's height) as disabled, hence entitled to federal civil-rights protection.

In other words, if you're just a little hefty, you can be discriminated against with impunity. If you want to win the civil-rights raffle, stuff yourself with tacos and Twinkies until you reach the nirvana of victimhood.

What we've got here is a genuine movement with plenty of room to grow (an estimated thirty-eight million Americans are on the chunky side). Fat activists, call them paunchy panthers, have their own organization, the National Association to Advance Fat Acceptance.

They've even got a chant. Demonstrating in front of the White House last year, 150 NAAFA members chanted: "Two-four-six-eight, see the person not the weight." No word on whether our portly president (whose thighs thunder from beneath running shorts) is sympathetic.

How far will the push for fat acceptance go? Will the Ford modeling agency be forced to display three hundred–pound women in strapless evening gowns? (Aren't large ladies entitled to think of themselves as sexy and glamorous?) How about aerobics instructors who can't see their toes, never mind touch them?

A 1993 study published in the *New England Journal of Medicine* found that obese women had a 20 percent slimmer chance of marrying than their svelte counterparts (11 percent less for corpulent men). Perhaps what's needed is equal-opportunity dating. Make Shannon Doherty step out with a chub for every hunk she dates.

Life is manifestly unfair. Most people aren't physically attracted to the grotesquely overweight. Being fat limits an individual's mobility, flexibility, and endurance. The cellulite crowd is automatically excluded from certain occupations (ballerina, commando, the romantic lead in movies).

Tipping the scales at over three hundred pounds increases the risk of everything from heart attack to diabetes. Reality is discriminatory. Perhaps fat activists would like us to repeal the laws of nature for them.

After fat acceptance, what next? (On the frontiers of antidiscrimination, there's always a what-next.) Equal rights for the obnoxious (the courtesy impaired), who are tragically stigmatized, or quotas for those who bathe infrequently (the hygienically challenged)?

It's hard to empathize with the fat acceptance movement even if, like me, your waistline and age appear to be on a parallel course. True, there is a genetic component to obesity. But it's usually overstated. Some geneticists think the heredity factor accounts for only 25 percent of weight problems.

The rest is due to our national affinity for sugary cereals, midnight snacks, and junk food fixes. Our destiny isn't in our stars. It's written in hot fudge, Happy Meals, red meat, and four-toppings pizzas. If gluttony and sloth merit civil rights protection, why not the other deadly sins as well?

## Tolerance: Not What It Used to Be
*May 23, 1995*

Tolerance is highly overrated. I don't mean tolerance in the classic sense, but tolerance 1990s style—which often is nothing more than a covert assault on what the late Russell Kirk called "things permanent."

When I'm in a particularly masochistic mood, I listen to National Public Radio's *All Things Considered*. Earlier this month, I caught a segment on tolerance that typifies the kind of woolly thinking that has become its specialty.

"Our civic culture calls for tolerance, but what does that mean and what are the limits of tolerance?" co-host Noah Adams inquired.

Included in the segment were interviews with a gay writer who said we shouldn't tolerate homophobia (i.e., Judeo-Christian morality) and Father Richard John Neuhaus who said—look, reasonable, decent people can disagree on these matters. You can't tell one side of the debate to just shut up.

Notably absent from the discussion was any consideration of the corruption of the concept and how it's used to stifle dissent.

Tolerance originated in a religious context. For our Founding Fathers, it was both sensible and humane. Their perspective was shaped by the experience in Europe, where for hundreds of years people killed each other over doctrinal differences.

This, they determined, was decidedly uncool. As a result, the new republic did not have a national church or a religious test for public office.

Difficulties arose when a standard formulated for religious, and later racial, minorities was applied to attitudes, preferences, and lifestyles.

The meaning of tolerance also began mutating. Tolerance used to mean I'll leave you alone (won't initiate force against you), and you'll leave me alone. Now, tolerance is nonjudgmentalism—don't criticize me or point out the obvious consequences of my conduct.

Increasingly, to tolerate is to affirm. For you to suggest that there is something wrong with my behavior is bigoted. It means you hate me and probably want to hurt me.

Pleas for social tolerance obscure a crucial reality: In the culture war, one side will triumph. Someone's values will be written into law, taught in the public schools, and validated by the culture.

The position of NPR's gay spokesman is revealing. In the public schools, should we try to accommodate divergent views on homosexuality, the interviewer asked?

Certainly not, said the writer. "It comes down to a level where there is a battle and someone will win." "What people are saying who argue for the inclusion of information about homosexuals in the schools is simply that homosexuals not be left out of the discussion." From this perspective, as we don't allow teachers to make anti-Semitic or racist remarks, comments that homosexuality is immoral or dangerous should not be allowed.

But Middle America never acquiesced to the notion that homosexuality is comparable to race or religion, is inbred, or deserves to be appreciated/celebrated. One man's "information" is another's propaganda.

However often the elite condescendingly tell us that they are willing to tolerate the odd, aberrant views of us benighted religionists, they are still indoctrinating our children, forcing us to subsidize their vision, and legislating their ethics.

Truth is, in the land of the loose, we already tolerate far too much—a sex- and violence-saturated media, indolence, promiscuity, and celebrity immorality. According to a 1993 survey by the Family Research Council, 56 percent of the public believes a woman who wants to have a child out of wedlock should do so without reproach.

Here, tolerance borders on social suicide. Illegitimacy is a major factor in creating the crime, drug abuse, and welfare crises. Thanks to an increasingly tolerant climate, by the year 2000, 40 percent of births in this country will be out of wedlock.

The inner cities—with roving gangs of juvenile predators,

welfare-baby farming, and rampant addiction—are shining monuments to tolerance at its most misguided.

NPR itself recently provided a stunning example of the dead end of tolerance. Though it reversed course under fire, the network had intended to allow a cop killer on death row to do a regular commentary on prison life. Doubtless, it reasoned that to exclude the voice of murderers from the crime debate is, well, intolerant.

While publicly paying homage to the new tolerance, when their families are at stake, Americans find other values more appealing. In the aforementioned survey, respondents also were asked where they'd rather live with their children, in a place "very tolerant of non-traditional lifestyles" or one that "strongly upheld family values." The latter won by a landslide (76 percent).

You don't have to be Tomas de Torquemada, he of the auto-da-fé, to believe this tolerance thing is getting out of hand.

# chapter eleven

# CAN'T TELL RIGHT FROM WRONG

## Watch Out When Con Turns Crime-Fighter
*March 24, 1994*

Liberalism has found a new voice in its antipunishment crusade—a brutal killer, model prisoner, and slick little con artist.

*Time* magazine graciously provided Wilbert Rideau with a full page in its March 21 issue for his meditations on our penal system ("Why Prisons Don't Work"). Rideau is somewhat of an expert on the subject, having spent the past thirty-two years as a guest of the state of Louisiana at its Angola penitentiary.

As the title suggests, the literary lifer has a low opinion of law-and-order appeals. "Getting tough has always been a 'silver bullet,' 'a quick fix' that doesn't work," he declares.

Rideau offers Louisiana as a case in point. The state has a high lock-up rate and imposes severe penalties but still has the highest murder rate in the nation. "Prison, like the police and courts, has a minimal impact on crime because it is a response after the fact, a mop-up operation," the essayist sagely informs us.

Louisiana has a high murder rate because it has a large minority population, widespread poverty (the habits of the heart that foster poverty also breed crime), and a culture of violence. Absent its lock-up rate, Louisiana would be the South Bronx, Cajun-style.

Rideau disputes the deterrent effect of punishment, asserting that most criminals are so "emotionally desperate or psychologically distressed" that they don't think they'll get caught or don't care. Emotional desperation, psychological distress? How well this facile hustler has mastered liberal jargon.

"There are some prisoners who cannot be returned to society—serial killers, serial rapists, professional hit men." As for the rest, Rideau advises, incarcerate them only until they mature. In his professional opinion, the average prisoner who has been behind bars fifteen or twenty years poses a threat to no one.

The author describes himself as one of thirty-one murderers sent to Angola in 1962, all "unskilled, impulsive, uneducated misfits who did dumb, impulsive things."

Rideau's impetuosity took the form of robbing the Gulf National Bank in Lake Charles, Louisiana, and taking three employees hostage. But the youthful hijinks didn't stop there. The hostages were driven to a secluded area and shot (how dumb). Two survived. Rideau not only shot Julia Ferguson, but he stabbed her in both the windpipe and side with a heavy blade that pierced her heart and liver (how impulsive). She died. In a better world, Rideau would be pushing up daisies, not writing essays for national newsmagazines.

The problem with prisons is their underutilization. The average violent offender is sentenced to just under eight years in prison but serves a little less than three. The median sentence for murder is 15 years; the median time served is 5.5 years.

The longer these conscienceless creatures can be segregated from society, the less trauma they can inflict on the innocent. For most, their parole papers double as hunting licenses. A three-year follow-up of 108,850 state inmates released in 1983 found 60 percent of violent offenders arrested for another felony or violent misde-meanor within three years.

Given that many parolees who commit crimes aren't caught, the actual percentage of ex-cons who rejoin the predatory class prob-ably approaches 100 percent.

The social cost is staggering. The average thief commits forty to sixty robberies a year. A survey by BOTEC Analysis Corporation of Cambridge, Massachusetts, tries to calculate the total cost of crime by adding the dollar value of pain and suffering to property loss and medical expenses. It estimates the net benefit of keeping a career criminal behind bars for just one year between $172,000 and $2,364,000.

Sometimes the cost of misguided compassion and blind faith in rehabilitation is incalculable. Say you're a member of a parole board asked to consider the case of a man who has spent nearly fourteen of the past eighteen years in prison.

He's thirty-six years old, long past his terrible teens and tumul-tuous twenties, when hormones are in high gear and the male of the species is given to excesses.

The prisoner isn't a killer, though he has demonstrated a marked propensity for savagery and deviant behavior. You take Rideau's advice and release him to make room for younger, more violence-prone malefactors.

Congratulations, you've just freed Richard Allen Davis, the confessed killer of twelve-year-old Polly Klaas. It took Davis about three months from his release from the California Men's Colony at San Luis Obispo to locate his latest victim.

On the evening of October 1, 1993, Davis took the child from a friend's sleep-over and subsequently strangled her. Try telling the Klaas family that long-term incarceration serves no useful purpose.

Would that Davis's were an isolated case. A few days ago, Rus-sell Obremski was arrested in Eugene, Oregon, for sodomizing a four-year-old girl. Obremski had been paroled in November after serving twenty-four years for a double murder.

The ancient Phoenicians sacrificed their children to fertility gods. We sacrifice ours to bankrupt theories of crime and punishment propagated in the pages of newsmagazines.


## Singapore Was Right About Fay
*August 11, 1994*

Singapore has been vindicated. Is it flogging a dead horse—so to speak—to note that Asia's favorite whipping boy was back in the news last week, in a way that confirms the fitness of his punishment?

Michael Fay, who was given four strokes on the buttocks with a wet rattan cane for vandalizing cars in Singapore, is progressing to more serious offenses.

The nineteen-year-old, who added a new dimension to the expression "smart-ass kid," came home drunk the other night and—according to the police report—attacked his father.

Fay had returned to the states to live with pop. When the latter objected to junior's "visibly intoxicated" condition and grounded him, Michael reportedly threw down his cigarette, bellowed "let's go," and charged his old man. George Fay held his son down until the police arrived.

If a child would assault a parent, what would he do to a stranger?

Recall the hand-wringing from the compassion crowd, President Clinton included, when Fay was in Singapore awaiting caning. State torture, a punishment that scars and maims—all for an offense against property—they whined.

Ignored was the fact that many Singaporeans were born poor in the Third World. Their success was by dint of hard work. Owning a car in Singapore is expensive.

Along comes this spoiled American brat who thought it would be hilarious to spray paint their autos. The authorities had every right not to be amused.

It's hardly surprising that a punk who starts with vandalism would quickly graduate to assault. Property is an extension of self. The society in which property rights are routinely violated will soon degenerate into one where human life is cheap. What begins with graffiti often ends with gang rape and multiple homicide.

The media were shocked by opinion polls that showed a majority of Americans siding with the Asian ministate. Mail and phone calls to Singapore's Washington embassy overwhelmingly favored not sparing the rod in the Fay case.

Only a totally detached elite would fail to understand how passionately the public cares about crime. Clinton's own pollster has advised Democrats running for reelection in 1994 to drop health care as an issue and concentrate on law and order.

The United States "dares not restrain or punish individuals," says Singapore's senior minister, Lee Kuan Yew. "That's why the whole country is in chaos."

Especially regarding its young. The Woodstock generation gave its values (anarchic individualism, defiance of authority) to its progeny—with predicable results.

From 1985 to 1991, the number of fifteen-year-olds arrested for murder rose 217 percent. A glance at the juvenile justice system tells why. Over 60 percent of all cases of youthful violence that make it to court are either dismissed or result in probation—four strokes with a flaccid noodle.

A year ago, the *Washington Post* ran a civilization-is-sinking-fast story. "In classrooms and school hallways throughout the Washington area, many students are 'going off' on teachers and administrators, cursing them and calling them names without regret or restraint," the paper reported.

Teachers who criticize students in front of the class, ask them to sit down or stop talking are frequently answered by a string of obscenities. Even more shocking was the letter to the editor in response to the article from a teacher who rationalized this behavior.

"Teachers need to seek cooperative solutions to problems. Respect cannot be dictated," the lobotomized liberal lectured. Wrong. Children can and should be taught manners. (As our grandparents understood, when all else fails, a razor strap can be a marvelous motivational device.) Ours are culturally conditioned to be obnoxious and inconsiderate.

Instead of making progress toward creating an atmosphere of safety and civility, we make excuses. Juvenile barbarism is attributed to TV violence, lack of parental supervision, poverty, alienation—anything but flawed human nature and the absence of punishment swift and sure.

Teens who kill their peers get a few years of detention in a youth facility. Slap your snotty sixteen-year-old, and you'll be hauled into court for child abuse.

Charles Colson put it so well: "We are witnessing the most terrifying thing that could happen to society: the death of conscience in a generation of young people."

It's adults who killed their moral sensibility—by telling them everything is their right and nothing their duty, by giving them too many things and too little guidance, by not having the courage to discipline.

In this regard, perhaps Singapore does go a bit overboard. But the average American would infinitely prefer that punks be punished with a wet rattan cane wielded by a martial-arts expert than a bundle of lame excuses in the hands of a sympathetic social worker or permissive judge.

# Try Dresden Approach to Drugs
*April 10, 1995*

A ctor Carroll O'Connor is a grieving father. William F. Buckley, Jr., is a syndicated columnist. Both have thought about drugs— and reached the wrong conclusion.

Two weeks ago, O'Connor's son Hugh, an addict for sixteen years, took his own life. According to the man who played Archie Bunker, his son was despondent over his addiction. Hugh chose a bullet in the brain to a fourth stay in a rehab center.

O'Connor dropped a dime on his son's alleged pusher, who will be tried later this month. "These dealers, they kill people," the actor tearfully charged. Even so, perhaps it would be better to legalize drugs, O'Connor mused. "It's not going to create more addicts, it's just going to put the crooks and criminals and killers out of business."

While stating his position more elegantly, Buckley reaches the same judgment. In his pro-legalization column-of-the-month last week, the sometimes-conservative assessed the costs of our war on drugs—law enforcement, the judicial system, incarceration, etc. Bottom line: $205 billion annually, every penny of it wasted.

Legalizing drugs doesn't imply social sanction, Buckley assures us. "We license the publication of *Hustler* magazine even as we gag at the knowledge of what goes on within its covers."

Having flipped through that odious publication, I heartily concur. But how many lives has *Hustler* destroyed? How many suicides have been caused by the magazine? How many babies are born brain-damaged due to a mother's addiction to viewing salacious pictures?

At least Buckley doesn't contend that legalization won't increase addiction. As criminologist James Q. Wilson replied to economist Milton Friedman (another legalizer): "I suppose that we should expect no increase in Porsche sales if we cut the price by 95 percent?"

Around 1.3 million Americans regularly use cocaine. If that number were doubled or quadrupled, the consequences would be staggering.

Cocaine is responsible for 20 percent of the highway fatalities in New York. Each year, thirty thousand to fifty thousand crack babies are born to addicted mothers in this country.

Narcotics account for 75 percent of child abuse in Michigan's Wayne County (which includes Detroit). All of these tragedies would increase exponentially if drugs were legalized.

Cocaine use isn't just a disgusting habit, like reading a "men's magazine." It's not merely a health hazard, like nicotine. It causes crime and the abuse of family members. Most binge users can't hold jobs. Those who do eventually injure themselves or others. It robs the user of his will. It corrodes the soul. Even in the short run, it's lethal.

There are no successful legalization experiments. In the nineteenth century, Britain forced the opium trade on China. By the turn of the century, one-third of the nation was hooked. Still haunted by memories of the experience, today the People's Republic executes drug dealers.

The United Kingdom had its own field test. In the 1960s, heroin was dispensed by prescription to junkies. Over a decade, it's estimated the number of addicts increased thirtyfold.

Dutch law prohibits prosecution of retail sales of marijuana and hashish. The police ignore street sales of all drugs. Cocaine use has risen to 5.8 percent of the over-fifteen population in Amsterdam, compared to less than 0.5 percent here.

Consider a few of the costs of addiction: lost productivity, medical services for addicts and their families, highway fatalities, police to protect us from the ravages of adolescents on crack or PCP, hospital costs of babies who acquired their habit in utero. Multiply the total by two, three, five, or more. That's the tab for legalization.

But this is a cold calculation. How do you put a price on the life of a man like Hugh O'Connor, age thirty-two, with a wife and a two-year-old son?

The elder O'Connor turned in the man reputed to be his son's pusher. If convicted, Harry Perzigian faces a long prison sentence. If drugs were legal, what could O'Connor do? Drop Perzigian from his Christmas-card list? Snub him at parties?

Legalization isn't the only radical approach to drugs. On April 2, Saudi Arabia beheaded three drug smugglers. A week earlier, Singapore executed some.

You won't find many crack houses in Riyadh. Even in the poorest neighborhoods, Singapore's streets aren't littered with used hypodermics and addicts looking for their next fix.

As O'Connor says, dealers are killers—just as surely as the thug who puts a gun in the face of a convenience store clerk and pulls the trigger. Instead of running up the white flag, why not apply the Dresden approach to the drug war?

## Die, ASAP
*March 2, 1994*

H arry has had it up to here.

"From this day forward, I no longer shall tinker with the machinery of death," Supreme Court Justice Harry A. Blackmun declared in a dissenting opinion last week.

His honor was not referring to *Roe v. Wade*—the decision he crafted twenty-one years ago, which to date has served as a death warrant for twenty-eight million unborn children—but capital punishment. His *cri de coeur* came in an appeal for a stay of execution that the court rejected.

Pronouncing the death penalty a "failed experiment" that can't be equitably applied, the justice mused: "It seems the decision whether or not a human being should live or die is so inherently subjective... that it inevitably defies the rationality and consistency required by the Constitution."

Blackmun and his colleagues have devised a neat, self-neutralizing formula. On the one hand, they have decreed, the death penalty must be applied consistently. On the other, juries must be allowed maximum latitude in weighing the circumstances of each case.

Having helped to establish these mutually exclusive standards, Blackmun is dismayed to discover the death sentence unevenly utilized. Good collectivists that they are, liberals are obsessive about equality. Whether it's reward (wealth) or punishment (capital), unless it can be uniformly distributed, they want none of it.

The *New York Times* amplified Blackmun's complaint with full-page coverage and excerpts from his opinion. A week earlier, it devoted the same hype to an indictment of the defense in one capital case.

It described the killer, one Jimmy Davis, as "accused of murdering a sales clerk in a robbery attempt," even though a jury of his peers had already convicted him. What does it take for the *Times* to acknowledge guilt in such cases?

The paper evaluated Davis's court-appointed defense and found it, if not wholly inadequate, "lackluster." No evidence was offered of the defendant's substandard intelligence, it complained. "No experts were put forward to address his mental competence or discuss the effects of his harsh childhood."

Generally, opponents of capital punishment are root-causers and rehabilitators, who disdain punishment of any sort. The day of Blackmun's dissent, Jesse Jackson—that consummate utopian—blasted life sentences for third-time offenders before a congressional committee. "Sounds American. Fits on a bumper. Postures tough, but essentially unworkable," the reverend pronounced.

On another element of the congressional crime package, Jackson said, "More jails are not the answer." You'll be amazed by the ingenuity of his solution to the crime contagion—more spending on child care, education, and job training. Who would have guessed it? The creep who raped your grandmother was set on the road to ruin by the lack of an enriching day-care experience.

I have a news flash for Justice Blackmun, the Reverend Jackson, and the *Times* editors: They may be losing sleep over the "arbitrary, capricious nature" of capital punishment, we're not—we being the 75 percent who have supported the death sentence in every poll for the past twenty years.

Capital punishment is a lottery? Too bad. The killer had a rotten childhood? Tough. Do the people who get it deserve it? That's all that matters. An exhaustive examination of every execution between 1938 and 1988, published in the *Stanford Law Review,* finds not one in which credible evidence exists that an innocent person was put to death.

The average capital defendant doesn't get the sort of legal alchemy that resulted in a hung jury in the Menendez case? We don't care. We don't believe every killer is entitled to have Clarence Darrow, Johnnie Cochrane, and Alan Dershowitz for the defense. We'd prefer to pay for better police protection for potential victims than try to provide the best shysters money can buy for those who prey on us.

Not that we're satisfied with the status quo. Since capital punishment was reinstated in 1976, about 300 people are sentenced to death each year. To date, only 228 have been executed. There is a far greater likelihood you'll become a crime statistic during your lifetime than of a condemned killer being executed.

The day Blackmun bared his soul, two men were arrested in Florida for the murder of a hiker and the rape of his sister. The murder victim was beaten, struck on the head, bound, and had his throat slashed. The woman was repeatedly attacked, then tied between two trees.

One of the two suspects was recently released from prison, after serving less than eighteen months of a five-and-a-half-year sentence. If the pair is convicted and sentenced to die, I for one will sleep like a babe on execution eve.

Unlike Justice Blackmun and the *Times* editors, Middle Americans can't afford to agonize over the fate of brutal killers. We don't live in guarded condos. We aren't chauffeured to and from work. Our children don't attend elite schools. Unlike them, we're on the front lines.

Our paramount concern is for the killers to die as expeditiously as possible.

## NRA, America's Premier Civil Liberties Group
*May 29, 1995*

America's oldest, largest, and most effective civil liberties group concluded its 124th annual convention in Phoenix last week. To the cheers of twenty-two thousand delegates, leaders of the National Rifle Association vowed not to slacken their defense of constitutional liberties.

The 3.3 million-member organization is dedicated to the preservation of a basic freedom—the right to self-defense.

Like most civil liberties groups, the NRA is controversial. Recently, it came under fire for its excessive criticism of federal agents.

Huffing and puffing and acting as if he actually believes in something, former President George Bush resigned his NRA membership over a fund-raising letter that described minions of the Bureau of Alcohol, Tobacco, and Firearms (those wonderful folks who brought you Waco) as "jackbooted government thugs."

Sensing a foe he could challenge with impunity and seeking to forge crime-fighting credentials, President Clinton spent the days leading up to the convention berating and misrepresenting the gun group.

By pretending "police officers are the enemy," the NRA was giving "aid and comfort" to criminals, Clinton charged. If our first president couldn't tell a lie, the latest will not tell the truth. The NRA wasn't slamming the cop on the beat but a rogue agency that is to law enforcement what the Hiroshima bombing was to urban renewal.

How ironic. Former antiwar activist Bill Clinton is now implying it's immoral to caustically question the operations of a federal agency.

True, the NRA went too far. However, semantic overkill in pursuit of donations is common enough. The Democratic National Committee frequently engages in outrageous hyperbole in its predictions of the cataclysmic consequences of Republican legislation.

You don't have to be a gun nut to fear the progressively reckless operations of the federal fuzz.

A January 10, 1994, letter to the president—signed by a host of organizations that usually support him, including the ACLU and National Association of Criminal Lawyers—called for an investigation of these agencies.

Noting that federal cops now comprise 10 percent of the nation's total police force, the letter expressed grave concern over the "improper use of deadly force," "use of paramilitary... units or tactics without justification," and "entrapment."

In describing the initial assault on the Branch Davidian compound, the *Wall Street Journal* editorialized that the BATF showed up with "two cattle trucks full of agents in battle gear and a plan for 'dynamic entry.' " Will Bush cancel his *Journal* subscription?

In his report for the Justice Department on the debacle in which eighty cult members died (after a blitz with tanks and CS gas), Harvard law professor Alan Stone wondered rhetorically: "Did a military mentality overtake the FBI?" Isn't this a discreet way of suggesting some agents became jackbooted government thugs?

Even the *New York Times,* which is enjoying the NRA's current discomfort, in a May 4 editorial charged the BATF "is badly in need of internal reform. Waco was merely the most spectacular in a series of lapses in which the BATF became too aggressive and publicity conscious."

Is the BATF merely overzealous, or has the Clinton administration given federal agencies the green light to harass gun owners in an effort to create a climate of fear and squelch the legitimate exercise of a constitutional right?

The NRA calls Clinton the most anti-gun president in history. With a federal waiting period to purchase a handgun and a ban on so-called assault weapons under his belt, it's a fair description. Of course, neither measure will do a blessed thing to disarm criminals.

Clinton thinks he can ride a wave of anti-gun hysteria to reelection. But as our society continues to unravel, Americans increasingly appreciate their Second Amendment rights.

In 1993, according to the FBI's Uniform Crime Reports, 455 felons were shot to death by police officers. Almost as many (356) were killed by armed citizens.

Recognizing this reality, twelve states are considering proposals to make it easier to carry handguns. Two weeks ago, Texas Gov. George Bush, Jr., signed a measure to allow citizens of his state to carry concealed firearms.

The American people support their local police and know that federal law enforcement agencies contain many decent, dedicated individuals. But we insist on maintaining our first line of defense against crime and see an ugly specter rising from the ruins of the Koresh compound. Stick to your guns, NRA.

chapter twelve

# THE YOKE'S ON US

## Balance Thy Budget, Sayeth the Bible
*September 22, 1994*

**H**erb Stein charges the Christian Coalition with misleading the public by implying that God is on the side of a balanced budget. Does heaven favor fiscal responsibility, or has the economist caught the religious right in a lie?

In a piece in last week's *New York Times*, the chairman of Nixon's Council of Economic Advisers claimed that by endorsing a balanced budget amendment to the U.S. Constitution, the coalition suggests Christianity ratifies the reform.

Stein began by admitting: "I am not an expert on Christian doctrine—or on Jewish doctrine either, for that matter," then proceeded to prove the point.

"I have consulted a concordance on the Bible," Stein said. "Apparently, the word 'budget' does not appear in either the Old or the New Testament. The work 'balance' does appear about eight times, but never in connection with fiscal policy."

But this is akin to saying that because the word "rights" is absent from Scriptures and "gay" is used only in relation to levity that the Bible is silent on homosexuality.

Not content with this logical fallacy, the economist proceeded to construct a biblical rationale for deficit spending. The Fifth Commandment says honor your father and mother, Stein noted. But there's no comparable mandate to honor our children and grandchildren.

Thus "One might say that the commandment not only sanctions but even requires running a budget deficit as a way for younger generations to sacrifice for older ones."

I seem to recall the Decalogue also containing a general prohibition against theft. Says Rabbi Daniel Lapin, "The law of robbery isn't set aside if the thief is the parent and the victim his child. What are budget deficits other than parents robbing their offspring?"

On the other hand, the deficit shouldn't be viewed strictly as a generational transfer, Stein cautions. "If we can leave our children a country free of the danger of war, with safe streets, reduced racial hostility... and an elevated culture," that will more than justify a mountain of debt, he mused.

Bet you didn't know a $5 trillion national debt has bought us a crime-free America, racial harmony, and a cultural renaissance? Neither did I.

Actually, the Bible has a lot to say about debt, none of it favorable. "The borrower becomes the lender's slave" (Proverbs 22:7) and "The wicked borrow and do not repay" (Psalms 37:21).

In Deuteronomy, among the blessings God bestows on Israel is the following: "You will lend to many nations but will borrow from none." National debt is considered a curse.

The Scriptures consistently urge prudence, hard work, and thrift. In Jesus' Parable of the Talents, the master praises the servant who invested money entrusted to him and rebukes the one who buried it in the ground, with no resulting return.

What if the latter, instead of merely preserving his master's wealth (but not augmenting it), had gone on a spending spree—presumably on the master's behalf? What if he'd run up debts in his master's name that even his progeny couldn't repay? Debts that grew day by day? Debts that took 20 percent of the family's income just to service?

The Bible stresses that everything ultimately belongs to God and we are its stewards with a responsibility to preserve and—where possible—increase our heritage for future generations. "A good man leaves an inheritance to his children's children" (Proverbs 13:22).

In this regard, we have been very bad indeed. Because we lacked the will to order our fiscal affairs, we've placed a staggering burden on the shoulders of posterity.

In just a decade, the national debt grew from under $1 trillion to almost $5 trillion. Today, interest on debt (the second largest item in the budget) accounts for one-fifth of federal spending. The percentage is rising. Thanks to our improvidence, future generations will be forced to devote an ever greater portion of their resources (money that could go to their roads and schools and public safety) to debt service.

An American born today will pay an extra $130,000 in taxes just to cover interest on the current debt, to say nothing of what the remainder of the Clinton years will bring.

Former U.S. Sen. Paul Tsongas, a Democrat, says we've accumulated debt "without any observable sense of regret. We've had one helluva time, and they [our descendants] will have to pay for it. Good luck kids. Hope you make it." This is stewardship?

In a way, debating the matter is a losing proposition. A secularist like Stein asks what the Bible has to do with a balanced budget. You explain it to him, chapter and verse. Then he does an ACLU, telling you that since we live in a pluralistic nation, the Judeo-Christian perspective is irrelevant when it comes to public policy.

Still, some of us view the Bible not as mythology or poetry but as a guide to successful living. Yes, Herb, He who split the Red Sea certainly has something to say about the sea of red ink that threatens to overwhelm us.

## Is Today's Welfare State Kosher?
### January 12, 1995

An Orthodox rabbi has forced the liberal Jewish establishment to debate the welfare state on his terms.

Through his fledgling organization, Toward Tradition, Rabbi Daniel Lapin and fifty of his colleagues ran an ad on the editorial pages of the *New York Times,* hailing the advent of the Republican Congress ("Mazel Tov, Speaker Gingrich—We Know All About 10-Point Contracts").

If that weren't cheeky enough, they proceeded to argue that Judaism is "a conservative... religion" that "values private property and the ethical marketplace" and "requires charity to be administered locally and for it to never foster dependency."

The broadside was a *casus belli* for an establishment accustomed to a monopoly on political discourse within the community, which fired back a *Times* ad of its own.

Responding as the Ad Hoc Jewish Coalition for Social Justice, the signers included many of the movers and schleppers of organized Jewry, among them a past president of the American Jewish Congress and the current head of the Union of American Hebrew (Reform) Congregations.

Pronouncing Toward Tradition unkosher, the ad insisted that a commitment to "social justice" is Judaism's political message. It pointed with pride to the Jewish vote in the 1994 congressional election—78 percent Democratic—as confirmation that liberalism is as Jewish as chicken soup and just as nourishing.

The Contract with America was caustically dismissed as a "mean-spirited turn from a politics of justice, equity, and compassion."

The editorial section of the *New York Times* is the Torah of the liberalism-and-lox set. By using this hallowed forum to dispute its worldview, Lapin has committed what must seem an act of desecration.

Is the Jewish position on a given issue to be determined by a head count, even among the most Jewishly ignorant generation in history? Lapin asks: "If 78 percent of American Jews had Christmas trees, would that, too, be in keeping with Jewish tradition?"

The rabbi has his own demographic challenge. "There's a very large number of Jews in America today who study the Talmud on a daily basis. What does it tell you, that the overwhelming majority of them are political conservatives?"

Members of the Ad Hoc Committee contend that a system responsible for the crisis of the inner cities—mothers without husbands, children without fathers, youth without hope—is the paradigm of the Jewish concept of loving kindness.

They speak in lofty terms of the prophetic tradition. Rarely will one of them quote the Mishnah, Maimonides, or another sage or source to prove his point. Woody Allen is the closest most can come to a rabbinical authority.

For them, Judaism is a philosophy, an ethical culture, or a folkway. Not divine revelation. It's interesting, even meaningful, but never binding.

They are wise to avoid a serious discussion of Jewish law. While not completely congruent with free-market economics, the Torah offers broad support for individual initiative, personal responsibility, and compassionate capitalism.

The Bible commands us to open our hand to the poor. But it also places a burden on recipients, something Jewish welfarists deliberately ignore. "Make your Sabbath [meal] plain as [those of] a weekday, and don't ask others for help," the Talmud enjoins.

Maimonides maintained that the highest form of charity is teaching a poor person a trade so he will no longer be dependent on the community. What's Hebrew for workfare?

In the Book of Samuel, the prophet warns that a king over Israel "will take one-tenth of your seed and of your vineyards... he will take one-tenth of your sheep and you will become his servants." Today, the American whose tax bill amounts to 10 percent of his income would think himself fortunate indeed.

Rabbi Meir Tamari, former chief economist of the Bank of Israel, notes another aspect of Judaism's political message neglected by social-justice Jews. "Men are free, and the mass of state intervention takes away their freedom. Therefore, we would have to limit the state to protect the freedom of man created in God's image."

Like modernists of other faiths, Jewish liberals have transformed a religion into a social-action program. Judaism does have political implications, but they can't be reduced to indiscriminate alms-giving by a monarchical government that's made citizens its servants.

Toward Tradition doesn't oppose aid to the needy, nor do resurgent Republicans. But—in the name of a thirty-three hundred-year-old tradition of philanthropy—it questions a welfare system that destroys initiative, families, and neighborhoods, and disputes those who condone the resulting ruin in the name of Jewish values.


## Where Is God on the Poverty Front?
*November 27, 1995*

God likes multigenerational poverty. God favors indolence. God thinks illegitimacy and fatherless families are swell. God wants more drug abuse and gang violence.

These conclusions may be deduced from a statement by the

National Council of Churches and the Religious Action Center for Reform Judaism that opposes ending welfare as an entitlement.

"The very moral fabric of our nation would be torn" if government reneges on its "60-year-promise to be protector of last resort" for the poor, reads the manifesto of the aforesaid groups.

"Unholy legislation that destroys the safety net must not be signed into law," the ersatz prophets thunder. That sanctified safety net has served us so well—increasing the rate of out-of-wedlock births 600 percent since the inception of the war on poverty, at a cost of $5 trillion, a sum exceeding the national debt.

The federal government isn't "the protector of last resort" but the sugar daddy of first choice. Lush subsidies create lifelong dependency.

In a September 28 *Wall Street Journal* column, Michael Tanner and Stephen Moore estimate that, based on the six most common assistance programs (AFDC, food stamps, Medicaid, housing, nutrition assistance, and energy subsidies), a New Jersey resident would have to earn $12.74 an hour to equal what a family of three on welfare collects.

Working Americans can accept the religious obligation of charity and still resent the twenty-year-old with three out-of-wedlock children who has turned taxpayers into her slaves.

The position of religious leaders who oppose welfare reform is based on a kneejerk understanding of commandments to succor the less fortunate.

Far from being a social-service handbook, the Bible is pro-work and anti-indolence. From Genesis on, we are told that man was put on this earth to labor. "By the sweat of your brow you will eat your food."

Sloth is excoriated. Proverbs comments, "The sluggard's craving will be the death of him, because his hands refuse to work." Surveys suggest almost 70 percent of adult welfare recipients aren't even looking for jobs.

Numerous biblical passages enjoin the haves to share their bounty, in the knowledge that ultimately all is from the Creator. "A generous man will himself be blessed for he shares his food with the poor" (Proverbs 22:9).

Mosaic law required landowners to leave the corners of their fields unharvested and the top branches of fruit trees unpicked, so the widow and orphan would have sustenance. But collecting these alms required physical labor on the part of beneficiaries (harvesting is strenuous), an Israelite forerunner of workfare.

Scriptures distinguish between the deserving poor (that quaint, Victorian notion) and others. In the New Testament, Paul advises Timothy to "give proper recognition to those widows who are really in need," not those who have families to fall back on, younger women who could remarry, and widows who become "idlers," "gossips," and "busybodies."

Charity is when *you* reach in your pocket to help the needy. When government performs the extraction (and shares half the proceeds with the bureaucracy), it has a less savory designation.

Kindness is the scriptural standard. Don't cheat the poor. Don't deny them equal justice. Help them when they are incapable of helping themselves.

How can our current welfare policies conceivably be thought of as compassionate? Are they kind to the 80 percent of inner-city children born into single-parent families? Are they kind to the society on which these kids, raised without parental discipline, will one day be inflicted? Thanks to our thirty-year-old war on poverty, youth offenses are the fastest growing crime category.

Are they kind to the young women who are doomed to an existence on the margins of society, to men who will never know the dignity of honest labor?

The modern welfare state isn't biblical; it's satanic. I don't mind religious leaders messing with politics, but I must object when they take positions that are both unbiblical and nonsensical.

# Litigation Madness: Good for the Greedy, Bad for the Rest
*September 12, 1994*

Two logic-defying judgments and a new movie demonstrate that litigation madness—and its rewards—apparently know no bounds.

The Steve Martin film *(A Simple Twist of Fate)* is an updated version of *Silas Marner*, with one significant difference.

In the George Eliot novel, when Godfrey Cass tries to claim Eppie as his child and she rebuffs him, he sadly but gracefully withdraws. In the Martin movie, the biological father does what any self-respecting citizen of the Republic of Pre-trial Discovery would do—launch a legal action, in this case a custody suit.

Not only is resort to the courts a commonplace of contemporary life, the outcome is increasingly bizarre. Earlier this month, a San Francisco jury awarded a record $7.1 million in a sexual harassment suit. At least it's comforting to know that this time a law firm was on the receiving end of the legal process.

Though employed by the firm as a secretary for less than two months, Rena Weeks apparently suffered sufficiently from the "clumsy gropings and crude remarks" of a partner to justify receiving the equivalent of several lifetimes of earnings.

Last month, eighty-one-year-old Stella Liebeck got $2.9 million from McDonald's Corporation for spilled coffee. The woman scalded herself with the beverage heated to 180 degrees. Her cagey lawyer convinced the jury that, in terms of negligence, this was the liquid equivalent of the Coconut Grove fire.

Was the pain worth $3 million? What about lost earnings? As a result of her injury, will the octogenarian Liebeck now be precluded from dancing with the Rockettes?

Unless Weeks's nemesis was a combination of Howard Stern and Andrew Dice Clay, how does two months of being subjected to crass behavior justify a $7 million award?

But that's the beauty of punitive damages (and why the legal community will fight to the last litigator to defend them): They're not necessarily related to actual harm. The criteria for determining punitive damages include the egregiousness of the conduct and the perceived deterrent effect of the award.

In other words, if the jury feels really sorry for a plaintiff, really dislikes a defendant, and/or believes the behavior in question was really outrageous, it can express its pity/indignation by giving the injured party a ton of money the beneficiary really doesn't deserve. Whatever happened to the common law ideal of making an injured party whole?

The quest for the pot of gold at the end of a pleading is nourished by equal parts of avarice and liberalism's responsibility avoidance ethic. The latter teaches that someone else is always to blame for our misfortunes and it's up to the courts to rectify the injustice.

As a result, the legal system has flourished to the detriment of every other segment of society. Each year, 18 million new suits are filed in this country. In constant dollars, attorneys' fees increased from $8.2 billion in 1960 to $47.5 billion in 1985. Between 1965 and 1990, the number of lawyers grew four times as fast as the population.

The total cost of our legal obsession (including higher insurance premiums and a decline in productivity) could approach $300 billion a year.

It's estimated that 80 percent of all board-certified obstetricians and gynecologists have been sued at least once. A quarter have reduced the amount of high-risk care they offer, and 12.3 percent have stopped practicing. Two-thirds of all medical malpractice claims are without merit.

One industry group reports that 47 percent of U.S. manufacturers have withdrawn products from the market for fear of litigation.

Don't look to Washington to solve the problem. The last administration tried. In 1991, then-Vice President Dan Quayle bearded the bar association beast in its lair. He proposed limiting punitive damages and requiring the losing side in litigation to pay the winner's legal fees.

You can imagine the reaction. In 1992, trial lawyers were the single largest group of contributors to the Clinton campaign. No threat of reform now. The American Bar Association must rejoice in the first two-lawyer family in the White House, with a president and first lady both dedicated to its interests.

How Clinton feels about legal reform may be seen in his nomination of H. Lee Sarokin for the federal appeals court. As a district court judge, Sarokin ruled that in evicting a nasty, noisy vagrant, a library violated his constitutional rights. The bum got $150,000.

The present system is too good to change—good for accident-prone old ladies, good for secretaries who can parlay offensive conduct into a $7 million judgment, good for the contingency fee crowd, good for the greedy and disgruntled. Bad for the rest of us.

## U.S. Courts: Time to Balance the Scales of Justice
*April 5, 1995*

The federal court system is a giant piñata—stuffed with privileges and tax-financed subsidies—that interest groups eagerly assault with litigation cudgels.

Last week, homosexual activists hit the jackpot as the treasure-trove disgorged yet another constitutional right that would baffle the Founding Fathers.

U.S. District Court Judge Eugene Nickerson, a Carter appointee renowned for his imaginative opinions, struck down the military's "don't ask, don't tell" policy on homosexuals.

The regulation is an intolerable infringement of free speech, his honor held. Nickerson heaped scorn on the theory that a declaration of homosexuality indicates a disposition to engage in homosexual acts. In the never-never land of judicial reasoning, no connection exists between assertions and intentions.

In February, U.S. District Court Judge Constance Baker Motley (sitting in Manhattan) ruled that Amtrak does not have the right to evict denizens of the pavement from Penn Station.

In a ruling more ideological than constitutional, her honor—a thirty-year veteran of the bench—jeered that Amtrak's policy was designed to spare travelers "the esthetic discomfort of being reminded on a daily basis that many of our fellow citizens are forced to live in abject and degrading poverty."

Forced by whom? Cruel capitalism? Reagan-era budget cuts? Jim Beam and Jack Daniels? Motley's views belong in a political pamphlet—not a federal injunction.

State judges too are afflicted by the mania to read their politics into the Constitution. In December, the New Jersey supreme court held that shopping centers could not ban leafletting.

Malls have assumed the aspects of the village green and city sidewalk, the majority declared in extending First Amendment rights to private property.

The court illogically limited its ruling by excluding speeches and demonstrations. Thus New Jersey shoppers, who generally don't go to malls to be pestered, will only have to dodge anti-fur fanatics and the legion of LaRouche handing out literature but will be spared their amplified harangues.

Increasingly, judges are telling electoral majorities to drop dead. In 1988 Arizonans amended their constitution to require that official state business be conducted in English. Last year California voters passed Proposition 187, denying most government benefits to illegal immigrants.

Both were recently pronounced unconstitutional. In Los Angeles, U.S. District Court Judge William Matthew Byrne, Jr., ruled that in the battle between illegal aliens and taxpayers, "there is a balance of hardship" in favor of the illegals. See the U.S. Constitution's balance-of-hardship article.

In overturning the Arizona measure, a panel of the 9th U.S. Circuit Court of Appeals (Carter appointees all) said language diversity enriches the "multicultural character of our society." By requiring state employees to speak English on the job, the Arizona amendment "provides no encouragement (for multiculturalism)... only coercion," the court observed. See Bill of Rights, non-encouragement clause.

National defense, a desire for cultural cohesion, and property rights all bow to the refined sensibilities of the federal judiciary. Even the lives of innocent children give way to civil-liberties fetishism.

In February, yet another Carter judge (wait till the Clinton judiciary hits its stride) in New Jersey threw out "Megan's Law" mandating neighborhood notification of the presence of released sex offenders.

The law (named for a seven-year-old girl who was raped and murdered by a neighbor twice convicted of sex crimes) creates a "lifelong albatross" around the necks of much-abused child molesters, U.S. District Judge Nicholas H. Politan ruled. The lifelong burdens of molested children apparently don't count for much.

The federal judiciary is making democracy obsolete. In all of the cries for congressional term limitation, only presidential candidate Patrick Buchanan is talking about limiting the terms of federal judges.

That would require a constitutional amendment. In the meantime, under Article III of the U.S. Constitution, our Republican Congress could remove the federal courts' jurisdiction over issues that evoke paroxysms of knee-jerk liberalism from the bench (homosexuality, homelessness, immigration, and welfare).

The current situation provides a cautionary tale. An accident of history, Jimmy Carter is still shaping government policy fourteen years after he was resoundingly rejected by the American people. In November 1996 voters will have a chance to indirectly choose judges who could balance the scales of justice.

## Big Government: The Yoke's on Us
*January 28, 1993*

One brush with the bureaucracy is worth a thousand angry stump speeches. Here are three: Real life stories of your wasteful, infuriatingly inefficient, outrageously unfair government in action, drawn from the Feder files.

FEDERAL: I needed to place a call to the Immigration and Naturalization Service. I had a routine question any middle-level functionary should have been able to answer. But try finding someone to ask.

After consulting a directory, I located a number that promised to provide information to the media. It took twenty-three minutes (I timed it) to connect with a nonmachine.

But first we did the recorded-message mambo. "Please hold on." "Your call is important to us." "I'll transfer you to the first available operator."

My hair got grayer. Cobwebs grew between my fingers. In deep space, new solar systems formed and disintegrated into cosmic dust. After a geologic age, at last I reached a person who informed me that I had the wrong department.

When I called the new number I'd been given, I got—another recording. "Please leave your name and number and we'll get back to you." Sure you will, when the mythical check in the mail at last arrives.

That was weeks ago. Still no word from the border boys. No wonder the nation is overrun by Peruvian nannies.

STATE: You can title this one Adventures in Cuomo-land. Last summer, while traveling to a speech in upstate New York, my wife and I were zipping through a Mayberry R.F.D.-type town at a dizzying five miles per hour when a cop standing in the middle of the main street—like a trout fisherman in a well-stocked stream—reeled us in.

Unbeknown to either of us, New York is a mandatory seatbelt state, and we were in flagrant violation of the law. "Just explain the situation to the town justice when you get your summons; I'm sure he'll understand," the cop assured us.

I did, informing the eminent jurist that we'd been driving in the state for two hours without spotting a single sign advising that seat belts are mandatory. Considering the circumstances, I was confident I'd get off easy. Not in revenue-greedy New York. Pay fifty smackers or you'll never guzzle gas in this state again, the court decreed. If we'd run over a diet doctor who'd jilted us, Cuomo probably would have issued an executive commutation.

LOCAL: I live in New England, which is to snow and ice what the Balkans are to community relations problems. In other words, winter precipitation is not wholly unanticipated.

We got a ton of the white stuff in December, eighteen inches or so. My town took three days to clear the streets enough so drivers weren't risking life and limb. Not that I'm complaining. I always wondered what it would be like to go tobogganing in a car. Many excuses with a resonant ring emanating from their interior were offered for the fiasco.

I mean, hey, isn't this what government is supposed to do, keeping the roads open—as opposed to all of the lunacy it shouldn't be doing, but does anyway? The money for plowing was probably siphoned off for AIDS education at our local high school. After all, why should government perform its necessary functions when there are so many more amusing ways to squander our tax dollars?

No big deal. All mundane matters. Nobody killed. No lives

ruined, industries vaporized, recessions prolonged, or Third World nations invaded. Just aggravating examples of the smother state in action.

The natives are visibly restless. Two indications of the level of popular discontent may be found in results of the 1992 election. Term limitation, which seeks to sever the careers of officeholders-for-life, triumphed in all fourteen states where it graced the ballot. The average vote for the reform was 66 percent—twenty-three points higher than President Clinton's national vote. So who (or what) has the mandate?

Ross Perot—that nerdy little guy from East of the Pecos, who ran the most bizarre campaign in electoral history (he's in, he's out, he's in)—drew 19 percent of the popular vote, the highest percent for a third-party candidate in eighty years, half the incumbent's total vote.

From public education to the postal service and health care to housing, from crime control (or lack thereof) to welfare follies—the failures of government litter the landscape.

Many of us have come to view our government as an occupation army, something to be endured. Like frantic peasants hiding their nubile women and chickens when the Cossacks ride through the village, most of us pray we can survive our rulers, that they won't plunder us too much, that someday God will make them go away.

And now we have another activist president—a man who believes body and soul in the redeeming power of big government (put your hands on the Treasury and you shall be healed), who carries a train of true believers into office with him.

Sometimes it's difficult to decide if American government is more comedy or tragedy. One thing's sure: When it comes to government, the yoke's on us.

# chapter thirteen

# NEW WORLD DISORDER

## UN: Globaloney Fit for the Grinder
*October 23, 1995*

This is "UN Week," the fiftieth anniversary commemorative edition of the General Assembly, when adulation of the world body will reach a crescendo.

To set the mood, the New World Order glee club has spent months harmonizing about the UN's half-century of progress, while predicting even greater triumphs to come.

But there's a storm cloud on the horizon. The United Nations is broke. In August, it was forced to borrow $98 million from its peacekeeping budget to help cover a $3.7 billion budget gap.

If "mankind's last, best hope for peace" goes into Chapter 11, blame the United States ($1.2 billion in arrears) and other international deadbeats, UN partisans complain.

In reality, American taxpayers have carried the UN's bloated bureaucracy on their sagging shoulders far too long.

We are assessed 25 percent of the UN's regular budget and 31.7 percent of peacekeeping costs. Yet our 250 million people have the same vote in the General Assembly as the 15,000 citizens of the Pacific island of Pelau.

Fairness aside, what exactly are we getting for our money? What has the world debating society contributed to peace since its founding fifty years ago?

Secretary General Boutros Boutros-Ghali claims the United Nations has helped resolve 172 regional conflicts. Wouldn't you just love to see that list? Most of these squabbles probably had the potential explosiveness of a border dispute between Belgium and Luxembourg.

From 1945 to 1990, there were more than eighty wars, which claimed more than thirty million lives. If that's success, failure must have a truly terrifying face.

The presence of a UN-peacekeeping contingent in Rwanda didn't stop the slaughter of five hundred thousand Tutsis by machete-wielding Hutus. In Bosnia, at least two hundred thousand have died since 1992, under the watchful eye of UN forces.

The United Nations prolonged the conflict with its self-defeating arms embargo and the gross incompetence of its diplomats on the ground.

In an article in the October issue of *Reader's Digest* entitled "The Folly of UN Peacekeeping," Dale Van Atta described UN military operations as distinguished by "incompetent commanders, undisciplined soldiers, alliances with aggressors, failure to prevent atrocities, and at times even contributing to the horror." Moreover, "the level of waste, fraud, and abuse is overwhelming."

Van Atta charged that some UN troops in Bosnia shared Muslim women kidnapped by Serbian forces and Kenyan peacekeepers sold twenty-five thousand gallons of gas to the Serbs.

After the UN's legion arrived in Cambodia in 1991, the number of prostitutes in Phnom Penh tripled (five thousand of the world gendarmes contracted venereal diseases).

While Somalis starved, UN forces stationed in Mogadishu spent

$56 million a year dining on such delicacies as fresh beef flown in from Australia and South American fruit. The boys in powder-blue helmets certainly know how to fight hunger—their own.

The behemoth on the East River may be a failure at peacekeeping, but it excels at bureaucracy building.

As of June 1994, the secretariat had a staff of 33,967. All supposedly are engaged in great humanitarian work—fighting epidemics, providing disaster relief, and working for the betterment of women and the rights of children.

Any good deeds done are purely incidental. Of the World Health Organization's $1 billion budget, 75 percent goes to salaries and much of the rest to conferences.

The United Nations is famous for its endless succession of summits—the Rio Summit on the Environment, the Cairo Conference on Population, the Beijing Conference on Women, to name but a few.

Each annihilates a few million dollars and produces chilling manifestos calling for more looting of capitalist economies, a further surrender of national sovereignty, and the transfer of authority from families to international meddlers.

We need the United Nations like the U.S. justice system needs another O. J. Simpson trial. Where necessary, peacekeeping is better handled by NATO. There are all sorts of frugal charities combating hunger and disease abroad. Nations of good will can always settle differences among themselves and nudge others in the right direction.

Fifty years from its founding, the United Nations is an unmitigated failure—morally as well as fiscally bankrupt. Time to say toodle-oo to this multinational white elephant.

## New World-Type Debates Bosnia
*December 4, 1995*

**D**ebate being a useful tool for clarifying issues, I've conjured up a proponent of U.S. military intervention in the Balkans—a New World orderly—and asked him to state his case.

Here are his arguments for deploying twenty thousand American ground forces on one of the bloodiest bits of real estate on Earth, and my responses.

Him: In Bosnia, more than two hundred thousand have died in the past forty-three months. We must stop the carnage.

Me: The latest Balkan war, while tragic, is sadly in keeping with a century in which not a year has passed without savage fighting somewhere in the world.

More than one hundred wars have been fought since the end of World War II. Many involved widespread atrocities against civilians and ethnic cleansing. (In 1994, five hundred thousand died in the Tutsi genocide in Rwanda.) Should we have intervened in all of them?

Him: As our president said, "We cannot stop war for all time, but we can stop some wars."

Me: And what a war he has chosen for his grand, peacekeeping adventure—one that has been fought intermittently for more than six hundred years by three hostile forces that have all demonstrated unparalleled brutality and scant desire for peace.

Please explain to me why marching into this loony bin bristling with arms is in our national interest.

Him: We have to stop the fighting from spreading. If America doesn't assume a leadership role, the NATO alliance will unravel.

Me: Where is the fighting supposed to spread? Serbia is the size of Belgium. It takes a vivid imagination to see Serbs, potent enough in their mountain passes, moving on Greece or Turkey. During the 1960s, when communism was advancing everywhere, antiwar activist Clinton scoffed at the idea of dominoes falling in Southeast Asia. Now, he sees them in the unlikeliest places.

NATO was formed to stop Soviet communism. The Kremlin was just sold at a garage sale. Is an alliance that was intended to protect the West against an imminent danger now to become a social service agency dedicated to promoting harmony among people who make the Mongol horde look like a peace march?

As Pat Buchanan puts it, "Does anyone believe that Europeans... will inform us that we may no longer protect them if we do not put twenty thousand troops in Bosnia?"

What a tragedy!

Him: Our mission won't be open-ended. There are specific goals and a timetable for withdrawal.

Me: A year ago, Clinton said our only conceivable role in the Balkans was to help evacuate NATO forces. Now, we're to be peacekeepers. Sure sounds like mission creep to me.

Clinton wants America to separate the belligerents, oversee arms reductions, and create a climate in which refugee resettlement and elections can take place—all in one year. A decade wouldn't be long enough.

Him: Our troops will have everything they need to do the job. We'll deploy a robust force, backed by Abrams tanks, Bradley fighting vehicles, and Apache attack helicopters.

Me: Most impressive. But have you considered the terrain? Bosnia's mountain roads are particularly ill-suited for armored vehicles. Our helicopters will be almost useless in the heavy cloud cover, low ceilings, and ground fog which come with winter in the Balkans.

In the December 4, 1995, issue of *Newsweek*, retired U.S. Army Col. David Hackworth described the territory our troops will be operating over as "steep and heavily timbered, with treacherously narrow and muddy roads and ruined or damaged bridges. It is a tightly compartmented landscape, where a patrol can easily get trapped and cut to pieces."

In Vietnam, land mines caused more than 60 percent of U.S. casualties. Bosnia abounds with millions of the devices.

Our forces will confront enemies who can traverse the terrain blindfolded, whose snipers are deadly marksmen, who have honed their combat skills in four years of ferocious fighting, and who specialize in hit-and-run tactics.

To date, 148 United Nations soldiers have died in Bosnia. British General Sir Michael Rose, former UN commander in Sarajevo, estimates that at least four hundred Americans will be killed in Operation Lost Cause. The operative words here are *at least*.

Him: Soldiers are supposed to risk their lives.

Me: When called upon, soldiers are expected to lay down their lives to defend this nation and its vital interests, not to undertake nebulous humanitarian missions. Bosnian intervention is insanity in the pursuit of a utopian vision worthy of a Rhodes scholar whose understanding of military affairs comes from playing the Parker Brothers' game Risk.

## Islamic Terror Continues to Spread
*December 19, 1994*

Here's a story just brimming with holiday cheer and good will toward men. According to a church official, four Catholics were crucified by Sudan's Islamic government this summer.

Speaking on Vatican Radio earlier this month, Bishop Cessare Mazzolari said the victims—converts to Christianity—were given one hundred lashes each, tied to crosses, and left to die in the blazing sun.

The day after this horror story emerged, the *New York Times* carried an article on Hassan al-Turabi, spiritual leader of Sudan's ruling Islamic party.

Turabi, the *Times* noted, studied law in Paris and London and says he respects Western culture, Christianity, and Judaism. "Moslems are not allowed to wage war, only resistance," the sixty-two-year-old cleric explained. "The Moslem has to relate to people peacefully."

In southern Sudan, this benign interaction takes the form of mass murder, starvation, and slavery. Two million have died in Khartoum's campaign to convert or annihilate Christian and animist tribesmen. More than twenty-five thousand children from the Nuba Mountains have been sold into slavery, most bringing the price of two chickens.

But Sudan (Bosnia with bad PR) is only the bloodiest example of the Jihad International. The past twelve months have seen the murder of three Protestant ministers in Iran; the assassination of a Christian charged with blasphemy in Lahore, Pakistan; the murder of five Coptic Christians, including two priests, outside a monastery in southern Egypt; and the Christmas-day bombing of a Philippine church by Moslem rebels (7 dead, 130 wounded).

Last week, the same group took responsibility for bombing a Philippines jet.

Dr. Walid Phares, who teaches international relations at the University of Miami, charges the Middle East's twenty million Christians "have been subjected to a gradual, systematic, and multi-level ethnic cleansing."

The situation is deteriorating as Islam straight up becomes the regional beverage of choice.

In Algeria, three hundred to four hundred die each week in a savage war of attrition between the nation's rulers and Islamist insurgents. In Morocco, long the most tolerant of Arab states, fundamentalists control student organizations at ten of the nation's twelve universities. Even secular Turkey has an Islamic Party that just elected the mayor of Istanbul.

Great Satan is no longer a neutral observer to Islamic green revolution. Sheik Omar Abdel-Rahman and his chemistry students were convicted of conspiring to deconstruct the Lincoln Tunnel, FBI headquarters, and the United Nations building, with the aid of Sudanese officials at the world organization.

A PBS documentary *(Jihad in America)* reveals the existence of a nationwide network of terrorist fund-raising and training camps.

The documentary showed a secretly filmed rally in New Jersey in November 1993, with a sing-along to the words: "We buy paradise with the blood of Jews." Nine months later, a substantial down payment was made when a bomb exploded at the headquarters of Jewish organizations in Buenos Aires, killing ninety-six.

Whenever I write one of my Joys-of-Islam columns, I'm barraged by letters from Moslems charging me with spreading hatred against their faith.

Yet in all of the agitation over the portrayal of believers in movies like *True Lies*, I have yet to hear one Moslem group condemn the atrocities regularly committed in the name of Islam.

I'm not looking for much, just a little press release to the effect that the Prophet's message isn't about blowing up buildings, assassinations, and crucifixions, and hey, we think it's really uncool.

Due to the exportation of the Middle East's surplus population, Islam is the fastest-growing religion in the West. France has four million Moslems. In a 1992 interview in *Le Point*, the founder of Hezbollah confidently predicted: "In twenty years, France will become an Islamic Republic."

In the Arab world, Christians are persecuted—militantly by militant governments, moderately by moderate governments.

In the United States, some Moslems feel free to abuse the liberties that would never be granted to minorities in Islamic lands to bring Beirut to Manhattan.

Western intellectuals are in a Cold War state of denial, maintaining the movement isn't monolithic, desperately casting about for moderates to deal with, claiming the sins of the West (encirclement, cultural insensitivity) are responsible for the rise of Islamic fundamentalism.

A row of crosses in southern Sudan should cast a shadow of doubt over proponents of peaceful coexistence.

## Rabin: A Metaphor for a Dying Israel
*November 6, 1995*

As his life ebbed away on an operating table in a Tel Aviv hospital, Israeli Prime Minister Yitzhak Rabin became a metaphor for his nation. Israel too is dying of multiple wounds, inflicted by the peace-at-any-price process Rabin's government doggedly pursued.

The assassination of Israel's elected leader was horrible—not just the murder of a man, but an attempt to kill democracy, using bullets to negate ballots.

But one can sincerely mourn Rabin's death while agonizing over what his Labor government has brought on the Jewish state.

Rabin was the 141st victim of the peace process to date. In the two years after he shook hands with Arafat, 140 Israelis were slaughtered in terrorist incidents the U.S. media barely deigned to notice.

After each atrocity, Rabin—who seemed increasingly detached from reality—declared that nothing would deter the nation from following the suicidal course he and Foreign Minister (now Prime Minister) Shimon Peres, had ordained.

In total disregard of the evidence, they had confidence in their peace partner, Yasser Arafat. Soon, almost 90 percent of the West Bank will be in his bloodstained hands and nearly 80 percent of Israel's population will be within mortar and shoulder-launched rocket range.

In 1991, Lt. Gen. Thomas Kelly, director of operations for the Joint Chiefs of Staff during the Gulf War, observed, "It is impossible to defend Jerusalem unless you hold the high ground.... I look onto the West Bank and I say to myself... 'I cannot defend this land [pre-1967 Israel] without that terrain.' "

Israel will be at the mercy of Arafat's Palestinian Authority, which routinely violates the three accords it's signed to date. These agreements call for a Palestinian police force of no more than nine thousand. Intelligence sources estimate the PA has more than seventeen thousand uniformed men toting automatic weapons.

Arafat permits at least five terrorist militias to operate freely in the territory he controls. Instead of keeping its covenant to disarm paramilitaries, the PA has issued gun licenses to senior personnel of Hamas and Islamic Jihad.

On June 14, members of Arafat's elite bodyguard unit were caught by Israeli border guards trying to smuggle five known terrorists into Gaza. After each car bombing, Palestinian police go through the motions of rounding up the usual suspects. Later, most are quietly released. The PA has rejected all ten Israeli demands for the extradition of suspected terrorists.

On April 2, Abu Middein, the PLO's justice minister, told the Arabic daily *Al-Quds*, "We and Hamas are complementing each other"—a totally superfluous admission.

In the aftermath of Rabin's assassination, the U.S. media has been playing a game of blame opponents of the peace process for creating an atmosphere in which such tragedies could occur.

Arafat is held to no standard at all. Speaking at Harvard, the PLO chieftain hailed peace with his "Israeli cousins." With Arab audiences, he drops the dove disguise and the vulture reemerges.

On these occasions, he puts current negotiations into the context of the PLO's 1974 "Plan of Phases," in which the destruction of Israel is to be accomplished in stages, "starting with the establishment of a Palestinian authority on any part of Palestinian soil... from which the Israelis withdraw."

His "Israeli cousins" become the "Zionist enemy." Arafat assures the Palestinians that "the intifada will continue until

Palestine is redeemed by blood and fire." Suicide bombers are revered as "martyrs."

Tel Aviv and Haifa will be "liberated," along with Jerusalem, and "whoever doesn't like it, let him drink from the Sea of Gaza."

When addressing Islamic women's groups, the Gandhi in a *kaffiyeh* eulogizes Dalal Magribi ("the star from among our heroes"), a female terrorist who participated in the 1978 bus attack that killed thirty-four civilians.

Among other feats of valor, Magribi threw a Jewish baby back on the burning bus after its mother tossed it to safety. With such heroes, the character of the Palestinian state is assured.

In actions and deeds, Arafat and his Palestinian Authority are a constant incitement to violence. Despite the damage done to the nation by a Jewish gunman, here is the real danger to the Zionist state.

Ironically, Rabin's death will probably strengthen the piece-meal-dismemberment process. An ex-general, Rabin at least had qualms and was a brake on the more perilous schemes of his party's radicals. Peres, a starry-eyed utopian, has no such doubts. The only thing more tragic than Rabin's assassination is Israel's slow death on the rack of gradual surrender.

## Vietnam: Why Let Sentiment Stand in the Way of Profits?
*July 17, 1995*

Regarding the normalization of relations with Vietnam, can we at least dispense with the tedious platitudes? America's international relations are driven by business interests, period—not morality, not human-rights concerns, not national pride or honor for our fallen heroes.

Only Bill Clinton, the dictionary definition of a hollow man, could have stood there last Tuesday and not gagged on his sickening platitudes.

Normalizing relations with Vietnam will bind old wounds and put the past behind us, the president said. Besides, the Vietnamese have been so cooperative in helping us account for the twenty-two hundred Americans officially listed as POWs or missing in action. But our quest for a final resolution will not flag, Clinton assured us (aided, no doubt, by having sacrificed our best bargaining chip).

Moreover—here, the ritual obeisance to human rights—legitimizing Ho Chi Minh's heirs "will advance the cause of freedom in Vietnam."

Sure it will. Constructive engagement has led to the flourishing of civil liberties in China. Just ask Harry Wu. The naturalized American was imprisoned for several months for exposing China's slave-labor program and its marketing of prisoners' organs.

While the president piously platitudinized, multinational corporations celebrated.

Since Clinton lifted the trade embargo against Vietnam a year ago, more than three hundred American firms have opened offices there. These corporate giants (who probably would have lined up to sell gas chambers to Hitler too) are salivating at the prospect of increased access to the world's thirteenth most populous nation.

Their next step will be to lobby for most-favored-nation trade status and subsidies from the Export-Import Bank. In international relations, money talks, morality walks.

Apologists for the move observe that after World War II we reestablished diplomatic ties with a defeated Germany and Japan. But imagine exchanging ambassadors with the Third Reich and the Tojo government had they stayed in power.

The regime we just recognized is the same criminal cabal that is responsible for the deaths of over fifty-five thousand Americans during the Vietnam War, the abrogation of the Paris Peace Accords, the murder of tens of thousands after its conquest of the south (many more were swallowed up in tropical gulags), and the flight of more than one million boat people.

In Freedom House's annual human-rights survey, Vietnam is regularly rated one of the most repressive nations on earth.

The Stalinist state still metes out long prison terms to democracy activists. Its latest victims include Dr. Doan Viet Hoat, sentenced in 1994 to fifteen years' hard labor for circulating a newsletter promoting peaceful reform.

Persecution of the United Buddhist Church, Roman Catholics, and the Cao Dai sect is relentless. Life in the socialist republic is so grim that riots broke out in refugee camps in Hong Kong and Singapore last month over the prospect of forced repatriation. Many exiles have said they'll commit suicide rather than be sent back.

The cold-blooded killers who brutally repress their own people have played a cynical game on the POW-MIA issue. Twenty years after the fall of Saigon, they have yet to account for more than three hundred American combatants known to be alive on the ground in Vietnam or Laotian territory they controlled.

Documentation on the fate of servicemen who fell into Hanoi's clutches is fed to us in dribs and drabs, whenever it seems advantageous to the ruling clique.

Make no mistake, we're dealing with war criminals every bit as evil as the SS troops who massacred captured GIs during the Battle of the Bulge.

In a February 1994 *American Spectator* article, former *New York Times* reporter John Corry noted the curious fact that among the 591 American POWs returned at the end of the war, there were "no amputees or burn cases; there was no one maimed, disfigured or blind. It is reasonable to believe that most afflicted POWs either remained in Vietnam or were murdered."

Now we are binding our wounds by caressing their killers. On the scales of international diplomacy, American dead, the sorrow of their families, and the oppression of seventy-three million Vietnamese are outweighed by business opportunities.

From his student-protest days to this loathsome act, Clinton has completed his betrayal of our fighting men. He might as well demolish the Vietnam War Memorial and sell the rubble to Hanoi for building material. Why let sentiment stand in the way of profits?

## The Mexican Conquest of America
*May 24, 1995*

**B**esides losing control of our borders, America has lost any semblance of national pride. Representatives of foreign governments feel free to insult us and meddle in our internal affairs.

At a Washington meeting last week, Mexican Foreign Minister Jose Angel Gurria launched into a denunciation of American xenophobia, supposedly manifested by California's Proposition 187, which denies government services to illegal aliens.

"With utmost concern, we observe the emergence of extremist tendencies, intolerant ideologies and hostile attitudes against Mexicans and people of Mexican origins," Gurria lectured his hosts. It's up to the political elite to educate us peons not to resent Mexico's annual underclass export, Gurria insisted.

Also last week, Teodoro Maus, Mexico's consul-general in Atlanta, said the state's attempt to make English its official language was reminiscent of the Ku Klux Klan. If so, Mexico's designation of Spanish as its official language must evoke images of the Inquisition.

Secretary of State Warren Christopher, who was present at the meeting with Gurria, didn't protest the affront. The Clinton administration, hustling Hispanic votes, is vocal in its opposition to Proposition 187.

"We will do all we can to curb illegal immigration, and at the same time, we are committed to facilitate the legal movement of people and goods across our border," Christopher soothingly replied.

Gurria's reprimand is particularly galling coming as it does from a representative of one of the most corrupt regimes in this hemisphere, run by a party that's maintained itself in power for sixty-five years by massive election fraud.

To give you an idea of what passes for democracy south of our border, the brother of former President Carlos Salinas is in jail, charged with masterminding the murder of a rival in the ruling Revolutionary Institutional Party. Perhaps Gurria would like one of Clinton's relations to order a hit on the head of the Federation for American Immigration Reform?

If we treated illegal immigrants the way it does, Mexico would have cause for complaint. While it encourages the unlawful exodus of 200,000 of its citizens annually to this nation, it deals brutally with those who cross its own borders illegally.

Mexico has its equivalent of Proposition 187. Medical and educational services are denied to those in the country illegally. In 1993, it deported 143,000 who had infiltrated its border with Guatemala.

Treatment of illegals by Mexican authorities is designed to discourage the influx. Human-rights groups are flooded with reports of the abuse of illegal immigrants in Mexico, including beatings, robbery, rape, long prison sentences (up to ten years for repeat offenders), and the deprivation of food and water.

As it pursues this ruthless policy, Mexico promotes what it calls the "migration" of Mexicans to America. After Proposition 187 passed, a bill was introduced in its legislature to allow dual citizenship for Mexican nationals living in the United States.

That way, they can take the citizenship oath here, to safeguard their welfare benefits, while maintaining their allegiance to the homeland.

Mexico views our border as a safety valve for its growing population. It believes we owe it this small favor for territory acquired in the Mexican-American War of 1846.

The small favor costs us a small fortune. In 1992, illegal aliens accounted for 40 percent of births in California hospitals paid for with public funds. Over half a billion is expended each year to arrest and incarcerate illegals.

In his book *Alien Nation*, Peter Brimelow notes the Mexican government is claiming "what amounts to extraterritorial rights over Mexican immigrants in the territory of the [former?] United States."

It provides books and teachers to facilitate bilingual education in Los Angeles, "monitors" death-sentence cases involving Mexicans, and organizes informal leadership elections in the barrios. Every major Mexican political party now has offices in California.

Brimelow comments: "The plain fact is that this is a rational strategy for the Mexican elite. They can dump their poor in the United States—and become the tail that wags the geopolitical dog."

Before Americans put another immigration initiative on the ballot, perhaps we should submit the language to Mexico City for its approval. Or just maybe in 1996, U.S. voters will elect a president more concerned with our sovereignty than internationalism or bailing out Wall Street bankers.

## Controlling Our Borders and Our Destiny
*October 10, 1995*

Somebody throw A. M. Rosenthal a lifeline. The sometimes sensible *New York Times* columnist is in dangerous waters and liable to sink under the weight of his overblown rhetoric.

I thought opponents of open immigration were supposed to be the Chicken Littles in this debate. You wouldn't know it from reading "Hunt Them Down," his exercise in hysteria.

"When a nation sets out to persecute a segment of its population," Rosenthal wrote, "to hound them, mark them, deprive them of the human care it gives others, tells them they can not work to earn their bread, that nation takes a large step toward persecuting other groups who live within its borders."

The "them" are illegal aliens, or—as Rosenthal would have it—"residents… who have come to this country in search of work or refuge without securing admission papers." And a burglar is one who enters my dwelling without prior permission.

These negligent folks are attacked by a "mean-spirited referendum" and abused by "self-serving politicians." Why, there are even base propagandists who spread the "falsehood" that our uninvited guests are a burden. Rosenthal cites an Urban Institute study which claims illegals contribute $25 billion to $30 billion more in taxes than they take in public services each year.

It's hard to argue economics here. Both sides can produce reams of reputable studies to validate their positions.

The following is indisputable: (1) As a *New York Times* article (May 19, 1994) notes, twenty years after the great influx of legal immigrants from Southeast Asia, 30 percent of their households are still on welfare—compared with 8 percent of households nationwide.

(2) Hordes of illegals are drawn here by the world's greatest welfare manna. In California, the cost of public health services for illegals jumped 1,800 percent between 1987 and 1992.

(3) Each year, in excess of one million legal and illegal immigrants reach these shores, the greatest population intake in history. Over 90 percent are non-Europeans. Against the wishes of the majority, they are changing our culture and national identity.

The cost of uncontrolled immigration can't be tallied in dollars and cents alone. I guess I'm one of the xenophobes who has set out to persecute a segment of the population. Funny, I don't feel like a fascist.

This is an unaccustomed role for the grandchild of immigrants (on both sides of the family). But the immigrants of the 1990s aren't like my grandparents.

My forebears didn't come here to go on welfare. They didn't insist that the nation adapt to them—accommodate their language, glorify their culture, teach their children in their native tongue, allow them to establish shtetl enclaves across the United States.

In Dade County, Florida, in 1993, the Hispanic majority threw out an ordinance requiring that public business be conducted in English only. The predominantly Third World city of San Jose, California, has raised a twenty-five–foot statue to the Aztec god Quetzalcoatl (with $500,000 in public money)—whose sect practiced human sacrifice—to celebrate the richness of Mexican culture.

The publication *Border Watch* reports on a prize-winning high school essay: "What Cinco de Mayo Day Means to Me." The author, a California student, declares he's a "Mexican and an American," not a Mexican-American—and note the order of precedence.

Of this Mexican national holiday, the teen writes: "My impulses and desires are linked to this day." (Not to the Fourth of July or Thanksgiving, which probably hold no emotional significance for him.) "Cinco de Mayo represents my birth, who I am and will become." This represents not nostalgia for the Old World, but ethnic/cultural separatism.

A 1993 survey of the attitudes of the children of new immigrants found little desire to assimilate. In 1991, the author of a three-year study done under the auspices of UCLA predicted: "We could come back in 100 years, and Latinos will not have assimilated in the classic sense."

For a chilling preview of what's in store for us, look not to the south but the north.

In French–speaking Quebec last month, separatists who won a majority of seats in the provincial assembly insist they will conduct a referendum on secession from Canada. More than one country has been ripped apart by binationalism.

What Rosenthal was saying, whether or not he realizes it, is that Americans have no special stake in America—that everyone in the world has as much right to be here as those who've lived in this nation all of their lives, whose families have sacrificed for America over decades or centuries. And, as a corollary, that we have no right to control our borders or our destiny.

---

Postscript: Quebec voted on secession on October 30, 1995. Separatists were narrowly defeated (by a vote of 50.6 percent to 49.4 percent). They have vowed to try again.

## Human Rights—Carter-Style
*June 21, 1993*

C ertain words seem to naturally go together, like "inefficient" and "state industry," "hard-line" and "communist regime," "Clinton" and "indecision," "Carter" and "confusion."

The accident of history who occupied the Oval Office from 1977 to 1981 is once again boring the nation with his muddled moralizing.

As the guest of honor at last week's UN Human Rights Conference—the Third World, three-ring circus in Vienna—the ex-president felt compelled to balance his critique of the atrocities of China and Iran with criticism of his own country.

We, too, are human-rights abusers, Carter confided to *USA Today*. Because there is poverty and income inequality in America, because some lack "food and clothing, a place to sleep and something to do that's productive," we are barely better than the dictatorships of the communist and Arab worlds.

*USA Today:* "You're saying homelessness is an example of a human rights abuse?"

Carter: "That's correct, and also when people don't have adequate food to eat or equal treatment in the courts." The one regret of my life is not having a column to call my own during the tragi-comical Carter years—a conservative commentator's nirvana.

Carter poses a dotty moral equivalency between the freest nation on earth and the most repressive societies. Thus by Carteresian logic, both the U.S. and People's Detention Center of China are oppressors. They torture political prisoners; we deny the homeless their "right" to shelter. They crush peaceful protestors under the treads of tanks; we don't spend enough on food stamps. Then why do one hundred thousand Chinese emigrate here illegally each year? Aren't they leaping from the communist frying pan into the cruel capitalist fire?

Among the many things Carter misses is the fact that approximately half of all government expenditures are welfare related. Since Lyndon Johnson's War on Poverty was launched in the 1960s, we've nearly bankrupted Middle America to realize the Democrats' redistributionist vision. Forty years ago, the average middle-class family paid 2 percent of its income in federal taxes. Today, Washington expropriates nearly a quarter of its income.

As the recent book *A Nation in Denial* demonstrates, the homeless are victims not of societal neglect but, quite often, of their own folly. Up to 83 percent are addicts, alcoholics, or mentally ill. Wherein does our mistreatment of them lie, in not preventing them from becoming drug or alcohol dependent, in not providing them with personal shrinks from birth?

It's no coincidence that Marxist states, established on the premise of economic rights—an inalienable right to certain material possessions—are among the worst human-rights malefactors. Witness China, witness Cuba, witness North Korea, witness Vietnam.

All are nations where breathing is prohibited without express consent of the authorities, and people are treated as mobile assets of the state. To speak of human rights in the context of these benighted lands is as incongruous as putting Woody Allen and "family values" in the same sentence.

It's such a beautiful dream—a world where no one hungers—
that becomes such a ghastly nightmare when government is the
principal instrument for achieving the same. The power to trans-
form society, to abolish the effects of natural differences in tem-
perament and ability, comes on the toe of a jackboot and the point
of a bayonet.

Ultimately, these states fail miserably at securing the only rights
they deem worthy of the name. In Cuba, all have a right to suffi-
cient nutrition. Pity the Cuban people can't eat that guarantee,
then they wouldn't have to ingest weeds and roadside plants to
avoid starvation.

Carter is symptomatic of a general sloppiness in rights rhetoric.
To the Founding Fathers and eighteenth-century political philosophers, a right was freedom from something—like censorship, religious coercion, or confiscatory taxation. If a Madison or a
Jefferson spoke of rights, they could always justify their position
with references to English common law, Locke, or the Bible.

Today, advocates postulate all sorts of spurious rights with no
philosophical foundation. Thus our ex-president's espousal of the
rights to food, clothing, shelter, and meaningful employment.

Where do such rights originate? The Constitution? The Magna
Carta? As a people, did we ever assent to them? At whose expense
will they be enforced? The rich? The middle class? Pharmaceuti-
cal firms?

The notorious "killer rabbit" who trailed *Motorboat One* on one
of Carter's presidential fishing trips was probably carrying a copy
of Von Mises's *Human Action*—a classical liberal exposition of
rights theory—in an effort to correct Carter's confusion. Too bad
they never connected.

chapter fourteen

# COUNTERATTACK

## Newt's Right: Savagery Grows...
*November 28, 1995*

H ouse Speaker Newt Gingrich is like a smart-bomb zeroing in
on the causes of social decay with uncanny accuracy. His comments on those grisly murders that took place in a Chicago suburb
last week could not have been more on target.

Two men and a woman shot and stabbed to death a pregnant
twenty-eight-year-old, slicing open her womb and removing the
child that was near term.

Jacqueline Williams, who couldn't conceive, hatched the bizarre
plot to kill Deborah Evans and take her baby. To demonstrate her
maternal instincts, after helping to butcher Evans, Williams proceeded
to kill the victim's eight-year-old son and ten-year-old daughter.

Incensed, Gingrich told a meeting of Republican governors,
"This happens in America... because for two generations we
haven't had the guts to talk about right and wrong."

The speaker pronounced the Chicago slayings "the final culmination of a drug-addicted underclass with no sense of humanity."
His statements quickly drew fire from those with no sense.

The sneering remark of White House spokesman Mike McCurry—that Gingrich "sounded like a community college sociology course"—was exactly what you'd expect from the snotty elitists who run this country. What was it Newt said about our national government being in the clutches of counterculture McGoverniks?

It's not just that the crime rate has exploded in the past thirty-five years, but crimes keep getting more savage and sickening.

In the July *Atlantic Monthly*, Adam Walinsky noted that in 1960, New Haven, Connecticut, had 6 murders, 4 rapes, and 16 robberies reported. In 1990, the medium-sized city (which lost 14 percent of its population in the interim) posted 30 murders, 168 rapes, and 1,784 robberies.

Stomach-churning atrocities have become ho-hum news.

In New York City on Sunday, robbers sprayed gasoline into a subway token booth, then created an inferno with a match (presumably for the pleasure of watching a man burn to death). A transit employee who suffered burns over 80 percent of his body later died.

Last weekend in Boston an honor student was shot to death by muggers who wanted his shearling jacket, Adidas sneakers, and a gold neck chain.

Last month, several Kansas City boys (two as young as ten) were arrested for kicking a recovering alcoholic to death.

In September, a family's car strayed into the wrong Los Angeles neighborhood. Gang members shot up the vehicle, killing a three-year-old girl and wounding her two-year-old brother.

Of course, liberals find Gingrich's comments offensive. They tilled the social soil where such barbarism flourishes and monsters sprout like mushrooms after a spring rain.

Let us speak of the cruelty of liberal compassion. We don't punish criminals too severely; that would be unkind. We don't crack down on drugs; someone's civil liberties might be violated. A woman on welfare can have any number of children out of wedlock, and each boosts her benefits. For government to do otherwise would be callous.

Value judgments are eschewed, and multiple lifestyles embraced. Liberal compassion is literally killing us.

Evans first became pregnant as a teenager. There followed welfare, seedy apartments, and a succession of children by different partners. This degrading existence, financed with your taxes, set the stage for the tragedy.

The two men arrested for her murder are probably not Wally and the Beav. Let me gaze into my crystal ball and make a few obvious predictions: Their families aren't the Nelsons. The schools they attended didn't emphasize virtue or even mention the word.

In the words of the Longfellow poem, their brows weren't wet by honest sweat. Prior to the murders, they were known to the authorities and well-acquainted with illicit substances.

Their clones are being incubated in welfare families across the country.

Here are a few statistics to elevate the hairs on the back of your neck. In the past decade, the number of minors arrested for murder increased 158 percent. Violent youth make up 61 percent of the California prison population, up from 44 percent in 1987.

Over 70 percent of the juveniles incarcerated for serious crimes come from single-parent homes. In 2010, there will be half a million more adolescent boys than today. By then, the number of youth arrests for violent crime could more than double.

Through welfare, the criminal justice system, and public education, liberalism has assiduously attacked the concept of personal responsibility and created a brutal, conscienceless, whim-driven subculture. That ugly reality, and not the budget or Bosnia, should be the main issue in the upcoming presidential campaign.

Say it again, Newt.

## Why Liberals Bad-Mouth Talk Radio
*January 26, 1995*

G rab the Valium, nurse. The liberals are flipping out over Rush again.

The titan of talk radio graces the cover of the January 23 issue of *Time* magazine, looking like a meaty Mephistopheles, smoke curling ominously from his cigar—a plutocrat of opinion and malefactor of rhetoric.

There are more than one thousand talk-radio stations in America today, the article discloses. "Listeners tend to be white, male, and hep to conservative ideas." Ah, the legendary angry white male.

This army of discontent, mobilized by master manipulators like Limbaugh, were shock troops in the GOP conquest of Congress, *Time* informs us, citing a survey showing hard-core listeners voted three-to-one Republican.

No offense to Limbaugh and his followers, but I think the power of talk radio is exaggerated. Unless the commander of the Dittoheads introduced the president's parents, I doubt Rush is personally responsible for the Democrats' 1994 debacle.

Why is the rest of the media so obsessed with talk radio? Because it's the one forum liberals don't control. They have everything else—network news, newspapers of record, and news magazines. The competition is driving them crazy. They want their monopoly back.

Whatever the sins of talk-show hosts, at least callers know they're getting opinion, unlike those who pick up *Time* and are proselytized and propagandized cover to cover in the name of news coverage.

*Time* has a glib explanation for conservative dominance of talk radio—liberals are too nice. It quotes with approval the observation of the general manager of WLS in Chicago that "liberals are genetically engineered not to offend anybody," a condition that renders them boring.

Liberals genetically engineered not to offend? Tell it to Robert Bork, Clarence Thomas, Oliver North, and other prominent victims of liberal smear campaigns. Only individuals desperately eager to please would imply that if you disagree with them on welfare policy, you're a creature of Dickensian darkness who wants to pack unwed mothers off to the workhouse.

Just imagine the level of invective from the left if liberals weren't the soft, cuddly, huggy bears *Time* insists they are.

The magazine's feeble rationale notwithstanding, conservatives do rule the radio airwaves. In any major market, the top talk show is hosted by a conservative—Bob Grant in New York, G. Gordon Liddy in Washington, D.C., and David Brudnoy and Howie Carr in Boston.

Conservatives are conspicuous here because the medium is highly competitive and finely attuned to public opinion.

Newspapers and network television can ignore the values of their audiences with near impunity. Most cities are one-newspaper towns. Even where there is competition, reporters and editors tend to be standard issue in their outlook.

If you don't like the slant on the CBS evening news, you can turn to ABC or NBC for the same bias.

Talk radio is different. The popularity of a host can be accurately gauged by the quarterly Arbitron ratings. With a half-dozen stations doing the same programming in each city, talk is too competitive to ignore the demands of the marketplace.

Most station managers are as liberal as their counterparts elsewhere in the media. No matter. If they want to stay in business, they must offer a marketable commodity. That's why Brudnoy has been on the air in Boston for nineteen years, Grant has been No. 1 in New York drive time for a decade, and Limbaugh is carried by 660 stations.

Liberals are genetically incapable of admitting the underlying cause of talk radio's popularity—their own increasing unpopularity. Like the results of the 1994 election, talk radio must be rationalized, psychoanalyzed, explained away.

It is an organizing principle of liberalism that since liberals are for the people, the people must be for them. Thus normally sober citizens, who've been beguiled by talk-show hosts playing on their fear and anger, will eventually come to their senses and join the Democratic National Committee in a rousing chorus of "Happy Days Are Here Again."

What liberals fail to perceive is how much ordinary people despise them.

People listen to talk radio not only for input and a sense of connection but because they want to hear liberals ridiculed, their foolish dogmatism refuted, their hypocrisy exposed, their pomposity lampooned, and their egos deflated. Half a century of liberal hegemony created the craze for conservative talk radio.

While Newt Gingrich speaks to a packed House and Limbaugh addresses twenty million weekly, increasingly, liberals are talking to themselves.

## If Liberals Walked the Walk
*August 15, 1994*

The moral pronouncements of Hillary Rodham Clinton remind me of something Teddy Roosevelt said about one of his opponents: "Every time he opens his mouth, he detracts from the sum total of human wisdom."

But "freeloading" is the one word I thought would never escape her lips. Yet Hillary has taken to talking about the "freeloading" small businessmen who oppose employer mandates in her plan to Swedenize medical care.

Forget that independent entrepreneurs were responsible for 80 percent of net job growth in the 1980s, and many know that mandates would kill them. Presumably, they are to cheerfully commit suicide to satisfy her passion for social engineering.

Yes, Hillary, let's talk freeloading—as in a yuppie couple that takes over a border state and proceeds to stick their snouts so far in the trough that it's doubtful they'll ever dislodge them. A governor and his missus who charge thousands of dollars of personal living expenses to the state's taxpayers (including a nanny for their daughter, listed on the roster of the governor's mansion as a security guard).

Let's talk about the wife of a political figure who turns a $1,000 investment into a $100,000 profit in a deal that looks suspiciously like a payoff. As first lady-to-be, she cashes out her partnership in a law firm hours before her husband's retroactive tax hike, legislated later, will go into effect.

After making Bonnie Parker look like the Welcome Wagon lady, Hillary has the gall to call others freeloaders. But this is so typical of the left, which Ms. Clinton epitomizes. There's no congruence—absolutely none—between what liberals say and what liberals do.

Imagine what the world would be like if liberals walked the walk as well as they talk the talk:

Democratic members of Congress would enroll their children in public schools. And not just any public schools, but—as evidence of their faith in the future of public education—in the most crime-ridden inner-city schools they could find, the very institutions to which their opposition to educational choice has doomed the urban poor.

Chelsea Clinton would bid farewell to the exclusive Sidwell Friends School. The daughter of the National Education Association's best friend on Earth could then experience the delights of the District's public school system.

Liberals with preschoolers would put them in day-care centers run by pedophiles to demonstrate that orientation doesn't imply behavior. Those with teenage daughters would present each with a condom as she left the house on a date, disease control being the only real issue in adolescent sexuality.

Affirming their commitment to affirmative action in the most tangible way, the white, middle-aged executives among them would resign their positions in favor of minority candidates. No longer would the burden of redressing the sins of the past fall exclusively on middle-class Caucasians.

To prove their allegiance to income redistribution, champagne collectivists would contribute 100 percent of their salaries above the national average to charity. No more BMWs or Mercedes for them. Instead of summer homes on Martha's Vineyard, they'd be catching the rays with the hoi polloi on a blanket at the nearest public beach.

To demonstrate their devotion to the creed of the American Civil Liberties Union, all would reside next door to crack houses in apartments without locks on the doors or firearms for self-defense.

No more handgun hypocrites, like Carl Rowan. The syndicated columnist's credibility as an anti-gun advocate was blown sky high by the episode at his suburban Washington home when he used an unlicensed pistol to pop a teenager trespassing in his pool.

Alternately, they would campaign for low-income housing in their neighborhoods or hire serial killers on work release to do odd jobs around the house, knowing how well rehabilitation works. Members of the now-I'm-a-dove, now-I'm-a-hawk Congressional Black Caucus would sign up for basic training at Camp Pendleton in preparation for the invasion of Haiti. Our draft-dodging commander in chief would lead the first assault wave to hit the beaches.

If the Clintons really cared about health care for all, they would have gone to medical school, moved to Appalachia, and opened a free clinic—instead of going into law, politics, and plunder.

But, of course, it's all a fantasy. Liberals have developed a knack for living their own lives as if the *Wall Street Journal* was their lodestar instead of *Mother Jones.* They drift through life mouthing pieties they never practice and denouncing others for their own flaws. Ask Hillary, the decade-of-greed centerfold who foams about freeloading.

## Middle Class Not Buying Class Envy
*May 8, 1995*

Am I supposed to sit in my modest, mortgaged-to-the-hilt dwelling, biting my knuckles in rage and frustration because Kirk Kerkorkian (who's trying to buy the Chrysler Corp.) has a bigger piece of the American dream than I do? That's what liberals expect, as they pound the drums of class envy.

It's as predictable as the flowers that bloom in the spring (tra-la): Republicans talk of cutting taxes, and Democrats respond with dire warnings about the rich making out like robber barons and the burgeoning income gap.

There's always an academic study to bolster the argument. This time, the research comes from Edward N. Wolff, an economics professor at New York University, who claims the top 1 percent of households (worth at least $2.3 million each) own 40 percent of the nation's wealth.

"We are the most unequal industrialized country in terms of income and wealth, and we're growing more unequal faster than other industrialized countries," Wolff warns.

Who's to blame? C'mon, you know—the decade of greed, Reagan-era tax cuts, and a decline of income-leveling transfer programs. To make matters worse, here comes the Contract with America proposing more "tax cuts for the rich." If the Democrats are to be believed, our society will soon resemble Bourbon France.

Wolff's statistics present a deceptive picture. Wealth isn't static. The people who were rich thirty years ago could be trailer-park residents today.

Folks like Donald Trump made a fortune in real estate in the 1980s and lost it in the 1990s. When last spotted, Trump was doing a walk-on in the movie *Home Alone 2.*

The class-warfare cadre points with envy to Europe. Wolff notes that even Britain, with its hereditary peerage, is more egalitarian than America. True, but you wouldn't want to be a twenty-one year old entering the job market in Britain.

Americans own one automobile for every 1.8 people. In Britain, it's one for every 2.8. It's one for every 2.2 in what was West Germany, 2.5 in France, and 4.2 in Japan. The living standard of Japan and most of Europe is 40 percent lower than ours.

During the decade of greed, the rich got richer—along with everyone else. Productivity, job growth, real wages, and taxes paid by the wealthy all increased. During the 1980s, the incomes of the top 20 percent of Americans rose by 13.6 percent; but the incomes of the bottom fifth went up 10.4 percent.

By reducing their marginal tax rate and encouraging the rich to be more productive, the portion of taxes paid by the top 5 percent of income earners increased from 36.4 percent in 1980 to 42.9 percent in 1990.

Before you get too resentful of the upper-crusty, consider a simple truth: Millionaires create jobs for assembly-line workers. The reverse is not the case. Income left in the hands of the filthy rich is used to start businesses, build factories, and buy stock. It creates jobs and generates wealth.

Taxed away by government, it stimulates a different type of production: out-of-wedlock births, welfare dependency, and social chaos.

From 1982 to 1990, the U.S. economy created 18.4 million new jobs. For the ten years from 1982 to 1992, the number of jobs grew

18.2 percent in this country. During the same period, job growth was 9.6 percent in Germany, 6.6 percent in the United Kingdom, 3.7 percent in France, and negative 0.6 percent in socialist Sweden.

Winston Churchill once remarked: "The inherent vice of capitalism is the unequal sharing of the blessings. The inherent blessing of socialism is the equal sharing of misery."

Bruce Bartlett, deputy assistant secretary of the treasury for economic policy under Presidents Reagan and Bush, acknowledges that there is a class conflict in America, but not the one liberals hype.

"Democrats don't have a clue about the real class-warfare issue in this country." It's not the middle class resentful of the rich but anger across the income spectrum directed at the parasitical poor.

This was brought home to me on income-tax day, when I listened to a local radio talk show while driving to work.

Not one caller complained about the much-touted income gap or blamed his tax bill on mythical underpayment by the rich. Complaints were all about congressional pensions, "welfare cheats," food-stamp fraud, and the like.

How is the left going to bait the rich, when the middle class won't rise to the bait?

## Liberals to Blame for U.S. Paranoia
*May 15, 1995*

One of the dumbest pieces of polemic to come out of the Oklahoma bombing is an ad by the American Federation of State, County, and Municipal Employees.

The broadside is a discreditable example of liberalism's penchant for exploiting such tragedies—including abortion-clinic violence—to stifle dissent.

After praising Oklahoma rescue workers ("public servants...

heroes"), the ad proceeds to censure the critics of big government. "Isn't it time to end the constant attacks on the people who serve us? Who knows what the twisted mind of a terrorist might think? Or do."

What's the point—that every time you complain about an officious bureaucrat, a meddlesome social worker, or an indolent postal employee, you risk detonating a human time bomb?

The ad concludes with an appeal: "Next time you hear someone viciously attack our government, and the Americans who work for it, tell them—Stop it. This is our government."

AFSCME doesn't like people dissing the welfare state or its pampered minions. The 1.3 million-member union represents those who gorge at government's banquet table. During the 1992 campaign, a banner on the union's headquarters proclaimed: "AFSCME is Clinton Country."

With typical liberal consistency, the union feels entitled to attack government when it suits its purposes. Its president, Gerald McEntee, accuses Congress of trying to starve "disadvantaged children" and victimize "the elderly and/or disabled."

Influenced by such invective, who knows what a maniac welfare mother or schizoid senior might think? Or do? The next time you hear someone viciously attack Newt Gingrich and the Republican Congress, tell them—Stop it. This is our government.

What is it the left wants: the emasculation of policy debate, campus speech codes applied nationwide, or simply to have its sacred cows declared endangered species and thus protected from the political hunt? All of the above.

If Oklahoma brought out liberalism's authoritarian instinct, it should prompt some critical distinctions on the right. It's time to articulate the authentic conservative position on government.

Conservatives aren't anarchistic or paranoid—sentiments often wrongly associated with the right by bunker-mentality kooks. We are not adverse to authority.

We want a government modest in size and means, respectful of the legitimate rights of citizens, and no more intrusive than necessary. But we recognize the necessity of government—that chaos is as undesirable as coercion and that the former invariably leads to the latter.

Being wary of political power is in keeping with the American tradition. George Washington voiced this Actonian skepticism when he noted: "Government is not reason; it is not eloquence; it is force. Like fire, it is a troublesome servant and a fearful master."

But the anarchist urge is alien to our national character. Alexander Hamilton expressed the founders' sense of balance when he observed that government is essential because "the passions of men will not conform to the dictates of reason and justice without it."

The difference between genuine conservatism and knee-jerk opposition to government is the difference between caution and paranoia. It's the difference between those who think Waco was badly botched, that incompetence and zealotry led to the deaths of eighty-five people, and the wackos who believe that federal agents intended to murder cult members.

It's the difference between those who think gun control is a natural expression of liberalism's inability to punish criminals (hence the need to demonize inanimate objects) and those who see it as a conspiracy to leave citizens defenseless, paving the way for one-world government.

Anxiety about government isn't confined to the right. In a Gallup poll taken shortly after the Oklahoma bombing, more liberals than conservatives (42 percent to 39 percent) agreed that Washington has "become so large and powerful that it poses an immediate threat to the rights and freedoms of citizens."

Mistrust of government is healthy, forestalling the sort of jack-booted horrors that have plagued this century. Implacable, irrational hostility toward the state could make representative government impossible.

Conservatives must disavow the verbal incendiaries. Liberals must understand that they nurtured antigovernment hysteria by creating a monstrosity that can't keep its hands out of our pockets or its legions from trampling our liberties.

## Shutting Off the Leftward Flow of Money
*February 27, 1995*

Forget the balanced-budget amendment and term limitation. The real job confronting the Republican Congress is defunding the left.

Since Great Society days, liberals have taken up residency in our hip pockets, there to propagandize, lobby, and litigate with our confiscated wealth. The federal treasury has become their megaphone, their lawyer's briefcase, their societal battering ram.

There is hope the GOP will hang tough here. In response to the persistent whining of the Public Broadcasting Service, House Speaker Newt Gingrich told a Washington gathering: "They still don't realize that the appropriation is gone, the game is over." Hooray and hallelujah.

While insisting on its right to our income, the Big Bird lobby is impervious to well-documented charges of bias. Its latest independent campaign expenditure for the Democratic Party—"America's War on Poverty"—featured a parade of apologists for the welfare state.

But the PBS empire, encompassing over one thousand TV stations, is only one province of the left's far-flung, tax-funded ideological empire.

By a vote of ninety-nine-to-one, the Senate recently denounced the National Endowment for the Humanities' National History Standards.

Produced by two UCLA academics, with $2 million from

NEH, the standards are American history through the eyes of Sheik Omar Abdel-Rahman. A teacher on an advisory panel for the project describes the standards as "unrelentingly anti-Western." Over ten thousand copies have been distributed to publishers and schools.

What does the NEH think it is—the Smithsonian? Veterans had to fight a second battle of Iwo Jima to force our national museum (annual budget: $383 million) to withdraw its revisionist exhibit on the end of the war in the Pacific, which cast Hirohito and Tojo as Third World victims of cultural imperialism.

Want more examples? How about the National Endowment for the Arts (annual appropriation, $170.2 million)? Its current head, actress Jane Alexander, wants to use the agency to "introduce people gently to gay themes." It's hard to imagine anything more subtle than HIV-positive performance artist Ron Athey's ritualistic bloodletting, brought to us by Alexander's ragtime band.

In 1993, New York's Whitney Museum got $200,000 from the NEA for an exhibit which sought, in the words of the catalog, to employ "methodologies adapted from feminism, queer theory... Marxism, and psychoanalysis" to "talk dirty in the institution and degrade its atmosphere of purity and prudery." Publicly funded political pornography. What better use of our taxes?

The left also litigates from our pockets. The Legal Services Corporation (current appropriation, $415 million) was established to provide representation to poor people in civil cases.

It didn't take long for the Kunstler-types who run the agency to politicize its mission. LSC is trying to overturn a New Jersey law that caps payments to welfare mothers who have additional children and is mounting a challenge to a California welfare residency requirement.

The Department of Health and Human Services has a $2 billion annual AIDS budget—money earmarked for research and prevention. Much of it finds its way to groups like the Gay Men's

Health Crisis, where it's used to make homosexual men more comfortable with their lifestyle.

Similarly, Planned Parenthood gets about $158 million annually for contraception. This frees up other funds for lobbying against restrictions on abortion.

The left is absolutely ingenious in devising ways to direct educational funds to activist groups. A Reagan appointee told me that when he was in the Department of Energy in the mid-1980s, money for community conservation was regularly diverted to Luddite environmentalists like the Natural Resources Defense Council.

When challenged on these blatant misuses of public funds, the left shifts into its favorite mode—indignation. Take away our money? Are you anti-culture? Anti-health? Anti-poor? Anti-planet?

Though they'd never admit it, they really believe they have a right to use our resources to defeat our values.

Other than union dues, money from Hollywood, and foundation grants, most of the left's funding comes from government. Without their federal ATM cards, they'd have to seek the voluntary support of individuals. Given their chances of success in that dubious venture, they will maintain their death grip on our wallets.

## Elites in a Tizzy Over White Males
*February 23, 1995*

"**A**re you an angry white male?" a *Washington Post* reporter earnestly asked me following my speech at the annual Conservative Political Action Conference.

This is the media's catch phrase of the hour. Angry white males (AWMs) drive talk radio—theoretically. Republicans captured Congress by appealing to racial or gender outrage—supposedly.

Here comes the legion of choleric, Caucasian guys—guzzling Coors out of Rush Limbaugh commemorative mugs, wearing

NRA caps, grumbling about sexual harassment suits. Welfare mooches, affirmative-action hires, and gyno-fascists, beware.

What makes the pale-faced gent so angry? Is his vexation justified or a temper tantrum of the overprivileged?

Columnist Ellen Goodman, dowager empress of political correctness, says the AWM isn't angry at all, he's just a scared little boy who is "worried about falling out of work, out of the middle class, out of power."

If it's possible to sweat and sneer simultaneously, that's what the establishment is doing over its latest *bête noire*.

Electoral rage, which liberals attribute exclusively to 39 percent of the population, isn't about to end. Even institutions ordinarily immune to politics are beginning to get the message. The Supreme Court is considering a case that could blow the whole minority set-asides scam right out of the water.

The California Civil Rights Initiative will be on the ballot in 1996. Spearheaded by two San Francisco-area professors (Ph.D.s with bow ties aren't your typical AWMs), the initiative would end quota hiring in government jobs and preferential treatment in state college admissions.

According to co-sponsor Thomas Woods, the outcome of the battle will determine "whether a person's rights will be independent of race, ethnicity, or gender or not, indeed whether the government will enforce group entitlements."

Liberals have done their best to fragment society: creating a racial/gender spoils system, casting some as victims and others as oppressors, stereotyping as they go.

The angry white male hypothesis fails on two grounds. First, it implies that anger is the defining characteristic of the conservative upsurge. Most of us have beliefs (in freedom, individual initiative, and traditional morality) that transcend whatever dark emotions we feel when listening to Barbra Streisand blather at the Kennedy School of Government.

The expression also implies that our indignation is directed at women and blacks. But it wasn't primarily women and minorities who got us into this mess. While doing his best to inflame race relations, Jesse Jackson didn't dream up AFDC or affirmative action.

Liberal white males who committed the Great Society, abetted by other LWMs in the media and academia, are responsible for reverse racism. It wasn't feminists but white male lawyers, legislators, and jurists who bestowed the blessings of no-fault divorce and legalized abortion on this nation. *Roe v. Wade* was decided by a Supreme Court that, with the exception of Thurgood Marshall, looked like the Union Club circa 1923.

Anger isn't confined to the melanin deficient and testosterone enriched. In the past election, 52 percent of married women voted for GOP congressional candidates.

California's Proposition 187, denying government benefits to illegal aliens—said to be the calling card of the AWM—passed with the support of half of black voters and one-third of Hispanics in the state.

Ward Connerly, a black member of the Board of Regents of the University of California and an opponent of racial admissions, declares: "I tell you with every fiber of my being that what we're doing is inequitable to certain people," which probably makes him an angry African American male (AAAM).

Affirmative action is an equal-opportunity victimizer. San Francisco limits the number of Asians admitted to the city's elite public high schools to maintain the proper pigmentation balance. Joe Gelman, a member of the Los Angeles Civil Service Commission, tells of a black male electrician—competent, bootstraps-type fellow—who couldn't get a job with the city's water and power department because he lacked the requisite genitalia to satisfy diversity worshipers.

You don't have to be an angry white male to see that affirmative action is evil or to know that sexual harassment has become a vehicle for bitter, chronically aggrieved individuals to vent their frustrations. You don't have to be an angry white male to understand that welfare policies beget the next generation of criminals, addicts, and parasites. And you don't have to be an AWM to perceive that multiculturalism is eroding our national fabric.

Liberalism's house of quotas is coming down. You don't have to be an angry white male to join the demolition crew.

# THE REAL AMERICA

## Why God Blesses America

G od blesses America.
Every church and synagogue in this land should dedicate at least one Sabbath a year to a service of thanksgiving for this great nation of ours. There was a time, in the late eighteenth and early nineteenth centuries, when such services were the norm. They should be again.

I searched my memory to recall the last time I heard someone say the words "I love America." It was six months ago. Sitting across from me in a Boston restaurant was a middle-aged man named Steve Ross. "I love America," he said with fervor and the faintest trace of an Eastern European accent. "It is a privilege to live here," he added.

He was wearing a short-sleeved shirt. As he spoke, I noticed blue numbers tattooed on his forearm. The survivor of five death camps, Ross was fifteen years old when U.S. troops liberated him from Dachau.

Perhaps one has to pass through fire to appreciate the blessings of this fair land.

What makes America special? In this century, we fought and defeated the worst political scourges to afflict humanity—fascism and communism, ideologies which between them murdered more than 100 million people. Were it not for America, the entire world would have been plunged into one of two alternative totalitarian nightmares.

We fought not for glory or territory or to spread an ideology. We fought evil. Following the Spanish-American War, we could have annexed Cuba. After World War II, we could have kept the Philippines, colonized Germany, and created our own empire in East Asia. We weren't even tempted.

The next time you hear an intellectual snob disparage this nation, remind him: America destroyed Nazism. America conquered communism. Could there be higher praise or a greater tribute than this?

But that's far from all. Our ideals inspired humanity. Our Constitution and laws served as a model for new nations. Our motto, "One nation under God, with liberty and justice for all," animated nation-builders around the world.

What does America mean? You know, it's strange that we should even ask that question. Yet millions do, both Americans and foreigners.

No one asks what France or Germany or Russia is about. They simply are. They are nation-states that occupy territory and have distinctive forms of government. Their customs, language, and historical consciousness evolved over millennia.

But they're not expected to mean anything. America is. It has from its inception. In the hearts of the best of us, it still does.

What then is the American ideal? Is it liberty, equality before the law, prosperity, productivity? All of the above and more.

Let me answer the question with a comparison. Throughout the course of history, only two nations have had meaning and a mission—or callings, if you will. One is the United States of America, the other was ancient Israel.

One started with twelve tribes, the other with thirteen colonies. In both cases, settlers came into the wilderness to establish a nation dedicated to an ideal.

Ancient Israel and America were unique in yet another way. They were the only two nations in the course of history where the idea preceded the land. The Israelites became a people, received their animating vision, while they were still landless nomads wandering in the Sinai.

The Pilgrims and Puritans were first inspired by that vision of a "shining city on a hill" while they were in Europe. The Mayflower Compact was signed before the Pilgrims landed at Plymouth Rock. At our inception as a nation in 1787, America occupied a sliver of land on the East Coast, a fraction of the territory it would one day possess.

At the outset, each nation was governed by a legal code in place of a monarch—a written constitution which served as its enabling document. One came directly from God; the other was man-made, but inspired by the wisdom of Scriptures.

Both understood that freedom is crucial, but that freedom is only a means to an end, that end being the service of the Creator.

It's as if ancient Israel stretched out its hand across millennia to establish another bastion on these shores, a new nation dedicated to the ideals of the Patriarchs and Prophets.

In turn, America came to the rescue of Israel's scattered remnant in this century and was instrumental in the birth of the modern state of Israel.

More than any other nation, America is about the quest for spirituality, the need to connect to the eternal.

It's there in our founding documents, from the Mayflower Compact to the Declaration of Independence with its observation that all men were "endowed by their Creator with certain unalienable rights."

It was there in the thoughts of the Founding Fathers, from Washington to Madison and Adams. The latter wrote: "Our

Constitution was meant for a moral and a religious people. It is wholly inadequate for the governance of any other."

This ethos is even reflected in our patriotic music. Our national songs make constant reference to God, beseech his blessings, and call on him for protection and guidance.

Listen to the spirit of America: "Then conquer we must, when our cause it is just, and this be our motto, in God is our trust."

"Our fathers' God to thee, author of liberty."

"Mine eyes have seen the glory of the coming of the Lord / He is trampling out the vintage where the grapes of wrath are stored / He has loosed the fateful lightning of his terrible swift sword / His truth is marching on."

"America, America, God shed His grace on thee. And crown thy good with brotherhood from sea to shining sea."

And that love sonnet to his adopted land written by a Russian immigrant who was born Israel Baline: "God bless America, land that I love / Stand beside her and guide her, through the night with a light from above."

Is there another nation whose patriotic music is thus infused with spiritual yearning?

Here is the secret of America's greatness. That most astute observer of our infant republic, the Frenchman Alexis de Tocqueville (who visited this country early in the last century), put it so well when he wrote: "America is great because America is good. And if America ever ceases to be good, she will cease to be great." Am I implying that God is on our side? The question misses the point.

During the darkest days of the Civil War, a reporter asked the same question of Abraham Lincoln. Our sixteenth president thoughtfully replied that what was important wasn't whether God was on our side but whether we were on His side.

As the Bible says: I will honor him who honors me.

In every generation, our nation has raised up men and women equal to the challenges that confronted us.

America needs the stout-hearted and the selfless, needs those of clear moral vision—as much today as she did in 1776, 1861, 1917, and 1941.

Our nation is under attack by a swarm of internal enemies, adherents to an alien philosophy. She is slandered and reviled.

In the spring of 1994, the Smithsonian Institution proposed an exhibit on the end of the war in the Pacific and the bombing of Hiroshima that cast America as the aggressor and, if you can believe it, the Japanese as victims of cultural imperialism.

Federally sponsored guidelines that seek to establish national standards for teaching history reek of political correctness. Lynn Cheney, chairman of the National Endowment for the Humanities under Reagan and Bush—which helped to underwrite the travesty—notes the guidelines have no less than seventeen references to the Ku Klux Klan and nineteen to McCarthyism but not a single mention of Alexander Graham Bell or Thomas Edison.

Anti-Americanism has been the reigning dogma on our college campuses for the past three decades and more. In the mass media, Hollywood in particular, constructive criticism has turned to mindless iconoclasm. Our national moles are magnified into mountain ranges. It's a long, dreary descent from Frank Capra to Oliver Stone.

We are raising a generation whose knowledge of our national past is filtered through a lens held by Benedict Arnolds of the spirit. Schoolchildren are indoctrinated in the dogma that the American saga consists exclusively of chapters on slavery, segregation, sweatshops, misogyny, genocide against native populations, imperialism, and economic exploitation.

They are told that America was founded on a contradiction, that while proclaiming liberty and the rights of man, our constitution tacitly allowed human bondage.

Their teachers somehow neglect to mention that slavery existed for roughly four thousand years before the birth of America and that the United States is the only nation on earth where a civil war was fought, and an especially bloody one at that, to end the awful institution.

It's time for the real America to rise up and say: Enough! We will not tolerate having our children's heads filled with lies. We will not allow the use of our tax dollars to libel brave servicemen and their families.

We know what America means, even if the cultural elite has forgotten. For more than two centuries, America has been the greatest force for good in the world. With the help of God, but only with His help, she will continue to be a beacon of hope in an often benighted world.

Thus, truly do we say: *God bless America, land that we love. Stand beside her and guide her through the night with a light from above. God bless America, our home, sweet home.*

## Norman Rockwell: Sonnets to the Prosaic
*January 27, 1994*

N orman Rockwell is a litmus test, a way of separating the snob elite from Middle America. An affinity for the Capra of canvas is an even better gauge of political incorrectness than a fondness for John Wayne, Ronald Reagan, or Rush Limbaugh.

February 3 marks the hundredth anniversary of the artist's birth. It has been seventeen years since his passing, but Rockwell is very much alive in the sentiments his work still evokes.

A 1993 *Newsweek* article on the opening of a new Rockwell museum in Stockbridge, Massachusetts, sneered that America's best-loved artist was the "Brueghel of the 20th-century bourgeoisie, the Holbein of Jell-O ads and magazine covers."

How they love to loathe him, the lumpen intelligentsia. He wasn't an artist but a lowly illustrator, they sniff. He was clichéd, banal, simplistic. He presented a cutesy-pie, storybook vision of America which, they insist (1) does not exist, (2) never existed, (3) could not exist.

On the other hand, many of them go into paroxysms of ecstasy over exhibits of artificial excrement and paintings that appear to be the work of a three-year-old with severe emotional problems.

Critics are driven to deride popular artists (Frank Capra, Irving Berlin, Steven Spielberg—before *Schindler's List*). For them, popularity is the cultural mark of Cain, a sure sign that the recipient of acclaim lacks subtlety and substance.

Never has there been a greater divergence of popular and elite opinion. For almost fifty years, Rockwell was the best-loved illustrator of America's favorite magazine. A *Saturday Evening Post* editor noted that in the 1950s a Rockwell cover meant an extra seventy-five thousand newsstand sales.

During World War II, the originals of his Four Freedoms paintings toured the country, generating $130 million in bond sales. A 1960s showing of fifty of his canvases was panned by critics and mobbed by the public. Every one sold during the preview, at an average price of $20,000. A book of his illustrations, published in 1970, has to date generated $10 million in sales.

Each year, more than three hundred thousand visitors flock to the Rockwell museum. An employee confessed that she "expected to see a bunch of blue-haired, little old ladies," but instead beheld couples with children in strollers reverently touring the facility.

In a troubled century, Rockwell's success reflected a hunger for the mundane. He celebrated timeless virtues: love, loyalty, friendship, pride in country. Before me is a book with all 332 of his magazine covers. Opened at random, it cannot fail to delight.

A doctor places his stethoscope to the chest of a doll held by an anxious little girl. A mother, with a yelping child across her lap and various broken objects at her feet, holds a hairbrush in one hand and a book on child psychology in the other, a thoroughly perplexed expression on her face. No one could capture the play of emotions across a countenance like Rockwell.

Waiting outside the principal's office, a pigtailed tomboy—disheveled, sporting a shiner—grins ear to ear. In a shabby rail yard restaurant, an elderly woman and her grandson bend over their meals in prayer, while tough yardmen look on.

My favorite Rockwell, the *Post* cover on February 16, 1929, was titled *The Age of Chivalry.* Here a plumpish, middle-aged man is asleep in his easy chair; a volume on chivalry rests in his lap. In the shadowy background, we glimpse the passing pageantry of a knightly dream. A beribboned cat stands vigil over its sleeping master.

Rockwell was the first to admit that his was a fanciful world. He once confided to an interviewer that he had unconsciously decided that if this wasn't an ideal world, it should be, and proceeded to make it so—creating on canvas an idyllic land without disease, deformity, or despair, where all women were virtuous, young men determined, and children at their worst mischievous, but more often supremely happy.

Problems were humorous and never too big. And yet in the silly dilemmas, misadventures, joys, and pleasures of his characters, viewers saw something of their own lives.

It's a perennial question: Should art mirror reality or idealize it? Today, much of what passes for the aesthetic celebrates the sordid, presents a perspective from the foot of a dung heap gazing up at oblivion.

I don't know if Rockwell was a religious man. His art was certainly reverential. His prolific brush produced affectionate portraits of exuberant youth, domestic contentment, budding romance—the best existence has to offer.

Thomas S. Buechner, former director of the Brooklyn Museum, wrote that Rockwell gave us "a body of work which is unsurpassed in the richness and variety of its subject matter and in the professionalism—often brilliant—of its execution."

He did much more. Rockwell painted sonnets to the prosaic

that America took to its collective heart. "People somehow get out of your work just about what you put into it," Rockwell observed. "And if you are interested in the characters you draw and understand them and love them, why the person who sees your picture is bound to feel the same way." Throughout this century, millions have and still do.

## This "Army" Fights to Make Us Care
*December 6, 1995*

I never pass a Salvation Army kettle without throwing in my change or a buck or two.

Those modest alms are partial repayment of a debt. My mother grew up in a poor immigrant family in Troy, New York. Every year at this time, she joined the kids in her neighborhood trooping to the local Salvation Army headquarters for a gift of oranges and nuts, and a warm knitted cap or mittens.

That was seventy-five years ago. But failing to recall a kindness done is bad form. And this army has done a lot of good over the past 130 years.

Soldiers who served in the trenches in 1917 saw the army's "donut lassies" dispensing food and hot beverages. During the Depression, in one week alone, Salvationists served thirty-four thousand meals in New York City. In World War II, they helped organize the USO and operated their own service clubs.

Today, the Salvation Army is America's favorite charity. An attempt to enumerate its humanitarian activities in the course of a year would fill volumes: operating 119 alcohol and drug rehab centers; serving 69 million meals; providing shelter for 9.5 million homeless; running AIDS hospices, day-care centers, summer camps, and parole halfway houses; distributing disaster relief and toys for poor children; and visiting hospitals and nursing homes.

Faith in action is this army's credo. Since Gen. William Booth, its first commanding officer, invaded the London slums in 1865 bringing a message of redemption to prostitutes, drunks, and thieves, the Salvation Army has pursued its dual mission of ministering to physical and spiritual needs.

The army is also a church. All of its officers are ordained ministers. "The paramount objective of the Salvation Army has always been to lead men and women into a proper relationship with God," an army pamphlet confesses.

But the scriptural message can't be heard over the rumblings of an empty stomach, through an alcoholic haze, or in the depths of despair. So Salvationists feed, clothe, comfort, counsel, rehabilitate—and preach.

The army's battle plan might be described as hard-headed soft-heartedness.

It believes in work therapy. Recipients who are able sort clothes, repair donated furniture and appliances, and ring bells during the Christmas season. In 1994, it made more than seventy thousand job referrals.

The red kettles, which first appeared on the San Francisco waterfront in 1891, make this pragmatic altruism possible. Between Thanksgiving and Christmas, sixty thousand grace—in both senses of the word—store fronts and mall entrances. Last year's receipts totaled more than $65 million.

But getting into the malls is "becoming more and more of a problem," says Lt. Col. Clarence Harvey, head of the national communications division. In the Boston area, only fifty stores and malls are letting the kettles operate this year, compared with sixty-three two years ago.

Harvey explains that the group has always had the support of local merchants with a stake in the community. But as more malls are bought out by distant corporate giants, cooperation diminishes correspondingly.

Such money-grubbing short-sightedness is typical of business bureaucrats. The kettles brew a Christmas spirit conducive to shopping as well as giving. They represent the charity that lies at the true heart of this overcommercialized season.

Many of us feel guilty about the enormous sums we expend on presents during this annual gift-giving orgy. Dropping a few dollars into the drum alleviates conscience pangs. Giving to those in need is somewhat of a sanction to go out and spend.

Harvey describes the kettle as one of the few symbols of trust left in America. Think about it: You're giving money to an anonymous stranger, trusting that the funds will go to intended recipients.

The kettles are something more. Besides all of the good the Salvation Army does for the hungry and homeless, alcoholics and addicts, unwed mothers and children, it also does something very special for donors.

It gives us a chance to fulfill the biblical mandate to clothe the naked and feed the hungry.

Charity is increasingly impersonal. A solicitation arrives in the mail, and a check goes out in a postage-paid envelope. Those kettles (may they multiply) provide the opportunity to reach into pockets or purses and make spontaneous offerings, to get the warm glow that comes from giving to a real person and getting a sincere "God bless you" in return.

Ringing bells summoning souls to acts of nobility and change ringing as it falls into kettles are among the most beautiful sounds of Christmas.

## How Far My Father Traveled
*July 12, 1995*

My father's life was too large to be encompassed in the eight hundred–plus words I am allotted here.

Harold Samuel Feder died on June 30. In his eighty-five years, he lived through most of this tumultuous century. When he was born, William Howard Taft was president. Horse-drawn wagons were more common than automobiles. It was barely six years since the Wright brothers defied gravity.

He lived through the Depression, two world wars (serving in the second), and into the age of flight, the space age, and the age of computers.

His journey started in the Williamsburg section of Brooklyn, New York. His parents, pathetically poor immigrants, lived in a four-room, cold-water flat. His "bedroom" was a cot in the kitchen, next to the stove. My father was seventeen when he first saw hot water issue from a faucet.

He grew up on the tough streets of one of the meanest tenement neighborhoods in the borough. Dad told me he had to fight his way to school every day. He always took on the biggest, toughest kid so—win or lose—the others would respect him.

His formal education ended with sixth grade. At fifteen, he left home. His parents had separated, and my grandmother worked as a janitress to support three other children.

He delivered hand mirrors from a factory to retailers, working a sixty-hour week for $12—barely enough for a bed in a flophouse, meals at the Horn and Hardart automat, and a scrubbing at a Turkish bath once a week.

Two years later, he was on the road (my father always had a wanderlust), hitching rides and seeing the country, stopping every few days to earn enough to go on. For eight years, he took the northern route in the summer and went south in the winter. Sometimes, farmers paid him with food and a place to sleep.

As he matured, the jobs got better—parking cars at a country club in Miami, waiting tables in New Orleans. In California, he made tents and awnings for MGM studios.

A broken arm from an encounter with the crank of a Model T truck forced him back to New York. The accident was fortuitous. The following year, 1936, he met and married my mother, proposing on their first date. Next June, they would have been married sixty years.

Before the war, he was a salesman for a biscuit company and worked for Metropolitan Life Insurance. He also learned to fly a plane, joined the Civil Air Patrol, and enlisted in the U.S. Army Air Corps in July 1942. He was discharged in October 1945.

After the war, he opened a ladies specialty shop in the little town in upstate New York where I grew up. The years in Johnstown were his happiest, with his own business, a house, and a new car every four years—usually one with tail fins that threatened to launch it into orbit.

Describing her childhood, a character in a 1940s film says her father was a man who never sought success. But as long as he was alive, she had a comfortable home, enough to eat, and a feeling of being loved and protected.

So it was with me. Everything my father never had as a child, he gave me—not the least of which was a father's love.

My dad was typical of his generation. He loved his family and country, believed in God and morality, and wasn't overly concerned with much else. He liked John Wayne movies (actually, anything with six-shooters), travel, pool, checkers, horse races, burgers, and an occasional beer.

Dad readily confessed to being a loner. Toughened by a solitary youth, he kept his own counsel and made his own decisions. Stubborn? When his mind was made up, moving a mountain was easier than changing his opinion.

My father taught me less by what he said than what he did. He taught me the value of work, self-reliance, honesty, kindness, commitment, and family.

In his last years, Dad lived not far from us. "How are my kids?" he always asked me, in reference to his grandchildren.

My father died of cancer in our home. Perhaps in recompense for his hardscrabble early years, fate was kind. When Dad passed away, everyone dearest to him was at his bedside. For a man who struggled most of his life, his departure from life was remarkably peaceful.

And it struck me, at the last, how very far my father had come in those eighty-five years—across decades and eras, through unimagined upheaval, from a tenement childhood to a middle-class neighborhood, from working for bosses who pushed him around to being his own boss, from gnawing loneliness to a loving family. How far he had come, and how much further he had made it possible for his family to go.

## Honoring Heroes Elevates Us All
*July 3, 1995*

We usually think of the Founding Fathers as characters in a painting, standing around Independence Hall in their wigs and buckle shoes. Good fellows, to be sure. Elegant writers, if a bit formal. But heroic?

Yes, the fifty-six delegates who signed the Declaration of Independence were heroes in the truest sense of the word. Given the prospects for American sovereignty, each knew he could be signing his own death warrant.

For love of country, the signers risked all they held dear. In the ensuing seven years, they paid dearly. One trained American guns on his own home, which the British were using as a command post. Another refused to recant even when the Crown imprisoned and tortured his two sons.

Those were the days when a Nathan Hale could be celebrated without guilt. The temper of our times is increasingly inhospitable to heroes.

In an act of stunning ingratitude, the British Education Ministry put out a video on the end of World War II, for use in the nation's schools, that devotes all of fourteen seconds to Winston Churchill, and that in the context of the Labor victory in the 1945 election.

Britain slighting Churchill is almost as incredible as the Smithsonian's original Enola Gay exhibit that slandered our servicemen and offered green tea and sympathy to the Empire of the Rising Sun. Heroes get scant respect in a climate of moral relativism.

Crucial to reversing our cultural decline is recovering a sense of the heroic. In his book *A World Without Heroes,* Hillsdale College President George Roche noted that the hero is distinguished by an act of courage in the service of a noble ideal.

Roche wrote: "The hero overcomes the ordinary and attains greatness by serving some great good. His example very nearly rebukes us; telling us that we fail, not by aiming too high in life, but by aiming far too low."

Heroes provide spiritual sustenance. We can draw comfort from the knowledge that giants walk the earth—individuals who strive greatly, who overcome the most appalling adversity, who think great thoughts, who do great deeds, whose life testifies to the truth that individuals make their own destiny.

I have three heroes. Among those foremost in my esteem is John Adams, wisest of the Founding Fathers, intellectual engine of American independence, a conservative revolutionary who declared: "Our Constitution was created for a moral and a religious people. It is wholly inadequate for the governance of any other."

Then, there's Theodore Roosevelt—naturalist, historian, rancher, war hero, and statesman. TR was a man of great physical courage, unwavering principle, and unassailable character, who preached the strenuous life and manly virtues and coined the term "Americanism."

Lastly, Churchill. When I think of fortitude, I see in my mind's eye a stooped figure in an overcoat, cigar clamped firmly in his mouth, growling at the horror of his age, "Never, never!" By his will, his wit, his eloquence, and his genius as a war leader, he held the ramparts of the West in our darkest hour.

Each of my heroes has this in common: They defied conventional wisdom—Adams the egalitarianism of the early nineteenth century and its infatuation with revolutionary France, Roosevelt the isolationism of the Age of McKinley, and Churchill the perverse pacifism of the 1930s.

Each risked his political future for principle. At a given point in his career, each was written off as a failure, psychologically unsuited to exercise power due to an uncompromising nature.

Each acknowledged being guided by a force outside himself.

A powerful statement of the hero's credo is contained in the new movie *First Knight*, a retelling of the Arthurian legend.

In Western tradition, the knights of the Round Table were prototypical heroes. As King Arthur, Sean Connery embodies the hero's commitment to an objective moral order and service to others. "God uses people like you," Arthur tells Lancelot.

In the climax, the villain (an antihero named Malagant) invades Camelot, announcing to the populace: "I've come to free you from the tyranny of Arthur's law and the tyranny of Arthur's God." The hero serves a transcendent order. Serving only himself, the antihero says—in effect—"my kingdom come, my will be done." Thus *First Knight* is the antithesis of Hollywood's usual message (do it your way, you've gotta be you).

We all can't be heroes. But in recognizing heroism—in honoring heroes, living and dead—we can aspire to greatness and become more decent and diligent in the process.

# A Piece of History to Hold in a Hand
*April 27, 1995*

Saturday marks the fiftieth anniversary of the liberation of Dachau. I hold in my hand a remembrance of that awful time—a thing fashioned by human hands in the fires of the inferno.

When it arrived in the mail from California, I stared at the artifact transfixed. Time seemed suspended. I still can't describe the emotions evoked by this poignant piece of history.

A wooden plaque, about four inches in diameter with bark around the circumference, it appears to be a cross section of a branch.

On a flat surface, the word "Jerusalem" is painted in black, Gothic letters. Above this, very faintly, are the Hebrew letters for the ancient city. Both sides are varnished.

The dead hands that made it seemed to reach across the decades and touch my soul, urging me to tell their story.

In the spring of 1945, an American infantryman with the 63rd Division, pushing into Germany from the Salzburg area, walked into a deserted labor camp.

The barracks might have held five hundred prisoners. He took the plaque from the commandant's office, along with a toy dog which he still has.

Aaron Breitbart, senior researcher at the Simon Wiesenthal Center, believes the camp could have been a satellite of Dachau. There were literally thousands of these nameless places where prisoners were worked, beaten, and starved to death.

The Nazis called this variation on the gas chamber "vernichtung durch arbeit," destruction through work—slower but more economical than Zyklon B.

An I. G. Farben employee, visiting the slave-labor camp at Auschwitz, jokingly wrote to a superior: "That the Jewish race is playing a special part here you can well imagine. The diet and treatment of this sort of people is in accordance with our aim. Evidently an increase in weight is hardly ever recorded for them. That bullets start whizzing at the slightest attempt of a 'change of air' is also certain, as well as the fact that many have already disappeared as a result of 'sunstroke.'"

Prisoners typically put in twelve-hour days of hard labor, exposed to the elements. Their daily rations often consisted of no more than six hundred grams (twenty-one ounces) of bread, ersatz coffee, and soup made from potato peels or turnip tops.

That people subjected to this found the energy and will to create is a testament to the human spirit. A survivor told me that at Auschwitz, an entire chess set was carved from bones.

At Mauthausen, the prisoners made an American flag, which they presented to the commander of the U.S. forces that freed them. It isn't accurate in every detail (there are fifty-six stars), but it's the thought that counts.

These artisans of anguish wanted to be remembered. Among the most common human emotions is the desire to leave behind something that tells our story—in this case, that lets posterity know that there were people who suffered and died in those man-made hells but never surrendered hope or faith.

Why was Jerusalem inscribed in English as well as Hebrew on my keepsake? Perhaps because the anonymous craftsman believed it would be found by an American or British soldier and wanted him to understand what it meant.

Is it presumptuous to speculate on the thoughts of the prisoner who chose that single word, "Jerusalem," for his token?

Two weeks ago, Jews concluded the Passover seder with the promise: "Next year in Jerusalem." The ancient city is more than a place on a map; it's the point where heaven and earth meet. It's a dream of a world free of pain, privation, and fear. It's a longing for reunion with the source of life and goodness.

This Jerusalem is located by the longitude of the spirit and the latitude of redemption.

In his monumental *History of the Jews,* British historian Paul Johnson observed: "No people has ever insisted more firmly than the Jews that history has a purpose and humanity a destiny."

Is history deliberate? Does mankind have meaning? Is it remarkable or intentional that this piece of wood—crafted by weary, hungry hands—would be acquired by an American GI and taken to his home in California? That it would be passed to his son and then given by him to a devout Christian woman with a deep love for the Jewish people, who in turn would send it across the country to a writer who would try to tell its story in a newspaper column?

That the man who fashioned my small signpost found his Jerusalem cannot be doubted. In the meantime, his creation remains on this dimension to point the way to a better world.

## The Pilgrims' Real Legacy
*November 24, 1994*

Last week, the secular left was thrown into a panic at the thought that God (in the form of school prayer) might be allowed through the classroom door.

Today we celebrate a national holiday that commemorates the settlers who brought religious values to these shores.

If you can tear yourself away from the cranberry sauce and gridiron contests, give a thought to the Pilgrims, those oddly dressed men and women in the pictures that hung in schoolrooms a generation ago—the men bearded and somber, toting blunderbusses, the women with bonnets and Bibles. They did something or other with turkeys and Indians, but we can't recall exactly what.

Our children will have even less acquaintance with these creatures seemingly from another planet. After Washington's new revisionist curriculum (the National History Standards) goes into effect, students will know more about Mansa Musa, a fourteenth-century West African King, than they do about William Bradford.

But the Pilgrims and their Puritan cousins had a somewhat more profound impact on America. They established our nation firmly in the Judeo-Christian tradition and took the first steps toward constitutional government.

"Pilgrim" was a term Bradford, whose *History of the Plimoth Plantation* chronicles their travails, gave his fellow congregants. They were separatists—devout Christians, appalled by the corruption of both church and state in seventeenth-century England.

King James I called them dangerous religious "fanatics" (foreshadowing the Democratic party's attack on the Christian right) "ever-discontented with the present government."

They were harried and imprisoned in England, exiled to Holland, and eventually sought refuge in the New World. A minority among the 102 passengers on the *Mayflower*, they endured a seven-week voyage and a "long beating at sea" to arrive at Cape Cod on November 9, 1620.

Bradford described the desolation that greeted them: land of a "wild and savage hue" where there were "no friends to welcome them, no inns to entertain or refresh their weather-beaten bodies, no houses… to repair to," their domain bounded on one side by the wilderness, on the other by an ocean that was "a main bar and gulf to separate them from all the civilized parts of the world."

During that brutal first winter, their numbers were cut in half. As Bradford noted, sometimes they died two and three in a day "in January and February, being the depth of winter, and wanting houses and other comforts; being infected with scurvy and other diseases."

Only faith sustained them. On disembarking, they fell on their knees and blessed "the God of heaven" who had watched over them.

They saw themselves as spiritual descendants of Israel, having fled the corruption of Babylon and "come to Jerusalem" to "build the Lord's temple."

When they wandered in the wilderness, the Jews were charged to make a thanksgiving offering from their first crops in the Promised Land. After the Pilgrims' first harvest, they had a ceremonial meal in remembrance of the commandment.

The origins of American government can be traced to the Mayflower Compact, signed by almost all the adult males of the company. Their enterprise, they declared, was undertaken "for the Glory of God and the advancement of the Christian faith." How monocultural.

They formed themselves into a body politic and pledged to enact "just and equal laws" by which they would be governed. Here is the wellspring of democracy, from which the Declaration of Independence and Constitution flow.

Our governmental tradition is founded on a recognition of divine sovereignty. Like the Mayflower Compact, the U.S. Constitution is a charter solemnly devised in imitation of the covenant accepted by the Jewish people at Sinai.

If the Pilgrims were around today, they'd be derided by the cultural elite as crypto-theocrats. "What's all this God-talk? Don't they know politics and religion don't mix?"

If they ran for school committee, they'd be exposed as stealth candidates. Multiculturalists would condemn them as (soon-to-be) dead, white European males who usurped the territory of an indigenous people. The Supreme Court might even declare them unconstitutional. At the very least, they'd be arrested for holding a prayer service at the site of their landing, now a public park.

Responding to House Speaker-to-be Newt Gingrich's school prayer proposal, Robert Peck of the American Civil Liberties Union pouted that such worship inevitably would be discriminatory, that a Moslem child won't have an opportunity to "teach his classmates to pray to Mecca or the little Santeria child to sacrifice a chicken in front of the class."

As I recall, the Pilgrims read the King James Bible, not the Koran. What chickens they had were for eating.

## Omaha Beach: Our Finest Hour
*June 6, 1994*

In June 1942, Hitler told his general staff that, having kicked the British off the continent once, he wasn't going to waste time worrying about them. Moreover, he relished the prospect of teaching the Americans a lesson. He got his chance—fifty years ago today.

Operation Overlord, the greatest amphibious assault in history, landed a force of Americans, British, Canadians, and Free French at five beaches on the rugged Normandy coast designated by the code names Omaha, Utah, Juno, Sword, and Gold. The first two were the American beaches.

The legion was transported in four thousand ships. An air force of seventy-five hundred planes softened the targets. Allied paratroops (some twenty-three thousand of them) dropped behind the beaches, attacked defenses, and generally created confusion among the enemy.

The invasion was, nonetheless, no beach party. The German commander, Karl von Rundstedt (one of the Reich's ablest generals), had sixty divisions at his disposal. By mid-May, the Germans had planted more than four million land mines and erected half a million obstacles.

The day before the invasion, the Channel weather was the worst in twenty-five years. On D-Day, the waves were still high, the undertow strong. While the invasion caught Hitler off guard, the Americans who landed at Omaha Beach (each lugging seventy pounds of wet gear) were met by the German 352nd Infantry Division, combat-tested troops at full battle strength. The cliffs the Germans held provided commanding positions from which to rain murderous fire on the invaders.

How did it feel to be one of those American kids—twenty years old, fresh off the Iowa farm or the sidewalks of New York—sitting in a flat-bottomed Higgins boat heading for the Normandy coast?

Unlike the British, seasoned veterans of North Africa and Italy, most were "green as growing corn," as an aide to General Eisenhower described them prior to the invasion.

They had to know there was a good chance they'd never make it back—some planners predicted 75 percent casualties—that they might drown in the heavy undertow, be blown to oblivion by artillery fire, or cut to ribbons by machine-gun emplacements. Many were.

What were they thinking, those young warriors? (Will I ever see the baby born after I left the States? Why didn't I tell my father I loved him?) Their emotions, perhaps, were a mixture of fear, confusion, pride, hope, and patriotism.

On that fateful day, Omaha Beach had the heaviest fighting and the highest casualties. In the 1st Battalion, 116th Infantry Regiment, every officer and sergeant was killed or wounded within ten minutes. Soldiers who reached the sand went back into the water to pull others ashore.

Lt. Gen. Omar Bradley, commander of the U.S. ground forces, recalled, "We started running the LCTs [landing craft tanks] up on the beach, and a lot of them were lost when they were hit by enemy fire."

On a high bluff, where half a century ago German guns pounded our GIs, sits the American cemetery at Normandy—9,368 crosses and Stars of David that bear mute witness to the price of "Bloody Omaha."

Still, by nightfall footholds were secured on all five beaches, and 156,000 men were ashore. There followed an expansion of the beachheads, the fall of Cherbourg, the breakout of General Patton's Third Army (early August), the liberation of Paris (late August), the Battle of Arnhem (September), the Battle of the Bulge (December/January), and the Rhine crossings (March 1945).

On April 12, 1945, Eisenhower (the Supreme Allied Commander), Bradley, and Patton toured the Ohrdruf concentration camp near the German town of Gotha. They saw the gallows, the mounds of corpses, and the skeletal survivors.

In the following days, U.S. and British troops walked into hell on earth, places with names like Dachau, Buchenwald, and Bergen-Belsen. Only then did we fully comprehend the enormity of the evil we confronted on that sandy stretch of Normandy coast.

If the Battle of Britain was England's finest hour, Normandy was ours. The New World came to the rescue of the Old. The land conceived in liberty arrived on the continent to liberate a slave empire and plunge a bayonet into the monstrous heart of Nazism.

During World War I, some of the British troops fighting at Mons swore they saw the ghosts of Henry V's archers of Agincourt shooting arrows into the German lines.

Normandy had its ghosts too. Every American who ever fought for his homeland—from the Minutemen to the Grand Army of the Republic to the doughboys of the Rainbow Division—slogged through the icy surf and struggled up the beaches shoulder to shoulder with their spiritual descendants.

## Every Book an Unexplored Continent
*February 2, 1995*

E agerly, I opened the book I'd just received, Martin Gilbert's *The First World War: A Complete History.*

I examined the cover, skimmed the chapter heads and perused the index, imagining the hours of pleasure awaiting me therein.

The Great War, whose carnage (fourteen million dead) was exceeded only by the second global conflict, cast its ghastly shadow across this century. Soviet communism and Nazism were born on its muddy battlefields. Its echoes reverberate down to the 1990s, in the streets of Sarajevo. I couldn't wait to start reading.

Every serious book is a virgin continent awaiting the mental tread of the literary explorer.

Some read for knowledge—because they're driven to understand who they are and whence they came—others for pure pleasure or to navigate life's rapids and traverse its doldrums.

Someone once described a woman as a young man's lover, the companion of one's middle years, and an old man's nurse. Books too play many roles—storyteller, teacher, counselor, companion, consoler.

Whenever I visit a home for the first time, I always look for books and am disappointed if I find none. I want to know what my host is reading and—by extension—thinking, the far horizons his mind has wandered. More than the eyes, a library is a window on its owner's soul.

I wish I could rightly claim the title of voracious reader. I'm more of a steady nibbler, a slow, deliberate reader. Still, a day without at least a few pages read seems incomplete.

The best books are often unexpected finds—something snatched from a sale table. Browsing in a bookstore, I found *In a Dark Woods Wandering,* a medieval novel by Dutch writer Hella Haasse. Published just after World War II, it tells the turbulent tale of the man whose son became the first Orleans king of France. The words fairly sang off the pages; sentences gleamed like sunshine through a stained-glass window.

Reading and greatness are linked. Between them, John Adams and his son, John Quincy, acquired 11,789 volumes at a time when books were a precious commodity.

Lincoln—who had only a few months of formal education—was self-taught from books. Norman Rockwell's famous painting shows the young president-to-be leaning on a cracker-barrel as he pores over a text, a look of intense concentration on his face.

As a soldier in India, Winston Churchill decided his education was woefully inadequate and spent the languid siesta hours, when his follow officers snoozed, in a rigorous reading regimen. Britain's most famous prime minister was also one of the century's eminent historians.

For reading, these are the best of times and worst of times. In an age of cable television, interactive TV, Internet, and CompuServe, there are still readers—enough to generate a projected $20.8 billion in book sales this year.

Quality is another matter. The current *New York Times* best-sellers crop has everything from Pope John Paul II's *Crossing the Threshold of Hope* and the controversial *The Bell Curve* to Dolly Parton's autobiography and something called *Don't Stand Too Close to a Naked Man*, described as "anecdotes and meditations on life by the star of *Home Improvement*." The philosopher-emperor Marcus Aurelius has nothing to fear.

Sadder than the consumers of celebrity biographies and the sludge of supermarket romances are those who cannot read (estimated at sixty-six million in this country) and those who will not read.

The latter read, if at all, out of a sense of duty, for their studies or careers or to annihilate time on a plane.

They deny themselves one of life's chief pleasures—the ability to transcend time and space, to learn at the feet of Aristotle, to argue politics with Machiavelli, to experience the grandeur of decaying Rome with Edward Gibbon as a guide, to know the beauty a great novelist can fashion.

Good movies are fine but over far too soon and leave too little scope for the imagination. An interesting book can last for weeks and let the mind travel byways even the author never imagined.

After my service in the trenches, where to next? Perhaps Gerhard L. Weinberg's massive history on the Second World War *(A World at Arms)*, which proceeded with lethal inevitability from the first. Or backward in time to a survey of nineteenth-century nationalism, where the long march to No Man's Land began. Or perhaps a detour to Mesopotamia or a novel of Renaissance Italy.

In books, there's never a dull moment—none of the infirmities that come with age are apparent. The mind is enriched, and the spirit roams free. For a few hours, beauty, adventure, and wisdom are at our fingertips.

## On Rosh Hashanah, Here Comes the Judge
*September 5, 1994*

If Lincoln and Washington have public birthdays, why not the world? This evening marks the beginning of Rosh Hashanah, the Jewish holy day that commemorates Creation.

It may be 1994 to you, but as far as the Jewish calendar is concerned, it's the year 5,755 from the beginning of the world.

The expression "Jewish New Year," the holiday's secular designation, is misleading, evoking images of the revelry that accompanies New Year's Eve—silly hats, noisemakers, and popping champagne corks. Rosh Hashanah is fun only if your idea of a good time is spending sixteen hours in a synagogue over the course of two days.

Leviticus enjoins: "In the seventh month, on the first day of the month, you shall have a rest-day, a day of remembrance, horn-blowing, and holy assembly."

Day of remembrance? Rather enigmatic, that. Who is to remember what?

Rosh Hashanah is the day God recalls His creatures for good or ill, when humanity's final arbiter issues His decrees. In the words of the Talmud, on this day: "All that comes into the world pass before Him like flocks of sheep."

Rosh Hashanah's themes are royalty, reflection, and repentance. We acknowledge God's sovereignty, weigh our deeds, and ask forgiveness. It's a solemn, yet hopeful time, in that there's always the possibility of redemption.

According to tradition, on Rosh Hashanah, each person's fate for the coming year is decided; the judgment is written. On Yom Kippur (the Day of Atonement), the decree is sealed. Hence, the traditional New Year's greeting: *L'Shana Tova Tikatevu*—may you be inscribed for a good year.

During the ten days of penitence—starting on Rosh Hashanah and ending at sundown on Yom Kippur (jointly, the Days of Awe)— the evil decree can yet be annulled by (in the words of the liturgy) *tefilah, tshuvah, tsadakah*—prayer, repentance, and good works.

Rosh Hashanah is profoundly countercultural in that it embraces a worldview our culture emphatically rejects.

Judgment implies responsibility. The ability to shape our destiny, to avert punishment, presupposes free will. All of this the culture disdains as Republican rhetoric and bourgeois bunk.

If you're bad, the culture says, it's because your environment made you so. You were an abused child. You were raised in poverty. You are a member of a despised minority and have internalized society's negative assumptions. You have the wrong genes.

The O. J. Simpson case is classic. The racial rationalizers insist that even if Simpson is guilty, he's not responsible.

He was driven to this desperate act, the theory goes, by the alienation caused by trying to "act white." If there was a Grand Prix for creative exculpation, this would take the trophy.

Far from excuse making and blame avoidance, during the Days of Awe, we even take responsibility for things we didn't do. (How's that for Jewish guilt?) On Yom Kippur, the congregation in unison confesses to a litany of sins most didn't personally commit.

This is an acknowledgment of our responsibility to the community (another conflict with the culture, which prizes autonomy). If we didn't try to dissuade the sinner, we share his guilt.

Here is an answer to those who demand that we refrain from trying to "force our morality" on them. We are specifically commanded to be moral buttinskies by the highest authority.

We're told to live our values, an injunction that runs contrary to the unholy crusade to expel religious conservatives from the political arena.

The whole idea of marathon services, of taking responsibility for our actions and making a commitment to change, is that we are not to leave our ideals behind when the door to the synagogue closes, but take them into the world.

How can Catholics, religious Jews, Mormons, or any other community of faith accept the dictum that their deepest values are not to affect a process whose every act involves moral distinctions?

Hebrew National hot dogs used to run a cunning commercial that showed Uncle Sam about to bite into a wiener. The announcer remarks: "The government says we can put bone meal in our franks—but we don't. We have to answer to a higher authority."

And that is Rosh Hashanah's central theme—that there is, in the words of the Declaration of Independence, a Supreme Judge of the World. Executive orders, laws passed by Congress, administrative actions, editorial opinions—all must bow to His edicts. As comedian Flip Wilson was wont to say: "Order in the court 'cause here comes the judge."

# chapter sixteen

# ABRAHAM, ISAAC, JACOB, AND FAMILY VALUES

When *Book of Virtues* author William Bennett released his second annual "index of leading cultural indicators" in February 1994, it made depressing reading for those who believe that the traditional two-parent family is an essential institution of civilization. A few highlights from this gloomy document:

If the present trend continues, by the year 2000, 40 percent of all births in this country will be out of wedlock.

The number of single-parent households increased from fewer than 10 percent of all families with children in 1960 to almost 30 percent in 1990. For a white child born in 1950, there was an 81 percent chance he would live with both of his biological parents to age eighteen. Of white children born in 1980, only 30 percent could expect to reach the age of majority in an intact family.

Children from single-parent families are two to three times more likely than children from two-parent families to have emotional and behavioral problems. They also are far more likely to do poorly in school, to drop out, (if girls) to become pregnant as teenagers, to engage in premarital sex at an early age, and to abuse drugs and alcohol. Welfare, crime, addiction, and the decline of learning and productivity—all are intimately related to the break-down of the family.

This brings the debate over family values into sharp focus. Like every other organism, families need nourishment. If the family ethic is withering and dying, look to the social climate in which families struggle to survive.

Here, as elsewhere, the pro-family movement is at loggerheads with the dominant culture, where the emphasis is on the maxi-mization of personal freedom and self-fulfillment.

How often have we heard it said: "With so many types of fami-lies, each with its own unique composition and lifestyle, how can we possibly speak of values that pertain to all of them?"

Typical of the assault on traditional families is Stephanie Coontz, a faculty member at Evergreen State College in Olympia, Washington. Coontz is the author of the 1992 book *The Way We Never Were: American Families and the Nostalgia Trip.*

The author emphatically asserts that our concept of the normative family of the past (cohesive, supportive, and nurturing) is seriously flawed.

She maintains, in effect, that families have always been dysfunc-tional, that our vision of normalcy is a myth concocted by 1950s prime-time television—via such popular sitcoms as *Ozzie and Har-riet, Father Knows Best, Leave It to Beaver,* and the *Donna Reed Show,* and foisted on an uncritical public. Coontz claims such families existed only in the maudlin imagination of television scriptwriters.

Not surprisingly, the professor is a junior-league Hillary Clin-ton, a fervent feminist who thinks day care, two-career families, and social parenting are swell.

Such revisionism must not be allowed to go unchallenged. Fam-ily values are real. Their absence is real too—as Bennett's index so compellingly demonstrates. "Family values" has a dual meaning. It's about those moral values that traditional families foster and the political values that promote family stability.

Sorry, Stephanie, but family values have a slightly more distinguished lineage than the Andersons and Nelsons. They started with one family all right, and it happened to be a Jewish family.

Most of the first book of the Bible (Genesis from chapter 12 to the end) is a family history. It's about a Jewish family—a man named Abraham (the first Jew); his wife, Sarah; their son, Isaac; his daughter-in-law, Rebecca; his grandson, Jacob; and Jacob's wives and children. Each of the episodes in this family's history reflects a moral principle with universal application.

In this book, which has had such a profound impact on Western civilization, the family was established on an eternal foundation. It is here that we learn of the proper relationship of husbands and wives and parents and children, as well as those virtues the family is intended to inculcate.

In the very first chapter of Genesis, God does something that no government agency has ever duplicated. He creates a family. The explanation is contained in chapter 2. "God said: It is not good that man should be alone, I will make a helpmeet for him" (Genesis 2:18). At this point, an obvious question arises: Why is woman the solution to man's loneliness?

In the late 1970s, when the gay-rights movement came on the scene, Anita Bryant reminded us that "God created Adam and Eve, not Adam and Steve." We either grinned or grimaced at this witticism, depending on our politics. But the humor reveals an important truth.

God could have created another man as a companion for the first, or—one supposes—an intelligent/talking animal. Why did it have to be a woman? Here is the Bible's first great lesson, that by themselves men and women are incomplete, that each has psychological and spiritual attributes the other lacks, that in order to be whole (to live the harmonious existence intended by their Creator) men and women need each other.

This theme is repeated time and again. When the first Creation was destroyed by a deluge, God commanded Noah to fill his ark with families—male and female of each species—as well as his own household.

"For this reason," says the Bible in one its most evocative passages, "man leaves his father and his mother and clings to his wife, and they become one flesh."

In his book, *Can Families Survive in Pagan America*, Rabbi Samuel Dresner, a professor at the Jewish Theological Seminary of America, elucidates the threefold meaning of "one flesh."

The rabbi explains that besides the obvious sexual union of husband and wife, the expression refers to "the shared intimacy of home and family, that is the single home they now inhabit, and the single family they now constitute."

Additionally, says Rabbi Dresner, if the couple is blessed with a child, their flesh literally becomes "one flesh" in their offspring.

Thus the pairing of men and women isn't merely a time-honored social convention, or a regulatory mechanism of bourgeois society, but an indispensable aspect of the divine scheme.

The lives of the great men and women of the Bible demonstrate family values in action. When Sarah tells Abraham to dismiss his concubine Hagar and her son Ishmael, Abraham is troubled. After all, Ishmael is his first-born. And God reassures him: "Let it not be evil in your eyes because of the lad and your handmaiden; in everything that Sarah says to you, harken to her voice, for in Isaac shall seed be called for you."

Like so much in the Bible, this admonition, "listen to the voice of Sarah," has a universal application. The mother has an intuitive understanding. In family matters, her voice must be heeded.

The Talmud, or Oral Law, tells us: "God counts the tears of a woman"—meaning that women have a special sensitivity to the world's suffering that men lack.

In the next generation, in Isaac's family, a mother once again intervenes to change the course of history. Knowing that Esau is unworthy, Rebecca works to transfer the patriarchal blessing to

Jacob, the man of peace. Isaac gave the blessing, but it was Rebecca who decided in whom seed would be called for him.

How should a husband regard his wife? The rabbis enjoin a man to "love his wife as himself and to honor her more than himself."

The first land owned by a Hebrew in Israel was the field of Makhpelah that Abraham purchased in Hebron to bury his wife Sarah. This act, more eloquent than words, is a silent tribute to spousal devotion.

In traditional Jewish households on Friday evening, with the family gathered around the Sabbath table, the husband recites a section of Proverbs known as "A Woman of Valor." According to our tradition, this was Abraham's eulogy for his beloved wife. Listen to a few of the verses:

> A good wife, who can find? She is more precious than corals. The heart of her husband trusts in her.... She arises while it is yet night and gives food to her household.... She examines a field and buys it, with the fruit of her hands she plants a vineyard. She girds herself with strength, and braces her arms for work.... She opens her hand to the poor, and extends her hand to the needy.... Strength and honor are her garb.... She opens her mouth with wisdom, and the teaching of kindness is on her tongue.... Her children rise up and call her blessed.... Grace is deceptive and beauty is passing; a woman revering God, she shall be praised.

No romantic vision of Hollywood ever equaled the beauty of this exultation of femininity.

After Sarah's death, Isaac takes a wife. Genesis offers a chronology that seems out of sequence. "And Isaac brought her [Rebecca] into the tent of his mother Sarah. He married Rebecca, she became his wife, and he loved her, and only then was Isaac comforted for his mother."

This is a reversal of what our society has come to accept as the natural order, where love (often mere infatuation) precedes marriage. How often two people, who declare themselves to be madly in love, marry and—after passion has had a few years to congeal— go their separate ways. We are told they "grew out of love." Perhaps the Bible is telling us that love is something to grow into, rather than an emotion to outgrow.

Why did Isaac bring Rebecca to the tent of his mother? According to Jewish tradition, Sarah was a woman of great spiritual endowments. The lamps she lit on Friday evening would give light for the entire week. A small portion of her bread would satisfy the most acute hunger.

Isaac wanted to see if Rebecca was a woman like his mother, a woman of valor. When he learned she was, he married her, and then he loved her.

The Bible takes marriage very seriously. It is a covenant between two people, often compared to the covenant between God and Israel at Sinai—where mutual promises were also exchanged, an event often described with matrimonial allegories, where Israel is likened to a bride and God to the groom who takes her with promises to love and cherish.

Marriage is viewed not just as an undertaking between a man and a woman but a relationship affecting the entire community. These vows are not to be taken lightly, but as the most solemn of commitments. The Talmud teaches: "Whoever divorces the wife of his youth, even the altar [of the Holy Temple] sheds tears for her."

From the union of a man and a woman come children (again, his flesh and hers become one). The very first commandment recounted in the Bible, given to the first family, was to procreate. "And God blessed them [Adam and Eve] and said to them: Be fruitful and multiply and fill the earth and subdue it."

In other words, people—the continuation of humanity from generation to generation—are an essential component of the divine scheme, a way of helping God to complete his work. The Talmud says there are three partners in the creation of a child: the mother, the father, and God. With each birth, God miraculously repeats the Creation, making another Adam or a new Eve.

Jewish tradition does not esteem celibacy or voluntary childlessness. In ancient Israel, a man without children could not become a member of the highest religious court. Families were thought to have a humanizing effect. In biblical Hebrew, there is no word for bachelor.

Rabbi Aryeh Kaplan, in his book on marriage, *Made in Heaven*, comments: "In Judaism the single life is regarded as a misfortune." The Talmud explains that in the World to Come (the Hereafter) the first three questions which will be asked of a Jew are: Did you buy and sell in good faith (were you honest in your business dealings)? Did you have a fixed time for Torah study? And, did you raise a family?

Zero Population Growth, Planned Parenthood, and the singles lifestyle find little support in Scriptures, one reason ideologues of the left have done their utmost to divorce religious principles from the public policy debate.

In the Judeo–Christian tradition, children are viewed as both an endowment from God and an obligation. To emphasize this point, throughout the Bible we find cases of infertility corrected by divine intervention. Sarah is ninety years old, Abraham is a hundred, when Isaac is born in fulfillment of God's promise.

Hannah, who is barren, offers a fervent prayer for a child and is rewarded with a son named Samuel who grows up to be the prophet who anoints King David. On this point, the Bible is quite emphatic: Children are not accidental—a choice to be taken or rejected—but a gift to be cherished.

Thus in the most profound sense, there are no unplanned pregnancies. Every conception is intended.

But childbearing is merely the beginning of parental responsibility. Parents are indispensable to moral education. In Deuteronomy,

God tells the nation Israel how his law, delivered unto Moses, is to be spread. "These words that I command you today shall be upon your heart, and teach them diligently to your sons, and speak of them when you sit in your house and when you walk upon the way; when you lie down and when you get up."

Teach them to whom? To your friends? To your neighbors? Teach them to your children. When? All the time. When you sit in your house and when you walk on the way. The law is to be inscribed not on the portals of your business but on the door posts of your home.

What do children owe their parents? Here the revelation at Sinai speaks unambiguously. The first Ten Commandments are divided into two categories.

The first grouping speaks of man's obligations to God: Know that God is God. Remember the Sabbath day and keep it holy. Don't take God's name in vain and so on.

The latter concern man's responsibilities to his fellow man: don't murder, don't steal, don't bear false witness, and the like. In the very middle stands the Fifth Commandment: "Honor your father and your mother so that your days may be long upon the land which God, your God, is giving you." Out of the 613 positive and negative commandments in Mosaic law, it is one of only two for which a reward is specified in this world, and implied in the World to Come, thus emphasizing its importance.

The fifth is the bridge commandment because it concerns both man's obligations to God and to humanity. Parents are God's earthly surrogates. Remember the old greeting-card doggerel: "Because God couldn't be everywhere, He created Mothers." Of course, God (omniscient and omnipotent) is everywhere. Still, that sentimental verse alludes to a powerful truth.

Parents are the transmitters of divine law. They bear the primary responsibility for inculcating godly virtues. As such, they merit both obedience and respect.

It's no accident that of all creatures people have the longest period of adolescence. Where it takes animals months to mature, humans need decades. The reason is quite simple: Animals are born with instincts, with all of the knowledge they need to survive. Children need time to learn life's lessons.

The family is their classroom. Mother and father are the tutors. This is why, when a school gives a child a condom it not only violates the dictates of common sense, but undermines the divine basis of social stability as well.

In Orthodox Jewish homes, the father gives a blessing to each of his children on Friday evenings. For sons the benediction is: "May God make you like Ephraim and Menasseh," the sons of Joseph adopted by the Patriarch Jacob. For daughters we say: "May God make you like Sarah, Rebecca, Rachel, and Leah." It's important that children understand that blessings come through their parents, that father and mother are their link with the Eternal.

In Judaism, the home is a minisanctuary. Far more than the synagogue, the home is a substitute for the Holy Temple in Jerusalem. From kindling the Sabbath candles and lighting the Hanukkah menorah to observing the Passover seder and building a tabernacle on the holiday of Shavuoth, the home is the site of our most important ceremonies, again emphasizing the centrality of family.

It is in the family that we learn life's most important lessons: how to be charitable, the importance of hospitality and harmony, and the value of labor, obedience, and piety.

In his book, *Toward a Meaningful Life,* the late Rabbi Menachem Mendel Schneerson, the leader of the worldwide Hasidic movement known as Lubavitsch, described the indispensable role of the home in moral development.

The rabbi wrote:

> Home is where we learn to cope and be productive,
>    to work and play, to be comfortable with ourselves and

others. Most important, home is where we learn about happiness and wholesomeness. Think about the warmth you feel when you come home after being away a few months or even a few days. How different that warmth is from what we experience in the outside world! Our home is a secure base that gives us the confidence to explore the terrain of an unpredictable and often dangerous world.

On the third day after his circumcision (at age ninety-nine) Abraham sat in the doorway of his tent ("in the heat of the day," as the Bible recounts) waiting for travelers. When they appeared, he ran to greet them, ushered them into his dwelling, washed their feet, and fed and entertained them. Compare this to the hospitality of Sodom, which was much closer to the norm for those times.

In the ghettos and shtetls of Eastern Europe, it was considered particularly meritorious for a family to invite a poor person to share their Sabbath meal. Even the most impoverished home had a *tsadaka* box (a charity box), in which children were encouraged to deposit a few small coins from time to time.

The home is where we also learn about tolerance and patience. The Talmud says: "Anger in the home is like worms in grain." One of the most important family values is *shalom beit*—a peaceful home. In the stories of Cain and Abel, Jacob and Esau, and Joseph and his brothers, we learn the often tragic consequences of family strife.

In an age in which ferocity and power were prized, the Bible stresses the value of loving kindness, again, relating it to the family.

When Abraham sends his servant back to his own land to fetch a wife for Isaac, the retainer—standing at the gates of the city— prays for a sign. "So let it come to pass that the girl to whom I will say: 'Please tilt your pitcher so that I may drink,' and she will say;

'Drink, and I will give your camels drink also,' let her be the one whom Thou hast appointed for Thy servant, Isaac" (Genesis 24:14).

Bear in mind, filling a bucket with water and raising it from a well by hand, and drawing enough to satisfy camels, isn't a common courtesy—like holding a door for someone whose arms are full—but an arduous act of generosity that bespeaks nobility of spirit.

Isaac's wife is to be recognized on what basis? The young lady with the finest clothes, who's obviously from the best family? The wittiest? The most intelligent? The most attractive?

For the woman who is to take Sarah's place, compassion is the key virtue.

These are family values and this is their source. How different they are from the values of contemporary society. A family as a man and a woman, whose union is sanctified by God, making a life commitment versus the family as any random conglomeration of individuals sharing two rooms and a bath.

Procreation as a choice versus childbearing as an obligation. Children as gift from God or children as a disposable commodity who serve primarily as a means of parental gratification.

Gender equality versus gender differentiation. Individual happiness as the highest good or the well-being of the family and community. Honor your mother and father, look to them for wisdom and guidance, or Hollywood's disparagement of parents as knaves or well-meaning fools.

Family values are biblical values. They come not from a television ministry, or a sociology textbook, or a party platform, or the industrial revolution, or a 1950s prime-time television series. Their origins lie in the very beginnings of human history. Without them, man would never have risen out of savagery to build civilizations. Unless our society can recover them, it is doomed to continue on its current decline.

Family values come to us from the highest authority. They were ordained by Him who gave humanity its nature, which is why they work so well.

No, it didn't start with Ozzie and Harriet, but with the first words which God spoke to the first man and woman. Its institutions were built into the order of the universe.

# INDEX